Paolo Marrone

SPIRITUAL AWAKENING

The Practical Guide to Use the Law of Attraction and Mindfulness Techniques to Stop Overthinking,

How to Become the Alchemist of Your Life with the Principles of Quantum Physics

Spiritual Awakening
by Paolo Marrone

© Paolo Marrone 2021. All rights reserved. The content contained within this book may not be reproduced, duplicated or transmitted without direct written permission from the author or the publisher.
Under no circumstances will any blame or legal responsibility be held against the publisher, or author, for any damages, reparation, or monetary loss due to the information contained within this book. Either directly or indirectly. This book is copyright protected. This book is only for personal use. You cannot amend, distribute, sell, use, quote or paraphrase any part, or the content within this book, without the consent of the author or publisher.

TABLE OF CONTENTS

Introduction	1
The Strange World of Quantum Physics	7
The World Appears Only When Needed	10
But Who Is This Observer?	14
What if It Was Due to Temporal Entanglement?	18
That Weird Experiment on Time	21
Have You Ever Wondered How Big You Are?	25
Is Reality a Large Quantum Computer?	28
Matrix: Discover the Flaws of the System	32
The Probability of Something Happening Depends Only on Us	36
When Rationality Is Only Low Superstition	39
The Importance of Expecting the Unexpected	42
Cause and Effect Work in Reverse	45
The Magic of the Uncertainty Principle	48
Relax, You Are Only Dreaming	52
You May Not Know That You Are Living in the Past	56
Relax, Creation Is Over	59
It Is Impossible to Be Wrong	62
Like the Flutter of Butterfly Wings	65
"Actuators" of a Divine Design?	68
The Mind as a Means of Expressing the Divine Idea	72
The Universe Has No Will of Its Own	76
Responsibility as a Means to Create Reality	79
You Wrote This Chapter	82
Karma and the Law of Attraction	86
The True Nature of the Law of Attraction	89
Be Careful What You Ask For, Because It Will Be Given to You	93
Your Defense Is Your Real Danger	97
Ladies and Gentlemen, Make Your Choice	100
Perseverance and Willpower Are the Keys to Wealth	103
The Role of the Will in the Creation of Reality	106
We Use Free Will to Control Our Lives	109
A Gateway to Conscious Creation	112
The Unconscious Does Not See with Our Eyes	115
Learning to Dialogue with the Unconscious	118
Choose Who to Be and Become It	121
I Will Only Be Happy When...	124
A Song to Make Our Wishes Come True	127
Emotion Is a Place	130

THE FACTORY OF EMOTIONS	133
INSIDE OUT, THE OTHER SIDE OF EMOTIONS	136
THE POWER OF IMAGINATION	139
INSTILL LIFE INTO YOUR DESIRE	143
HAVE FAITH. HERE IS THE SECRET INGREDIENT	147
THE ART OF ASKING THE UNIVERSE	150
IMPERSONATE THE ROLE OF THE CONSCIOUS CREATOR	153
I AM NOT GETTING UP THIS MORNING UNTIL...	157
YOUR WISH IS GRANTED INSTANTLY	161
APPRECIATION AS A POWERFUL MEANS TO CREATE	165
THE TRAMPOLINE TO MATERIALIZE OUR DREAMS	168
GRATITUDE STRENGTHENS OUR POWER OVER THE WORLD	171
TRAIN YOUR GRATITUDE	174
FORGIVENESS AS A MEANS TO HEAL ONESELF	177
THE WHOLE UNIVERSE WAS CREATED FOR YOU	180
BECOME A CONSCIOUS CREATOR	183
BECOME THE HIGHEST IDEA OF YOURSELF	186
A PRACTICAL MANUAL OF CONSCIOUS CREATION	189
YOU CANNOT HAVE WHAT YOU ASK FOR, ONLY WHAT YOU HAVE	192
THE LAW OF ATTRACTION WORKS FOR EVERYONE	195
THE LAW OF WEALTH	198
LIFE IS A GAME. LET'S LEARN TO PLAY IT!	201
SHARING AS A POWERFUL TOOL FOR CREATION	204
LEARN TO ASK THE RIGHT QUESTION	208
ATTENTION IS THE WEAPON OF THE CONSCIOUS CREATOR	211
SELF-REMEMBERING TO BE THE MASTER OF YOUR OWN LIFE	214
THE ALCHEMICAL WORK THAT TURNS LEAD INTO GOLD	218
AWARENESS AS A MEANS TO ESCAPE TIME	221
DEMANDING RESPECT FOR OURSELVES AND FROM OUR INNER VOICE	225
NEVER USE WORDS AGAINST YOURSELF	228
BEYOND MECHANICALNESS, TRUE LIFE BEGINS	231
IF DOING WERE EASY	234
FREE YOUR MIND TO FREE YOUR LIFE	237
THE EGO, YOUR BEST ALLY	241
THE MOST PRECIOUS ASSET YOU HAVE	245
THE WORLD YOU SEE IS YOU	248
THOSE DEMONS? JUST A DIRTY TRICK	251
A DIFFERENT READING OF CHRIST'S LIFE	253
DOES THE SOUL MATE REALLY EXIST?	257
TRUE LOVE AND NEED DO NOT GET ALONG	260
THAT'S WHO WE REALLY ARE	263
DISCOVER THE WARRIOR WITHIN YOU	266

THE BEST DEAL OF YOUR LIFE	269
YOU DO NOT HAVE TO LEARN ANYTHING, ONLY REMEMBER	273
THE ROAD TO AWAKENING	276
DOES ABSOLUTE TRUTH REALLY EXIST?	279
IT IS NOT ENOUGH TO KNOW THE RULES OF THE GAME	283
I DIDN'T SAY IT WOULD BE EASY	287
ESCAPE YOUR PAST TO FREE YOUR PRESENT	290
REINTERPRET YOUR PAST TO CHANGE YOUR FUTURE	293
THE TRUE STORY OF THE ORIGINAL SIN	297
THE UNCONSCIOUS IS THE SEAT OF OUR GUILT	299
THE HIDDEN TRUTH BEHIND PINOCCHIO'S STORY	302
APPENDIX: MIND-BODY ALIGNMENT TECHNIQUES	305
ANGER IS YOUR DRUG	306
DISCOVER HOW META-MEDICINE HELPS HEALING	310
HEAL YOURSELF. NOW IT IS POSSIBLE WITH EFT	313
AN ALMOST MAGICAL PURIFICATION SYSTEM	316
MAKE THE LAW OF ATTRACTION WORK WITHOUT LIMITS	319
A DEMONSTRATION OF THE POWER OF HO'OPONOPONO	322
BIBLIOGRAPHY	325

Spiritual Awakening

Introduction

Spiritual Awakening is a somewhat unique book. It is a book that collects my notes and my thoughts that I have developed over several years, with the sole purpose of putting together my ideas and create a place where they can be reread and re-elaborated, in order to use them as a springboard for new thoughts.

A notebook, then, and should be considered as such. It is a collection of articles that appeared in my blog (www.campoquantico.it) over a span of about eight years, from 2012 to 2020. During my research, I have read many books, followed several teachers and attended countless seminars of many diverse disciplines and schools of thought. While advancing in this intricate journey, I realized that I was in front of something immense, an ocean of notions and ideas that left me completely lost, unable to come to terms with that infinite amount of concepts, sometimes even contradictory. Therefore, the first strong need was to put down on paper what I had come across and to put order in that tangled thicket of notions so as to draw a picture that was as consistent as possible and find a common thread that would allow me to make sense of the path I was undertaking.

So, opening a blog was the most obvious solution I could think of to put all my notes in order. That's how Campo Quantico was conceived, and the first article I wrote is the first chapter of this book. I must say that it worked, because having to expose the various topics to a community of readers, I had to work hard to describe the various concepts in the clearest and most coherent way possible, an effort that most likely I would have never done if those notes had been confined into a drawer. I don't know who wrote it, but I have to admit that the phrase "if you want to learn something, teach it" definitely worked for me. Later on, as I went further in my studies, I also discovered why this statement was true. It comes from a quantum concept, and in one of the articles in my blog I explain the underlying reasons of this eternal truth.

Regarding quantum physics, I believe that it was my passion for this scientific discipline that allowed me to elaborate most of the concepts expressed in this book, and I owe a lot to it, since it has covered, at least in the early days, the fundamental role of a lighthouse that guided me throughout my research path. I have been studying quantum physics since high school and I have always been convinced that thanks to it I would finally be able to discover one day the "Ultimate Truth" about the world. That idea never left me, and thanks to that firm conviction I never let it go, even when I was assailed by discouragement when I could not see any progress in my growth path. Not that today I have reached who knows what Truth, but I know for sure that this extensive work has allowed me to see the world with different eyes, and to face the vicissitudes of life with greater awareness.

Quantum physics had the role, at least for me, of a "picklock" through which it was possible to break the resistance that the rational mind placed every time I faced a particularly difficult issue that was going to clash strongly with all the burden of false beliefs that I always carried with me. The fact that a scientific experiment was able to demonstrate conclusively the truth of some physical phenomenon that was in sharp contrast with my previous beliefs has allowed me to go beyond and jump the obstacle represented by the natural inertia with which the rational mind is opposed to change.

Having written just over one hundred articles in more than eight years certainly does not place me among the most active bloggers. In fact, the average of about one article a month makes me a rather inactive writer, I must admit. But it is not laziness or unwillingness. The sporadic nature with which I have been updating my blog stems from the fact that I have rarely sat at the computer to deliberately write something new. Almost every article is the result of a sudden intuition, an idea that popped into my head when I least expected it, perhaps while I was doing or thinking about things that had nothing to do with the topics of my blog. When that intuition came, initially only as a vague idea, my mind was irresistibly dragged into a vortex of thoughts that led me to define and focus on the initial idea, until, once arrived at sufficient maturity, I felt the need to write a new article to define in an indelible way and give real consistency to the concepts thus developed.

Reading this book, therefore, means to retrace the history of my research, starting from quantum physics to elaborating concepts about the true nature of the world and ourselves. In this book, we will talk about many things, from how to apply the Law of Attraction, to how to improve ourselves through the knowledge of the mechanisms of our subconscious, but also more "esoteric" topics such as achieving inner peace through the work of alchemical transformation of negative emotions, and much more.

Although the topics covered are many, while reading *Spiritual Awakening* you will realize the existence of a basic concept on which is based almost every chapter of this book. The basic idea is that we are the only ones responsible for everything that happens. We are the origin of the world, and from this assumption derives the title of the book that you have in your hands. The fact that we are directly responsible for whatever happens in our lives is the fil rouge, the unquestionable idea that is never questioned, and that accompanies the reader throughout the discovery of the true laws that govern the world. The natural consequence is that the whole world is nothing but a mere illusion, a dream created by our mind, nothing that has real consistency. My studies, and consequently the blog from which this book derives, have always had the purpose of elaborating and dissecting in detail this concept trying to analyze the assumptions and reveal the most incredible and extraordinary consequences, laying the groundwork for a path to the discovery of our true nature, of which I was the first user, and that could be of support and guide for anyone who wanted to undertake the study.

I believe that the awareness that we are the only ones responsible for everything that happens is the first and indispensable step towards what can be called the "liberation" from the chains of the mind, a prison whose bars are not visible, but still not less binding. The castle of beliefs, mostly false, on which we have based our entire existence is the "golden prison" in which we have felt comfortable for a long time, but at some point, we began to perceive as limiting us immensely. This is the moment when we start looking for "something" that can relieve us from that sense of uneasiness that is the background to all things in life. We realize that we are ready to face the long and hard work of research when we discover that the "normality" to which we had become accustomed is no longer enough. At that point we find ourselves at a crossroads, where we have to make a decision from which we can no longer turn back. We have to decide whether to stay and live in that reassuring "normality" from which we feel completely estranged, or to take courage and leap over the ditch, to embark on a journey of self-discovery, a journey whose duration, complexity and final destination we know nothing about.

For me it has been of enormous help to collect my notes in a blog, since it has represented in a certain way, the track of the path taken, a bit like colored stones left along the way so as not to get lost in the forest, and I hope the same happens to the readers of this book.

After a first superficial analysis, the many topics addressed in these pages could seem somewhat disconnected from each other, but it is not so, since you cannot think of applying the Law of Attraction, for example, without having done profound work on yourself in order to limit the background noise represented by that little voice that speaks in our head and tells us of a world that does not exist, and in which we blindly believe. The world appears chaotic and uncontrollable precisely because it is nothing more than the reflection of what happens in our minds. The truth that will be revealed sooner or later before our eyes is that the Law of Attraction cannot be understood as the sole purpose of our research work. We will soon realize that if we approach the Law of Attraction with the sole purpose of obtaining material benefits, we will find ourselves back to square one. In fact, it will be very difficult to obtain results trying to apply it within our initial state of (un)awareness, but even if we succeed for some fortuitous combination to obtain results, we will soon realize that from the vibrational point of view the manifestation of a desire soon exhausts its effects, revealing the total impermanence of apparent happiness obtained through material gains. We would inevitably find ourselves again in search of the next dose of happiness, each time, forced to raise the bar to obtain even more.

What to do then? Should we suppress our every desire and give up on making our dreams come true? Absolutely not, let's welcome the study of the Law of Attraction, I would be hypocritical if I said otherwise, but let's do it with the knowledge that the only road that makes sense is the one of personal growth, the only one able to give us long-lasting satisfaction.

So, I tried to collect and order in this book the various articles of my blog with the aim of facilitating the reading in a manner that would follow a certain logic, grouping them within predetermined categories. Being scattered notes written over a very long period of time, however, it was not always possible to position each chapter according to a rigid logic of cataloging. This means that the different topics can sometimes appear in a not entirely congruent order, or the same concept could be repeated in several places, even if with different words each time.

Spiritual growth and personal growth are topics characterized by an almost infinite vastness, and each time you deal with a specific topic you can find a thousand other related topics that would be worth exploring. This book aims to serve, as it has served me, as a travel map, which will prevent us from getting lost and will allow us to realize the close correlation that exists between the various topics, even when appearances would suggest otherwise. Therefore, the most natural thing to do is to read the various chapters in the order in which they have been proposed in the book, but I cannot exclude that you could alternatively delve into one specific topic by reading only the articles related to it. Even if there is a path already traced, nothing prevents you from following the road in the order that suits you best.

I will leave you then with my notes, hoping you will find interesting food for your thoughts.

Paolo Marrone

The Strange World of Quantum Physics

In this first chapter, I will try to illustrate what science has discovered in recent decades and how these discoveries are revolutionizing the way of thinking of many.

Let's go in order, indeed no, let's start from the end, and that is, let's say immediately where I want to "go": the world as we see and perceive it does not exist, or rather, it exists only in our mind. Sounds crazy? It is, or rather, it may seem so because of our beliefs, rooted in our subconscious by hundreds or thousands of years of *common thought* (if everyone believes in one thing, it is easier to blindly believe, rather than question it).

Let's try to explain why.

Traditional or deterministic physics

Until the end of the nineteenth century, scientists were convinced that the world responded to *deterministic* physics, where the first rule was that every action was the natural consequence of a cause, whatever it was. For example, it is normal for all of us to accept that if we apply a force to an object, it begins to move with an accelerated motion, proportional to the force impressed. From this it follows that, knowing all the variables involved (mass, impressed force, air resistance, ...) one could easily determine the trajectory (in terms of position and speed) of the object at any subsequent moment. Extending this concept, deterministic physics states that, if we could measure all the properties of the elementary particles that make up the Universe, and having the necessary computational power available, we could accurately calculate the evolution of the Universe itself in any future instant.

Logical, isn't it? Too bad the truth is different.

In the 1920s, a new theory made its way among scientists, a theory that attempted to explain strange results that were being shown in scientific laboratories, which were in total disagreement with traditional physics.

Quantum physics (i.e., the world does not work as we imagined it)

In the early years of the twentieth century, some scientists (M. Planck, N. Bohr and others) developed a theory (supported by numerous real experiments) according to which the true nature of matter is not corpuscular (or at least not only), but has an intrinsic wave nature, where each wave describes the probability that a certain particle exists at a certain point in spacetime.

Probability??? Yes, every particle does not exist as we imagine it, i.e., as a small "lump" of matter (or as a ball, as erroneously drawn in many physics texts), but as a simple wave of probability. The particle *might* be here, but with a different probability it *might* be there instead. Or anywhere else, with different probabilities.

Okay, but who decides where exactly the particle should appear if a scientist tried to measure its position? Hold on tight: who decides is the scientist himself, through the act of observation.

In other words, as long as no one observes the particle, it exists only as a probability wave, while as soon as some "observer" decides to observe it, then the wave disappears (physicists say it collapses), and in its place appears the particle. Where is it? Exactly where the observer expects to find it.

Strange but true. Scientists are realizing more and more that the observer, unlike what was believed in traditional physics, has a central role in determining the effects of any physical phenomenon.

More exactly, the observer has a decisive role in *creating* the reality that surrounds us.

The Creator in Each of Us

At this point, the conclusions that can be drawn are absolutely shocking. If we determine, through observation, the existence of any particle, it is self-evident that we are the "Creators" of our reality. How do we create? The answer is astounding (at least apparently): believe it or not, we create matter with our mind by exercising our thinking.

We do it every day, unconsciously, simply by thinking about what our daily reality is, based on our beliefs about how reality should be.

Going a little further, we can hypothesize that the world out there does not exist until we imagine it, and by imagining it we create it.

Perhaps there is no concept of *out there* separate from *in here* (our mind), as everything must exist in our mind before manifesting out there. Reality is most likely just a projection of our thoughts.

But we will return to this very soon in other chapters.

The World Appears Only When Needed

Several times we have heard it said that "there is only the here and now", but perhaps we have never wondered what it really meant. Let's find out together in this chapter.

For those who have read my book "The monk with no past", we are in the last chapter, when after having dined with the disciples, the Master takes me to the great hall of the monastery to continue our talk, sipping tea, sitting on large purple cushions.

This is what the Master told me at a certain point, in response to my question in which I asked him if I could go back to that monastery and meet him again:

"You believe you are dealing with people who exist outside of you, and have their own history. You think that for all the people who have come into your life, but that's not the case. You are in a dream, and everything that is part of it materializes when needed…"

What did he mean by this sentence? In what sense does the world *materialize when needed?*

What the Master is simply telling me, perhaps in a simpler, more concrete and direct way, is that there is nothing but the Here and Now.

Ok, we have heard the affirmation that there is only the Here and Now who knows how many times, and now we take it for granted, no longer considering it as something strange or incomprehensible.

Perhaps you have not properly evaluated the real meaning of that sentence. The problem is that we take too many things for granted, and we have therefore lost the habit of asking ourselves questions to deepen the various concepts.

About the *Now*, there is little debate. But about the *Here*, how do we put it?

There is only the Here and Now. Well. Regarding the Now, or the present moment, probably few will have any doubts, because we have heard it many times that time is only an illusion, and that therefore past and future do not really exist, but are only our mental construction. The statement therefore, that there is only the present moment does not bother us, having somehow made friends with this concept. I do not want to dwell on why time is just an illusion, because it is a subject that is dealt with several times in this book, and I will deal with it again.

Let's dwell instead on the concept that there is only the *Here*. Have you ever wondered what this means? Fasten your seat belts, because we are about to embark on a journey that will lead us to draw some shocking conclusions, but don't worry, I will take you a little at a time, leading you by the hand, trying not to lose anyone along the way.

The title of this chapter should have already given you some clues, but there is a little voice inside your head that refuses to make it to the final conclusion. While it is the most logical explanation, it upsets every old logic on which you have based your whole life. Until now.

Anyone who has seen the beautiful film *"The Thirteenth Floor"* (if you haven't seen it yet, do it, it's worth it), will surely remember that one of the protagonists at some point undertakes a journey by car, to verify with his eyes if the idea that he was living in a computer simulation was true.

Well, our character at a certain point, after having violated a multitude of signals that told him to stop and not go further, finds the *"borders of his world"*, where beyond a certain limit only one "draft" of the world exists, consisting of a "wireframe" representation, like those of computerized images. Anyone who is familiar with video game programming knows very well that video games scenes are built when needed, representing only and exclusively the details that are displayed on the screen. In other words, when in the course of the game we leave an environment to enter another, the old environment is no longer "rendered", since it is no longer useful, it avoids wasting precious processing time to build objects and walls that are not are no longer displayed.

So, in a video game (as well as in the film I mentioned), the statement that there is only the here and now is fully valid and verifiable. Past scenes simply no longer exist. Only what is under the player's direct vision is created instant by instant.

But what actually happens?

Well yes, I am about to say it, even if perhaps you do not want to hear it:

Just like in a video game, even in reality only and exclusively the things that are under our direct perception are materialized.

Here I use the term "perception" because all five senses must be included, not just sight. I clearly hear that little voice in your head that is suggesting that this is all madness, and is urging you to leave this page, cursing the time wasted reading this far.

Stop, because I promised to lead you by the hand all the way, and that is what I am going to do. You have surely heard of the double-slit experiment, the one in which quantum physics managed to experimentally prove that matter only exists when it is observed. I would say "perceived", because as I have already said, all five senses must be considered in the same way. I will repeat, in case it is not clear:

When a particle is not observed, it simply does not exist. What exists in its place is only a probability wave, which indicates the probability with which the particle can appear at a certain point in spacetime when observed. No observation, no particle.

This means that if at this moment none of your senses have the perception of what is inside your house by the sea, 50 km away, for quantum physics that house, and all that it contains, simply does not exist. How is it possible that the house does not exist? But if I go there, I see it, and I can also go in, you will object. Sure, but when you go there, you are observing the house, and therefore you are materializing it when necessary. How can that house materialize always in the same, usual place, with the same color walls and roof? Simple, because according to quantum physics what you perceive is the materialization (or collapse) of the wave function that describes that house.

The wave function can be thought of as a "thought shape" that exists in our mind. The house is recreated moment by moment according to the *thought shape* or "idea" you have of that house.

In short, everything that is not under our direct perception simply does not exist, and is consequently materialized, when necessary, at the exact moment in which we perceive it. This is why, in addition to the now, there is only the "here".

But it could not be otherwise, considering that we live within a dream. If in a night dream you dream of a house, and then changing your dream or moving away from it you no longer see it, when you wake up do you believe that that house continued to exist somewhere even when it was no longer part of your dream? Of course not, it was just an image in your mind that you recreate when needed.

Well, consider that this world that feels so real to you is also an image in your mind, just in case you find it difficult to accept what I have just said in this chapter.

But Who Is This Observer?

We have been talking, or have often heard of the Observer. But who is he in reality? We tend to think that the Observer is the person observing, therefore ultimately ourselves, but you will be amazed to discover that perhaps it makes no sense to speak of an Observer.

I would like to start from a beautiful phrase by Søren Kierkegaard, a Danish philosopher and writer who lived in the 19th century:

What you see depends on how you look. Since observing is not just receiving, revealing, but at the same time it is a creative act.

A *creative act*. Let's dwell on this concept, and try to understand what it means to *observe*, so as to be able to understand who or what the Observer is.

In this book we have already talked about the experiment of the double-slits, through which science has been able to elaborate a new vision of the world, in which objects no longer exist regardless of who observes them, but in fact appear only and exclusively when they are observed. Without observation there is no world to experience.

This concept is still a source of great debate within the scientific community today, because it is clear that if the world does not exist when it is not observed, it is self-evident that it is **Observation** that actually creates the world we see. For official science, this goes far beyond what can be considered acceptable, because it would imply the introduction of the concept of creation, and therefore of human beings as creators of the world, which at the moment cannot find an official place within the rigid and *plastered* scientific thinking.

For, like it or not, it is creation. Without *observation* there is no matter, and therefore no world. It is from here that we start to understand who this elusive Observer could be.

Read again the words I used, because they have a precise meaning. I wrote that **observation** creates matter. Why didn't I use the word "*Observer*"?

Because maybe it does not exist, and we are about to find out why.

ATTENTION: What follows will not please your ego at all, which, seeing its existence put in serious danger, will introduce into your mind the thought "this is all nonsense", making you believe moreover that you are thinking it. If you identify with your ego, my advice is to stop reading here. I warned you, do not comment then that you cannot believe these things. It is not you who says it, but your ego. Disidentification begins with knowing how to recognize the true origin of our thoughts.

As two sides of the same coin

Let's start with the assumption (proven through laboratory experiments) that a particle appears only when it is observed. Well. Let's ask ourselves *healthy* questions now.

In our reasoning there are three apparently very distinct entities:

The Particle, the Observation and the Observer.

Let's see who depends on whom.

In the absence of the observation, does the Observer exist? Of course not. Don't tell me that an Observer exists apart from observation, because you are taking for granted something that is not. An Observer is an Observer only when he observes, otherwise he can be anything else: a plumber, a fireman, a teacher, etc.

Imagine arriving on the shore of a lake and seeing a man standing near the shore perfectly dressed in trousers, jacket, etc. When asked "is there a swimmer?", the only possible answer is no, because there is no one swimming in the lake. If that person at some point takes off his clothes remaining in his bathing suit, and dives into the water and starts swimming, the answer to the same question will be yes, of course. The swimmer is a swimmer only when **he performs the act of swimming**, otherwise he is anything other than a swimmer.

The same goes for the Observer.

Am I boring you? I hope not, because now comes the fun. So, if the Observer exists only when there is observation, we can say that the **Observer depends on observation**. You have probably believed the opposite until now, but this comes from the fact that we tend to take things for granted that are not at all.

We are getting closer in small steps. Let's go on.

The other question is: does the particle exist without observation? Of course not, but I do not think anyone has anything to say about this. There are scientific experiments that prove this to us. **The particle also depends on observation.**

Well. If the Observer and the particle exist only in the presence of **observation**, it goes without saying that all that exists is precisely *observation*. It's like a medal. Its two faces cannot exist without the coin itself, and therefore cannot be separated and have an autonomous existence. Have you ever seen the face of a medal without the medal? In fact, all three are one, just like our trio of particle, observation and observer.

There is only observation, therefore, the act of observing. And the Observer? It is only our supposition to believe in the existence of an Observer and an observed object. They do not have and cannot have a life of their own. Are you there? I repeat, there is nothing other than Observation (now I can finally write it with a capital letter). In other words, we take for granted the existence of things that, in fact, do not exist, but ultimately, we do not live in a world of people or things. **We live in a world of events.**

Observation is a very specific event, after which we hypothesize the existence of an observer and an observed object. I will give you an example.

If I look at a glass, everything that happens in my Consciousness is the event (or act) of Observation, which makes me experience observing a glass. All that exists is the event, because only the result of the act of Observation arrives in our mind. It cannot be otherwise, think about it. Following this, however, we are immediately led to believe that there is a subject (ourselves) that is observing, and an object (the glass) that is being observed. But both the first and the second in fact do not exist, because in the absence of Observation, they could not have any possibility of existing.

So, do you understand where the illusion of the existence of an 'I' (to which we desperately cling to build our own identity) and of an apparently distinct and separate "world" comes from? Not only are they one, but they do not actually exist. They are just the result of a supposition, made on the basis of a single event, Observation, which is the only thing that exists in our mind.

So, we are not the observer, because this is an abstract concept, deriving from our (erroneous) assumption that if there is Observation, then there must also be the observer. But if the observer does not have an existence of its own, independent of Observation, who are we?

We are pure Consciousness, within which *"events"* happen.

We can call these events **Observations**, if we like, or use any other term, but what matters is to understand that this is the only thing, I want to highlight, **the only thing that exists**.

Everything else is the result of pure assumptions. Call them illusions, if you like.

What if It Was Due to Temporal Entanglement?

What if quantum entanglement worked not only between two distant particles in space, but also for two events separated in time? Let's delve into this hypothesis and see its implications.

Some time ago I discovered on YouTube a beautiful video that exposes a very important quantum concept, in which the events of the future seem to influence past events in some way, materializing exactly those that are needed to reach the observed event.

The video uses the example of the sun's rays hitting the cells of a plant, allowing it to generate chlorophyll, an essential substance for its survival. Well, every ray of light, according to traditional physics, would have a very low probability of reaching the point in the leaf where it could trigger the chlorophyll transformation, given that along its way it could encounter thousands of obstacles represented by the myriad of other elements present in a leaf.

Yet photosynthesis is a real process, so much so that plants exist, and are able to live thanks to this extraordinary biological mechanism. What actually happens? It happens that according to quantum physics the infinite quantum states that represent all the possible trajectories of each photon are "superimposed", that is, they all exist simultaneously until observation takes place. The act of observation causes only one of all possible states to collapse (that is, to become real), and causes only that particular trajectory to be followed. So how is the right trajectory chosen? Well, it is the observation of the fact that the plant is alive, that allows only the correct trajectories to materialize.

In other words, the very fact that the plant is alive in the here and now ensures that only the trajectories of light rays useful for the realization of this *"fact"* are allowed, and therefore become reality.

It is as if the observed state affects its past, causing th
to adapt so that what is observed can be realized.

Thinking about this, I also thought about t
"influence" on the past occurs immediately, at zero ......
Universe "jumped" onto a different timeline. Which one? The one that contains in its past all the events that justify what I am observing now. What else?

What if temporal entanglement was involved?

Influence at a distance in no time? Um, this reminds me of something ... Think about quantum entanglement? For those who do not know what it is, I will explain it very briefly.

Entanglement is a physical phenomenon observed in scientific laboratories, in which if you make two particles interact with each other, and then make them travel away from each other, anything you do to one of the two particles immediately affects, at zero time, the other particle, regardless of their distance.

This phenomenon would apparently violate Einstein's relativity (so much so that the great scientist initially contested this theory), because in order to influence the other particle at zero time, the information would have to travel at infinite speed, which is impossible for Einstein's relativity, according to which the speed of light (about 300,000 km / second) is an insurmountable limit.

Then one of the two: either the theory of relativity is wrong, or the distance that separates the two particles does not exist, and is therefore only illusory. Well, the second hypothesis is the right one, and this principle gives a scientific justification for the affirmation of many Eastern doctrines that we are all One, and that separation is only a mere illusion. In fact, the two particles represent two different views **of the same thing.**

But returning to the hypothesis made at the beginning of this chapter, according to which the observed events affect in zero time the events of the past that are the apparent cause, here we perhaps find many similarities.

If everything is One, it cannot be only spatially, but it must be also temporally, otherwise what One would be?

So, do you see that entanglement operates not only spatially, but also temporally? In fact, we live in a spacetime continuum in which separation, both of space and time is only apparent. Each event affects the entire Universe, but not only at spatial level, but also at temporal level, determining the past, based on the observation that is made in the here and now. In the moment in which we observe something, (even with our thoughts), **an entire Universe is recreated**, with all its specific past, containing only the events that make "real" what we are observing in the here and now.

It is only my idea, of course, a bit of a bizarre idea that no scientist has ever hypothesized (although it has certainly something to do with the concept of syntropy by Luigi Fantappiè). But the more bizarre the ideas are, the more we like them, don't we?

That Weird Experiment on Time

Is it possible to change the past? Probably anyone, faced with this question, would answer no. Instead, there is an experiment in quantum physics that demonstrates that this is possible, and if you want to know more, you just have to read this chapter to the end...

You have probably all heard of the double-slit experiment before. In that experiment, particles were passed through a panel on which two slits had been opened (in the original experiment conceived by T. Young in 1802, the light of a candle was used, but then the experiment was repeated a century later using different particles, including electrons), and based on the image reproduced on the back wall it was possible to deduce whether the photons were behaving as particles or as waves.

The following image provides a fairly faithful, albeit simplified, representation of how Young's experiment was performed:

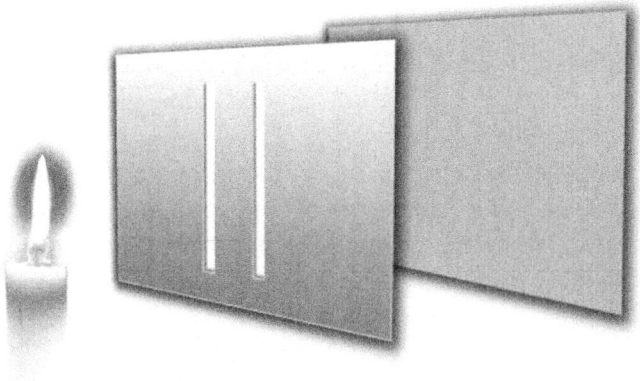

21

Normally several lighter bands are formed on the back wall (not just two as one would expect), and this demonstrates the fact that the particles behave like waves when not observed. I am not here to explain the reason for this, but those who want to know more can find on the Internet many pages that discuss it in more or less depth (e.g., on Wikipedia).

Scientists discovered that when a sensor is placed before one of the two slits, in order to "observe" which electrons pass through that slot, the figure projected on the wall changes, showing only two lighter bands, demonstrating the fact that electrons, when observed, no longer behave like waves, but like particles.

So far everything is normal, because this experiment has been performed countless times using electrons, photons, protons, etc. always obtaining the exact same result, which proves irrefutably that a particle behaves as such **only when it is observed**.

Things got really strange when, following an idea elaborated in 1978 by physicist J.A. Wheeler, some scientists from the Australian National University tried to investigate the phenomenon further, carrying out the so-called *delayed choice experiment*, through which they tried to understand how, but especially when, the observer influences the behavior of the particle he is observing.

The only difference compared to the previous experiment was that in this second version the sensor was no longer placed before the slit, but *after it*. This means that when the particle passes through the slit, **it cannot know whether it will be observed once beyond it**. Well, even in this case the figure that appeared on the back wall was made up of **only two lighter bands**, thus indicating that the electron had behaved like a particle. But what does this have to do with time?

It has something to do with it, because in order to make the two lighter bands appear on the back wall, the electrons would have to pass through the two slits as "particles". But from the first experiment we know for sure that when not observed, electrons behave like waves. In this second experiment, therefore, the sensor was placed after the slits, and the electrons still made the decision to pass as particles, as if they knew in advance that they would have been observed beyond the slits.

Basically, it is as if the electron, once in front of the sensor, was able to somehow warn itself in the past, so that it could change its behavior.

To make an analogy, it is as if, driving on a road in a car, after passing in front of a speed camera, we will warn ourselves in the past of the presence of those speed cameras, so that we can take our foot off the accelerator in time.

Is the past modifiable?

Is it therefore possible to influence our past in some way? It would seem so, and the experiment of the Australian National University proves it. But since we are not satisfied with appearances, let's try to really understand what this experiment would show us.

Of course, it is not possible to "warn" oneself in the past of something happening in the present. Probably to understand this experiment we need to get out of the normal canons with which we are used to reasoning and start to question what we think we know about reality, and in particular about time.

This experiment is perhaps the practical demonstration of the fact that time is only an illusion, and that therefore there is only the present, the here and now. **The past and the future are just wrong assumptions** about how the world works. Both of these concepts have nothing real, they are only mental constructions, and as such they exist only within our mind.

How then can we explain the delayed choice experiment we have just described? We can do this **only if we dismantle what we believe in the law of cause and effect**. We have always believed until now that the past irreversibly determines the present, in the sense that something is as it appears because events have occurred in its past that have determined its current state. This experiment completely overturns this concept, because we are faced with the demonstration that **the entire past is actually determined by the present**. In other words, whenever an observation is made, not only the current state of the observed object is determined, but its apparent past is also determined. But which past is chosen among the infinitely possible? Of course, **the one that justifies what you are observing**.

It is as if with each observation one enters a **parallel universe**, endowed with its own present (determined by the observation carried out), and with the corresponding past that justifies that present.

This conclusion can be the only plausible one, assuming that **all that exists is the here and now**. Everything else is only the result of an illusion, determined by what happens in the perceived here and now.

Change your worldview and the world will change

What is the conclusion? The world does not work as we have always believed and quantum physics can represent the way to escape from the mental cage in which we have lived until today, made up of false beliefs and limitations. Understanding that Ultimate Reality allows us to see the world with different eyes, and since we create that world, it appears exactly as we believe it should appear. This means that a different view of reality can only change the way that reality manifests itself.

Have You Ever Wondered How Big You Are?

Maybe you do not know how big you are. You are not only bigger than your body, but also bigger than the whole planet, let's say that you are as big as the whole Universe. Don't you believe it? Read and you will know why.

All of us are mistakenly convinced that we are limited by the confines of our body. In fact, we identify with the body itself, which for us represents the entirety of our being, believing that beyond the surface of our skin there is the rest of the world. Even those who believe that man possesses a spirit, usually imagine it within themselves, thinking that the spiritual essence is located somewhere in the body. These are only erroneous beliefs, I would dare to say stupid superstition, partly artfully constructed to prevent us from becoming aware of our true greatness.

If we want to evolve spiritually, we must necessarily get out of this erroneous and limited view of reality. Each of us is much bigger than our own body, and in this chapter, I will try to prove it.

Quantum physics has shown us, on several occasions, that in reality the world we perceive does not exist outside of us. We are the ones containing the world, not the other way around.

We are all more or less familiar with the double-slit experiment, which found that a particle simply does not exist until it is observed. It is the act of observation that makes it real. Without observation, and therefore in the absence of an Observer, any particle exists only as a probability wave, which is nothing more than a mathematical formula describing how likely the particle will appear at different points in spacetime, if observed.

Well, have you ever wondered what a mathematical formula is? A formula is just an abstraction, a way to describe a concept. Nothing tangible, so much so that no one has ever seen a mathematical formula wandering the streets of his city. A concept is something that exists only in the mind of the one who formulates that concept.

For this reason, we can say with absolute certainty that the world that appears so solid and real to us is in reality only the projection of our ideas or thoughts.

What does this have to do with our greatness? It has something to do with it, because it demonstrates without a shadow of a doubt that the entire Universe is contained within us, but as I say in my books, since the container cannot be smaller than what it contains, we must assume that we are necessarily as **large as the Universe itself**.

When you look at any star in the sky, it is you who, through the act of observation, are making that star real; if it were not observed, it simply would not exist.

I understand that it is difficult to believe what I am saying, but it is the reality. In short, the Universe cannot exist apart from an Observer who makes its existence possible.

Who is the Observer?

Here we enter into a very interesting discourse, which can reveal, in a truly surprising way, who we really are. We are close to a great discovery, do not give up and read on. The best is yet to come.

It is clear that we are the Observer. But it is also clear that at the same time we are the ones who are being observed. We can indeed observe ourselves, our body, our mind. In other words, we can "conceptualize", and thus observe, ourselves.

So, who is this Observer really? I would call it our True Self. One who is outside of time and space and represents **who we really are**.

What if we wanted to see it? In short, what do I do if I want to somehow get in touch with the Observer, and therefore understand who I really am?

But at this point another question arises: **can the Observer be observed?** The answer is no, because to observe something you have to look at it from a point outside of it.

But if the Observer is as large as the Universe, there is no point beyond which to observe it. And in any case, in order to observe the Observer, I have to construct an image or a concept of it to project and observe. However, when I make the Observer observable, it is no longer there, because I am only observing *the observed*, that is the part of me that I can conceptualize.

Here is the great discovery: **I cannot observe the Observer**, so the only thing possible is to *"become"* the Observer. In other words, if I start meditating to get in touch with my True Self, the only plausible thing I can do is to identify with it and through it contemplate myself and the nature of things.

You cannot see the Observer, you can only become one. The search for your True Self ends where you understand that you can never find it.

This is what the essence of meditation is. The only sensible thing you can do is **to merge with the Observer** and observe, with absolute stillness, the wonderful result of your Creation.

Is Reality a Large Quantum Computer?

Does the Law of Attraction really exist? How is it possible that in a world made of solid things, an evanescent and impalpable thought can have the power to change reality? There is only one possible answer to this and many other questions: we live in a quantum reality, and if you want to know how this can give you the answers you are looking for, well you just have to keep reading…

You have surely read many things regarding the Law of Attraction, and you have often heard it alongside quantum physics. You have been told that thought can change reality, and to justify this concept the double-slit experiment has been used, in which scientists have shown that matter does not seem to exist when it is not observed.

Okay, very interesting, but I bet you were left with a thousand doubts about the true meaning of all this, and the questions that float in your head are always the same: how the hell is it possible that a simple thought can change the reality I experience? And is this Law of Attraction really true? Well, among all the explanations you were given, perhaps the most important and fundamental one is missing, and strangely enough, the answer does not come from quantum physics laboratories, but from those of **computer science**.

Computer science? Yes, you got it right, the simplest explanation that can be given of the Law of Attraction comes precisely from the new discoveries in the field of computers, more precisely from **quantum computers** (well, to be honest, quantum physics always has to do with it, but here we are talking about it a little differently).

What is a quantum computer

Let's start by explaining what a quantum computer is and how it works. It should be noted that these computers are not yet available on the market, but only exist in prototype form in some research laboratories. You can find a more in-depth explanation on Wikipedia[1], but here we will try to explain it as briefly and clearly as possible.

A quantum computer completely distorts the concept of the computer as we have known it up to now. To understand it, we have to start from **traditional computers**, that is, those we all use for our work. In traditional computers, there is a central processing unit (the CPU), able to execute in sequence a large number of commands, or instructions, that a programmer has written within a program.

To give an example, if a traditional computer (the one inside your mobile phone, for example) has to find the shortest way between two points on a road map, it performs more or less these steps in sequence:

1. It searches all possible routes between the two points.

2. It calculates for each of them the distance and the travel time.

3. It puts them in order from the shortest to the longest, or from the fastest to the slowest.

4. It shows us the path that turned out to be the best.

This is what is called a **program**, and you need a programmer who has been able to identify all the steps necessary to solve the problem, and has transcribed them into understandable instructions for the computer.

In traditional computers, therefore, there must necessarily be a programmer who already knows **the way to solve the problem**,

---

[1] https://en.wikipedia.org/wiki/Quantum_computing

because the computer does not have the faintest idea of **how to solve it** without someone pointing it out. The computer on our desk, or in our smartphone, is just a **stupid executor** of instructions someone else wrote for it.

Now let's see how a **quantum computer** works. In this case there is neither a program nor a programmer who must know in advance all the necessary steps to arrive at the solution of the problem. In quantum computers, instead, all that needs to be provided are the "requirements" or "constraints" that must be respected. In our example, all we need to know is that we want to get from point A to point B on the shortest (or fastest) route.

The quantum computer exploits a property of quantum physics according to which each of its single computation units (called qubits, and there can be thousands or millions of them in a single computer) can simultaneously have several **superimposed states**. Such a computer could simultaneously consider all possible solutions to a given problem. According to the imposed requirements, the quantum computer will "settle" on a single combination of states that will satisfy these constraints. In our example it is as if all the computation units of the quantum computer can cross **simultaneously** all the roads that go from A to B, and based on the constraint imposed, the computer will "choose" the combination corresponding to the path that will turn out to be the shortest. Why does this happen? Simply because the final state, the one that solves the problem, is **the only one possible** among all the possible states, given the initial requirements. Everything else simply cannot happen.

With an analogy, it is like throwing water on a downhill boulevard. Among all the possible paths water will choose to channel in the only possible direction, that is, in the direction of the descent. Not because water can make decisions, but simply because according to the laws of physics it can do nothing else (in this case the constraint imposed is that of the law of gravity, which cannot be violated).

Let's summarize: in a quantum computer you do not have to know **how to** solve the problem, but all you need is to **choose what** you want. The quantum computer, among all the infinite existing solutions, will choose only the one that will satisfy the imposed constraints. Not because it is intelligent, nor because it already knows the solution, but simply because it is **the only thing it is allowed to do**, given the initial constraints.

You don't know, but you are living in a huge quantum computer

Well, scientists have discovered that the real physics that governs this reality is quantum physics, so it is as if we lived inside a huge quantum computer. The books dealing with the Law of Attraction have told you that you must **choose** your desire and then not worry about **how** it will be fulfilled. Do you understand now why? Read again how a quantum computer works, and it will immediately become clear to you that you live in a reality where all possible futures exist
simultaneously in a potential state. Which one will materialize? Only the one that meets the requirements, of course. The universe can do nothing else.

But what are these requirements and who decides them?

They are **your desires**, of course, and **you decide**, who else?

Matrix: Discover the Flaws of the System

If we really live in an illusory world, there must necessarily be flaws that reveal that we are inside an imaginary system. Let's find out together if these flaws exist, and what they are.

Those who work with computers know very well that sooner or later, any computer, even the most sophisticated, will show some flaws that reveal its artificial nature. For this reason, even today it is not possible to simulate complex behaviors on the computer, such as human thinking, because for an expert user it would be relatively easy to find some evident "symptoms" of the fact that what he is dealing with is not a real human being, but only a mechanized simulation (for those interested in learning more about these concepts, I recommend reading about the Turing Test[2]).

By now it should be clear to everyone that the basic idea I am describing in this book, deriving from some concepts of quantum physics, is that we live in an illusory world created by us, and that everything we see as apparently real is only the result of a great illusion, of which we have forgotten that we are the only creators and protagonists.

If so, there must be some "flaws" that could reveal the illusory nature of this world. Those who have seen the Matrix movie may remember that Neo at one point has the confirmation of being inside a simulation by noticing a cat that for two consecutive times performs the exact same gesture[3].

And in our world? Are there any flaws that allow us to realize that we are inside an illusion created by our mind?

---

[2] https://en.wikipedia.org/wiki/Turing_test

[3] https://youtu.be/z_KmNZNT5xw

Of course, they exist, but before revealing them, it is a good idea to make some useful premises.

Don't expect to see a cat appearing twice in the same spot performing the exact same movements (although in theory it would be possible). It is necessary to analyze one of the main properties of the illusion in which we are immersed in order to look into the right direction and have any chance of finding a flaw.

So, let's start with a quantum physics experiment, which reveals a fundamental property of the world in which we live. I am talking about Quantum Entanglement[4], a physical effect in which two particles that have interacted in some way, even when separated by enormous distances, continue to behave as if they were a single particle. Any measurement made on one of the two particles will determine **instantly** the state of the other, even if at that moment they are separated by billions of light years. This principle would apparently violate one of the postulates of Einstein's Theory of Relativity, according to which nothing can travel faster than the speed of light. The fact that two particles can communicate **in zero time over immense distances would**, in fact, presuppose that something can travel at infinite speed in order to alert the other particle of what is happening to its remote twin.

Assuming that the speed of light is really not surpassable (as demonstrated by countless experiments), it is evident that the two particles actually **are one**, and that the space that separates them is only an illusion created by our mind. This, if you will, is the scientific demonstration of the fact that **we are all One**, an idea so dear to some Eastern religions.

If we are expression of one thing, then the question that arises spontaneously is:

---

[4] https://en.wikipedia.org/wiki/Quantum_entanglement

Why do we see things separate from us? Is there any "sign" that can indicate the intrinsic reality of the world in which we live?

If we are expression of one entity, there could probably be something that could reveal *"the trick"*, this singular **"uniqueness"** of all things.

This flaw exists, it does exist. Indeed, there are at least two. Let's see them together.

The inviolability of the law of the mirror

You are probably already familiar with the law of the mirror, according to which all the characteristics we observe in others are only aspects of ourselves that we project outwards. Well, you might say, what does this have to do with the flaw we are talking about? The strange phenomenon that I am about to illustrate is just one of those "flaws" we are looking for.

One thing few people know about the law of the mirror is that **it is literally impossible to use it on others**. I will explain. For example, if you are trying to apply the law of the mirror to someone else's behavior (for example because they are criticizing a trait they don't like in some other person) and you think, *"See? He is criticizing a characteristic of himself that he does not know he has"*, in reality you have fallen into the trap of the law of the mirror yourself. The fact that you have noticed the propensity to criticize in the other, unequivocally reveals your propensity to criticize. It is the law of the mirror, there is no escape, in any way.

The fact that we are all One is revealed explicitly to us in the impossibility of being able to exercise *towards others* the law of the mirror. Why does this happen? Because *others do not exist*, of course, they are only our projections, and therefore **when we think of applying the law of the mirror to others, we are in fact applying it to ourselves**. A mirror always reflects, wherever you look at it. What I have just illustrated therefore clearly highlights the presence of this mirror, even if it is apparently invisible to us. So here is the first flaw revealed. Let's now look at the second one.

Do not judge, so that you will not be judged

Don't judge, so that you will not be judged. For in the way you judge, you will be judge; and by your standard of measure, it will be measured to you. (Matthew 7,1)

Here is the second flaw revealed even through the words of Jesus.

Imagine this scene: you are in line at the post office and the person they are serving in front of you is taking a long time to complete his operations. You then complain, snort, judging the other rude for the little consideration he has for the people who are waiting in line behind him. Then it is your turn, and for some reason (for example the printer jams), you too take a long time to complete your operations. At this point, even if no one is complaining, you feel embarrassed and uncomfortable, due to the fact that you sense the negative judgment of the people queuing behind you.

In reality, those people are most likely not complaining, so you would have no reason to feel embarrassed. What is actually happening? The reality is that all that judgment (which is nothing but negative energy) that you had previously expressed towards the one who seemed separate from you, was actually being expressed *towards yourself*.

All is one, and so when you judge someone else you are actually judging yourself. So here is another flaw that clearly and incontrovertibly shows us the fact that **we are all One**. Apparently, we see others separate from us, but the system always shows us behaviors that reveal their real nature. It is enough to have eyes to see them.

The world is within you, so stop fighting the world, because in reality you are just having a stupid fight with yourself.

The Probability of Something Happening Depends Only on Us

We have always been taught to believe that only some things are possible, and that the probability of them happening depends only on external factors. Let's demystify this misconception by looking at how things really are.

We have always thought, because this is how they led us to believe, that the world works with very precise and immutable rules, and that these rules determine the occurrence of events. On the basis of this belief, we are convinced that not everything is possible, and that in the context of possible things, the probability of events happening follows predetermined rules.

To give an example, we do not believe at all that the water inside a pot placed on a lit stove can freeze, or that a broken egg can be magically recomposed.

We deceive ourselves. But before we see why, let's try to understand the difference between **possibility and probability**.

When we think about the **possibility** of something happening, we normally think in terms of YES / NO or possible / impossible. This is correct from a mathematical point of view, and the difference with respect to **probability** lies precisely in the fact that the latter can have any value between 0 and 100, in percentage terms, or between 0 and 1 in absolute terms.

Apart from mathematical considerations, we can say that **possibility** tells us if something can or cannot happen in absolute terms, and only if the possibility is not zero, then the **probability** tells us how likely it is that that event will happen. To give an example, from a physical point of view it is possible that boiling water becomes a block of ice, but the probability of it happening is so small that it can be easily approximated to zero.

Our misconceptions about possibility and probability

Perfect. This is what, apparently, the functioning of every physical event seems to be based on. Now let's take it all apart by describing how things really are, for both of these concepts.

Let's start with the **possibility**. In fact, possibility is a concept invented by the limited human mind, which believes that there is a real world outside of it that respects certain rules; rules that would in fact "forbid" the occurrence of some events.

Quantum physics has shown that, by investigating deeper and deeper, matter does not actually exist, but it is simply a particular form of energy (remember Einstein's formula $E = MC2$). A table is solid not because its constituent particles are themselves solid, but because of the laws of electromagnetism, which are nothing more than a form of energy, impalpable energy.

Another shocking discovery is that all particles appear and disappear from the Universe all the time. Imagine an empty space (which is actually not empty) as an immense boiling broth, from which particles continually emerge, and then immediately disappear in the same broth. This phenomenon is called quantum fluctuation by physicists.

What's that broth? That broth is **quantum nothing**. Attention, nothing does not mean the absence of everything, but rather the presence of everything, in terms of potential only. I see your questioning faces, so let me explain. To say that quantum nothing contains all conceivable things, means that from that **anything** can potentially grow. So, returning to our concept, **anything is possible**. Anything, without exception.

And then, if there are no impossible things, the concept of possibility simply falls apart. It is a pure invention of the human mind, not supported by any scientific theory.

Ok, now we know that anything is possible. But who or what decides how likely a certain thing happens? Well, I am sure you already know the answer. The mind of the Observer, that is us, decides the probability. All the particles and forces of the Universe obey only and exclusively the rules that we give them, with our thoughts and our beliefs.

Our mind extracts from that broth only what it believes it is possible to extract. The particles of the chair on which we are sitting disappear continuously in that quantum nothing, and then reappear exactly in the same place where they disappeared, giving us the illusion of the existence of a chair that has always been there. Particles appear within that region of spacetime that we call a chair only because our minds do not accept as possible that a chair dissolves into nothing, suddenly changes shape or reappears 3 meters away.

Ok, so let's get to the practical conclusions. What can we do with these new concepts of possibility and probability? We can definitely begin to change the way we think, and that means we can begin to affect our reality. In the future, whenever you find yourself in trouble for any reason, start to think that **nothing is impossible**, and that the probability of finding the solution to the problem depends only on how much we believe it is possible to find it. Begin to use our mind in a different, more positive and constructive way, and you will see that the Universe can only indulge our new thoughts.

I will leave you with the words of James Jeans, astronomer and physicist:

The universe begins to seem more like a great thought than a great machine.

When Rationality Is Only Low Superstition

Believing in rationality and in the fact that the world works only on the basis of inviolable rules severely limits what we can achieve. Let's see how to overcome the limits we impose on ourselves.

Our mind works mainly by association. We filter everything that reaches our senses in order to bring to our awareness only what can somehow be traced back to something already known. We discard everything else.

Using **rationality** leads us to consider only a small part of what exists, in order to make us feel safe in the midst of what we can somehow recognize and catalog.

But we do not realize that in this way we condemn ourselves to living our past over and over again. Nothing new can happen if we do not abandon the rigid schemes imposed on us by rationality.

We think we are aware of everything that exists around us. Nothing could be more false. We live immersed in a huge ocean of energy, and our senses are traversed every moment by billions of different facts. What comes to our consciousness represents only an infinitesimal part of what true reality is. Salvatore Brizzi, in his "Draco Daatson's Book", explains this concept very well:

Your rationality is only **low superstition**. Whoever is still entangled in the logical and rational description of the world is only a primitive who believes in an idol.

Yes, it may seem counterintuitive, but in fact rationality is only low superstition, and relying solely on it to understand the world is pure madness. Madness that keeps us more and more prisoners of

39

the prison that we have built around ourselves, unaware of the infinite possibilities offered to us by the Universe.

If you have read the previous chapter, you are aware of what the real potential of the Universe is. In reality, the word impossible does not exist, it is only an invention of our limited mind. The use of rationality gives us access to a limited and unreal world, which is why Brizzi associates it with low superstition.

Beyond rationality there is an infinite sea of possibilities

We could draw on a myriad of different possibilities, but our rationality leads us to believe that the future is only a logical consequence of the past. Let's not fall into this sneaky trap.

If it is true, as quantum physics has shown us, that the potential contained in every cubic millimeter of space is simply infinite, then we should not limit our reality in the false illusion that nothing can happen beyond what our mind, guided by rationality, can conceive. **We are creators who, by believing in reality, are actually creating it.**

We assume that the Universe works in a certain way and then we do everything to confirm our belief, remaining prisoners of this superstition. In this way we deny ourselves access to a world, the real world, apparently paradoxical but possible, made up of infinite potential. In that world, miracles happen, and the limits imposed by our rationality simply do not exist.

Let's stop dreaming of a dream that is not ours and step outside the limits of what is rationally acceptable. The turning point comes when we accept our total responsibility for creating reality, and learn to shape our own projection. Then the Universe, which has no will of its own, can do nothing but adapt itself and make us live, be or have what we ask for.

I will leave you with the beautiful words of "A Course in Miracles", on which to meditate:

*Believing that reality is what you want it to be
depending on the use you make of it...
is unreasonable.*

The Importance of Expecting the Unexpected

We believe that everything is predetermined, and that there is no room for indeterminacy. Let's find out how wrong this way of thinking is.

We have always been led to believe that any future event cannot be anything other than the result of past actions, and that nothing absolutely unpredictable can ever happen. Even when something really unexpected happens, we tend to justify it immediately, linking the reason to chance, or to some cause that we had not taken into consideration.

This behavior is quite normal, and comes from the way our brain processes the information available. We must consider that the main purpose of our brain is to protect us from possible dangers, therefore we spontaneously tend to make a prediction of what could happen, based on the information we have memorized about the outcome of situations similar to the one we are about to face.

To this you must add that, for the same reason, the mind always tends to hypothesize the worst situation that could arise, in order to protect itself from potential danger.

Everything is fine with us in all cases where we have to face some really dangerous situation, or in cases where not evaluating the consequences of our actions, we could really endanger our safety or that of our loved ones. Unfortunately, the problem is that we have made this mechanism become a mental habit, which automatically is triggered in all situations, even when there is no danger to face.

You have surely faced a school exam with the fear of failing, or have found yourself in difficult situations - for example economic or professional - and thought that nothing and no one in the world could get you out of there, etc.

The world is not deterministic

At this point you will know for sure that the Universe has no will of its own, and that therefore we are the only architects of our destiny. Perhaps you also know that, even taking everything into consideration precisely all the variables involved, due to Heisenberg's uncertainty principle, it is absolutely impossible to determine what the evolution of any physical system will be.

It is not physically possible, believe it or not, to determine exactly the future, and this is amply demonstrated by several principles of quantum physics. The world is not subject to any deterministic laws, but the only rule that exists is that **any result is always possible**. Any, regardless of the current situation, and without any connection with what may have happened in the past in similar situations.

Creating Expectation for the Unexpected

The world is therefore not a place subject to rigid mechanical laws. This is believed only by those who do not know the latest discoveries in the field of quantum physics, but we must not fall into the opposite error either, believing that the world is a chaotic place where anything can happen without any control on our part.

The law of cause and effect exists, so it is not possible for something to happen without a trigger. But the real cause of everything, the first cause, is one and only one: **our thoughts**.

What does this mean? It means that, as the title of this chapter says, we have to create expectation. In short, we must **expect the unexpected**.

We need to understand that until we believe that anything can happen, we make the world a place where nothing new can happen. Our thoughts, and therefore our expectations, are inviolable laws for the Universe, therefore creating the expectation for the unexpected opens the door to the new, and makes anything possible.

Whenever we think that something is impossible, we must always remember that the probability that something could happen is up to us, through our beliefs. It is therefore important to **create the right expectation**, and to wipe out all the automatic thoughts that make us believe that everything can only go as common sense suggests.

Imagining a positive outcome is just as simple as imagining a negative one. The amount of energy needed is the same. It does not seem like that to us because we have always been pessimistic. So, let's break our mental patterns once and for all, and face all situations with positive expectations for the unexpected. Try it, you will see miracles happen.

I will end this chapter with a thought from Neale Donald Walsch:

*The Universe is happy to bring us the unexpected,
are we equally inclined to welcome it?*

Cause and Effect Work in Reverse

We are led to think that cause and effect are two entities that are correlated and temporally dependent on each other. This chapter shows you how false this is.

In this chapter, I want to discuss two apparently unrelated topics, such as thought and time, which on a deeper analysis are absolutely related. This chapter, I admit, is a bit 'tough' to digest, but if you believe, you will be rewarded.

We will start with the relationship between our thoughts and the events that happen in our life. As you know by now, we must hold ourselves responsible for everything that happens to us, whether good or bad. Responsibility comes from the fact that we are the creators of our own reality, and we constantly create, based on our innermost thoughts and beliefs.

If we want to change our life, we must necessarily change our thoughts and our deepest beliefs. We have an incredibly powerful tool, the mind, but we do not have a clue on how to use it to our advantage.

Ok, you say, we already know that it is we who create reality. The subject has already been covered in this book. So? What's the news? Nothing new. I just want to make you think about some concepts that, although you already know them, probably have not been analyzed thoroughly enough.

In fact, I also want to discuss time. Apparently, it does not have much to do with how we create reality, but if you follow me to the end, you will come to unexpected conclusions.

Cause and effect do not act as we think

What does time have to do with it? And what does it have to do with its **cause and effect**? They have something to do with it, because we think that time is a real and measurable physical entity. In fact, we think that the law of cause and effect exists in physics, and that the passage of time creates a temporal dependence between them. In other words, every effect must have a cause that precedes it in time.

Pious illusion. Nothing more false. We let ourselves be deceived by our senses, and we are convinced of the existence of physical entities, such as time, which have no confirmation in the reality of things. And we also think that cause and effect are temporally linked to each other. This is precisely the deception that keeps us prisoners inside the prison that we ourselves have built, and to which only we have the keys.

Let's see why. Listen to me carefully and hold on tight: **the only cause that exists in nature is thought**. Reread the sentence at least three times before moving on.

What does it mean? It means that cause and effect are not temporally linked as we believe. That is, there is no **effect** that does not derive from some form of **thought**. And it also means that what apparently may seem like a physical cause, it is not at all (reread the sentence above to be convinced of it).

Now let's see what the implications of this new concept of cause and effect are in our life. Everything that happens to us does not derive from previous actions or events, but only and exclusively **from our thoughts**.

What apparently seems like a cause is just what the Universe **is forced to make happen** in order for the effect imagined and created by our thought to happen. In fact, unlike what we commonly believe, cause and effect have reversed roles: the effect (whose true cause is represented by our mind) forces a particular cause to manifest itself, so that that particular effect appears in the present moment. It is the effect that generates its cause.

That's right, and once again I recommend that you read the sentence several times. Do you want different things to happen in your life? It cannot be until you change your mind about cause and effect. You have to change your thoughts and think about things you never thought about before. As long as you continue to rethink thoughts already thought, your life will not be able to change in any way.

Only by governing this important and fundamental law, can you become the master of your life. What do I mean by thoughts never thought of before? I mean thoughts not related to past events or beliefs. This only happens when you imagine any desired future event, without getting lost in imagining how that event might happen. Future events are created instantaneously when you focus your thoughts on them, and the Universe at that precise moment begins to build backwards all the events that, when the final events take place, they will seem like their causes to you.

Cause and effect are reversed: it is up to you to create the final goal, instead the Universe has the task of finding, immediately after, the path to take you there.

Do not make the mistake of imagining what causes led you (or did not lead you) to the desired events. You would actually be "thinking backwards" about how the Universe actually works, hindering its work. You would do nothing but "think thoughts already made" and in doing so drag your past inexorably into the future.

The cause is you with your mind. Leave the burden to the Universe to find **the apparent causes** that will lead you to see your dreams come true.

The Magic of the Uncertainty Principle

In nature there is a principle according to which it is impossible to know all the parameters of any physical event with the maximum precision. Let's see what the effects of this strange law of quantum physics are.

Perhaps this formula tells you absolutely nothing:

$$\Delta x \Delta p \geq \frac{\hbar}{2}$$

Yet this formula, which mathematically describes Heisenberg's Uncertainty Principle[5], contains **one of the greatest secrets** of quantum physics, and few, apart from the *"chosen few"*, are aware of the real implications of this formula.

Don't worry, I will not bore you with strange and incomprehensible principles of theoretical physics, but what I want to do is to explain in the simplest way possible the implications of one of the most important laws that govern the world in which we live.

What is Heisenberg's Uncertainty Principle

Let's start immediately by explaining what this principle is, which was studied in 1927 by the German physicist Werner Karl Heisenberg, and then demonstrated in the laboratory in countless physical experiments.

---

[5] http://en.wikipedia.org/wiki/Uncertainty_principle

Heisenberg states that it is physically impossible to determine with absolute precision both **the position** and **the velocity** of any particle. What exactly does it mean? It means that if you measure with extreme precision the position of a particle, you will not be able to know its speed with the same precision.

This effect can be easily explained with a visual example. Imagine watching a tennis match, and taking some photos of the match from the sidelines as it unfolds. Back home, while showing your friends the beautiful photos you have taken, you come across this image:

If one of your friends asks you "Nice picture! But how fast was the ball going?". You immediately realize that simply by looking at the image you are not able to give an answer to your curious friend. Here is an example of the uncertainty principle: in a photo you are certainly able to determine the position of an object, but the shot does not contain any information regarding its speed or direction.

Of course, this photo is just an example, but it certainly renders well what happens when a researcher tries to accurately measure both the position and the velocity of a particle within a scientific experiment.

Attention, the limit I am talking about **does not depend** on the imprecision of the instruments used or on the perturbation introduced during the measurement. The uncertainty of measurement is a physical property of nature, and is perfectly described by the formula you saw at the beginning of this chapter. In other words, **the world is just like that**, and the impossibility of knowing both the position and the velocity of a particle does not depend on how the measurement is made.

What does that little voice know...

Okay, you will say, that's all very interesting, but what are the implications of this strange physical principle? You would never imagine it, but the Uncertainty Principle has a number of implications that I am sure will leave you speechless.

First of all, the fact that you cannot determine in any way all the variables of a physical system means that it is not possible to accurately determine future evolution. What does it mean? It means that our stupid tendency to hypothesize our future based on the past or the present situation is simply meaningless. We cannot know all the variables involved, so how can we determine what will happen in the future?

And consequently: what the hell does it know, **that little voice in your head** that talks to you incessantly, telling you that your project will not be successful, or that thing will not happen?

It is physically impossible for that voice to know anything, so why do we always agree with it and follow its stupid advice? Let's meditate on this...

The Creation Formula

But the best is yet to come... The formula you saw at the beginning of the chapter is... the Creation formula. Yes, that's right. Let's see why.

If, as scientists mistakenly thought before quantum physics, every future instant was uniquely determined by the present situation, there would be no room for any kind of creation. In fact, if everything was already predetermined, there would be no free will, and we could not in any way intervene in modifying a destiny already 100% determined by the initial situation.

However, thanks to the uncertainty principle, we have great power in our hands. The fact that the future evolution of any event is not 100% determinable leaves just the necessary space for Creation to take place. As I said before, **the world is made like this**, and Who conceived it in this way created that **little indeterminacy** in order to leave room for the possibility of creating new things that do not depend in any way on the pre-existing situation.

So, all the theories on the Law of Attraction and the fact that we can determine our future acquire real consistency, thanks precisely to the fact that the existing reality cannot be completely determined, and that regardless of what the current situation may be, **any evolution is always possible**.

You cannot know your future, but you can determine it. I am not telling you **how** you can create your future, because I explained it extensively in other chapters of this book, but now you know **why** it is possible to do so.

Relax, You Are Only Dreaming

We believe we are separate from the world, and we do not realize instead that all the reality we perceive exists only within a dream created by our mind.

Here I am writing again about the Quantum Field, one of the topics that is close to my heart, convinced of its fundamental importance in understanding many of the other topics addressed in this book. The title might seem somewhat strange and pretentious, but if you have the persistence to go all the way you will agree with me about the truth of what I am about to say.

Let's start with some physical concepts concerning the perception we have of the world, obtained through the 5 senses. Nothing new if I affirm that images (but the same also applies to sounds, flavors, etc.) are perceived by our brain through the process of electrical signals coming from the retina located at the bottom of the eyeball and carried by the nerves. Science has located a specific area of the brain dedicated to image processing, behind our neck.

The key word here is *"processing"* of electrical signals. In reality our brain knows nothing about external reality. It's been locked up inside the skull since birth, and if you think about it, *it's in the dark*.

In fact, the brain never comes into contact with the world it tries to interpret.

But let's go a little further. If we connect the same area of the brain with electrodes to a computer, we could send electrical signals identical to those generated by the eyeball, and reproduce in the brain images (or sounds, smells, tastes, ...) that would be perceived as real. The brain could not in any way notice the difference between a so-called "real" image and one artificially generated by the computer. In a hypothetical experiment (which we hope will always and only remain hypothetical) we could induce a subject to live in a completely artificial reality, without the unfortunate person ever noticing the difference (the 3D glasses and gloves of some virtual reality applications are based more or less on the same principle).

In fact, we could make him live any type of experience, good or bad, completely imaginative, that is, not linked to any particular reality. We could make him meet "artificial" people and make him feel joy, hate, love, etc. towards them. If the subject lived like this from birth, he would never know anything about his artificial condition.

But think about it: what would his reaction be if someone tried to explain to him that everything he perceives is not real, and that the world he lives in actually exists only in his brain? He would categorically refuse to believe what is revealed to him. In fact, I am sure they would consider mad the one who is trying to reveal the truth to them.

Well, our normal condition is not that different from the hypothetical subject. Think about it: just like him we only receive and process electrical signals, and nothing and no one can assure us that *out there* the world exists exactly as we perceive it. We cannot have information about reality other than that which is provided to us through natural electrodes (nerve endings) with which Mother Nature has endowed us since birth.

Nothing and no one can give us information about the real existence of the world we perceive.

Ok, you will say, this does not mean anything, because in the same way, it is not possible to prove that the world out there does not exist as we perceive it.

Only probability waves, nothing else

Here quantum physics intervenes, realizing that in reality matter is made of... nothing.

Nothing? Yes, nothing. Or rather, nothing that can be traced back to something material and tangible. Matter cannot be explained with matter itself. In other words, if we go deep into the microcosm, and try to break down matter into its smallest compounds, we come to a point where nothing exists but *probability waves*.

And the seemingly most incredible thing is the fact that a particle of matter behaves in one way rather than another, solely based on the observer's decision or expectation. In other words, it is the brain that creates reality as we see it.

In fact, the world out there does not exist. Or more exactly, it exists only as a completely subjective representation of what we believe to be the real world, which in fact is composed only of energy and probability waves. This fact was revealed to us thousands of years ago by great Masters of the past, such as Buddha or Jesus himself, and today it is confirmed by quantum physics experiments conducted in the laboratories of universities around the world.

We make real what we believe

But do you know what the real problem is? Just like the hypothetical subject of our experiment, **we categorically refuse to believe all of this**. We think that what we perceive is a real world made of *solid* matter. We have always believed this, since birth, and **we gladly consider visionary** those who try to teach us the ultimate reality of things.

This is precisely the problem.

We suffer the vicissitudes of the world because we believe we are separate from it. This gives the world the power that it otherwise would not have. We are Gods, absolute masters of the world we are creating, therefore the Universe behaves **exactly as we ask**, through our beliefs and expectations, how it should behave.

There is no doubt that we create our world, with its joys and problems, dreaming of a reality that exists only within our mind.

We are the creators who got lost within their own creation, believing it to be real.

So, stop believing that the world out there has a life of its own, and that it is not possible to voluntarily create a different and better reality.

In other words, relax, you are only dreaming.

You May Not Know That You Are Living in the Past

It may seem strange to you, but all you see around you is just the crystallization of things from the past. In short, you are living in the past, and now you will find out what that means.

Let's immediately remove all doubts by revealing the basic idea of this chapter: what does it mean that **you are living in the past?** Simple, the reality is that you are living within the crystallization of your past thoughts and beliefs. Yes, that's right. The world you see around you simply comes from your past thoughts, which have "crystallized" into the reality you are experiencing right now.

If you have read the previous chapters carefully you know perfectly well that we all create reality through our innermost beliefs and thoughts. Whenever you express a thought that describes what you believe about reality, you are in fact creating that reality, which will materialize sooner or later in your life.

In the previous chapters we have seen that each particle, in reality, is representable only as a probability wave that extends up to infinite distances, and that the wave actually describes the probability that that particle has to appear in a certain point of spacetime. The particle will become real, that is, visible and measurable, only and exclusively when it is observed, and the point at which it appears is determined by the expectations of the Observer.

Okay, but how does this explain the fact that you are living in the past? I will try to make the concept as simple as possible. That famous probability wave actually tells us that the particle can potentially appear at any point in spacetime. In fact, since it is the observer who determines what that point will be, we can say that "potentially" as long as the observer does not interfere with the particle, it exists everywhere.

What does it mean that the particle is potentially everywhere? It means that, at any given instant, the observer can determine, among infinite possibilities, what the final result of his observation will be.

The analogy with the clay vase

Imagine reality as something that can be molded, exactly as clay that is modeled on a lathe by the skilled hands of an artist. Before we look at it, reality is like that fresh clay. The artist will be able to shape that vase in infinite different forms, just as we can shape the future with our thoughts.

Well, at the very moment in which the observer decides to observe the particle, this will assume only and exclusively a position in spacetime, thus making all the other positions impossible. It is like clay which, once placed in the oven, will solidify in the last form chosen by the artist, making any other form impossible.

We can then say that reality will have "solidified" (or crystallized) in a certain "form" which has been determined by the observer's thoughts.

This explains why you are living in the past

So, the reality you see is composed of particles of matter which, according to your past thoughts and beliefs, took a certain final shape and as such it showed itself to you, exactly like the clay pot after it has been cooked. In fact, you are living in a reality that is nothing more than the crystallization of your past thoughts. In other words, you are living in the past.

What does this entail? Well, the consequences are very, very interesting. In fact, we can finally know exactly what the notorious **here and now**, or present moment, is and how to relate to it.

The first important implication is that the present moment is what it is, and you have chosen it with your beliefs and thoughts, among all the infinite possibilities. This means that it is absolutely stupid and pointless to rebel against the current situation. If the present moment is in fact a crystallization of your past thoughts, there is no point in resisting it with anger, bad mood, complaints, etc. You would just make the situation worse. It is as if the artist, not happy with the final result, wanted to modify the shape of the vase using a hammer. He would achieve nothing but breaking his vase.

This is what quantum physics and so many enlightened people teach us, i.e., **we must accept reality as it is**, and we are responsible for it, so it makes no sense repudiating it. Repudiation and grievance towards the present moment has another negative effect. By complaining about our creation, we are effectively denying our nature as Creators. And since reality always reflects our beliefs, if we deny our ability to create... **we deprive ourselves of our infinite power.**

The other very important aspect is that we must realize that at all times we have the clay pot still fresh in our hands, it is still moldable at will. This means that **the future is in our hands**, and we decide what form it will take. The present moment (the here and now) must therefore be seen not as something to be repudiated, but as a point of strength from which we can and must intervene to shape our future. So, let's use all our imagination and creative thinking in the present moment to imagine the future we want.

Now that you know that you are living in the past, in a past crystallized and wanted by you, do not waste precious energy to oppose it, but instead harness that energy in a constructive way by using the present moment to imagine and create the future of your dreams.

Relax, Creation Is Over

Let's get rid of all doubts about how and why we can get everything we want from the Universe. Creation is finished, that is why we can have it all.

One of the biggest problems faced by people who try unsuccessfully to apply the Law of Attraction, is the apparent difference between the lived reality and the dream or longed desire. For this reason, innumerable doubts assail us as to how the present situation could ever reach the desired situation. But this is precisely the problem: whoever questions the infinite power of the Universe in bringing us what we ask for, actually prevents the object of desire from being reached.

It is for this reason that I have decided to write this chapter, in which I have promised myself to explain to you, more or less scientifically, why our doubts are completely unfounded.

Relax, creation is over

Is creation over? What the hell does it mean that **creation is over**? Don't give up reading, thinking that I am saying absurdities. Sometimes I like to provoke the reader with catchy phrases, but it is only with the benevolent aim of getting your attention. Read on and you will see that we will get to the pivotal point of the whole thing.

Normally, we are used to the fact that in life you always have to do something to achieve something else, and we are therefore convinced that the future does not exist, and that we or someone else must necessarily **build the desired things**. This is in our imagination and involves effort. Another absolutely wrong belief.

Two very important laws must be kept in mind:

The first law is based on the fact that time does not exist, being a mere invention of our mind due to our limited vision in three dimensions (scientists have discovered that the Universe has innumerable dimensions, maybe twelve or more, but our physical body is too limited to experience them).

If we could see all the dimensions at play, we will find that all the past, the present and future events exist at the same time. Where? In the here and now, of course. The here and now is made up of innumerable dimensions. As I said, if we had access to the other dimensions, we could see all potential futures.

The second law is based on the fact that each particle in reality cannot be represented as a small sphere which at any given moment has a precise position and speed. Not at all. Quantum physics tells us that a particle is nothing more than a probability wave, and that we, with our expectations, decide where and when the particle will appear.

What does this mean? Simple, it means that any particle, in its and our apparent future, can potentially occupy any position, and that we simply determine which one in particular of all the infinite possibilities we want to occupy.

And now the logical conclusions

If the whole future already exists somewhere, it is evident that the title of this chapter, namely that creation is over, acquires a very precise meaning. Future has already been created, so it is clear that creation is over. Imagine the grooves of a vinyl record. Imagine an infinite record with an infinite number of grooves. The needle represents the present that we perceive in this moment. All the grooves already exist, so, through our **free will**, we must decide on which groove to place the needle, and therefore which present we want to experience. This directing the needle on the desired groove can be done by means of probability waves. All existing futures are possible to some extent. What actually happens is determined by our imagination.

These are not far-fetched things. That is what quantum physics tells us, and the conclusions have already been tested and confirmed in scientific laboratories around the world.

How does it affect us that creation is over? Well, going back to what we said in the premise of our chapter, it does not take any effort to experience a particular desired future. That future is already there, engraved in the N dimensions of the universe as are the grooves of a record.

Here then perhaps everything is clearer. Creation is complete. Nobody has to create anything, everything already exists somewhere, and **no effort is needed**. The fact that we cannot see it is only due to the fact that our physical body was not designed to see in more than three dimensions.

The needle that plows through that record can be manipulated by us with our thoughts. All we have to do is to eliminate any doubts and train our mind to focus **only on the desired things**, so as to reach those grooves and live the corresponding experience, which is just waiting for us to reach it.

It Is Impossible to Be Wrong

Any decision we make is the right decision. It is impossible to be wrong, and in this chapter, we will find out why.

Surely you have had to go somewhere, and not know the way. Today, with the use of a GPS navigator, it is very easy to find the best route that leads us to our destination, just set the arrival address and follow all the information given to us to the letter.

Well, it may have also happened to deviate from the road indicated, either because you were forced to make some obligatory detour, or simply because you "missed" the indicated turn and therefore found yourself on a road that was not on the predetermined path.

Any good navigator, at this point, will rarely ask you to retrace your steps, but will almost certainly recalculate an alternative route that will lead you to your intended destination.

Well, what I am about to tell you is that, as it happens for the navigator, even in everyday life there is always the possibility of reaching the desired result, regardless of the decisions we make.

In other words, it is literally impossible to make the wrong decision. You got it right: it is **impossible from a physical point of view**, therefore it is one of the **Eternal and inviolable Laws of the Universe**.

It just depends on the thought

What makes me say such a thing? By now it should be clear to everyone that thought is the cause of any event that happens in our life, be it good or bad. In fact, nothing can exist without having first been imagined at thought level. Anyone who has read my books knows of the existence of the two levels on which any creation is based: the spiritual and the material level, and how these interact in the process of materialization of reality.

What is the key to this mechanism? To understand this, you have to change your point of view, and stop believing that the final result depends on the direction taken. Remember this fundamental concept:

The final result depends solely and exclusively on our ability to focus on the desired result.

In the case of the navigator, the only important thing is to have set the right destination. Nothing else is needed, because that single piece of information is more than enough to make sure that you can reach the desired goal. We can say that the navigator always succeeds in its intent because it is *"focused"* on the final result. It was designed to work that way, so nothing in the world will stray it from that purpose.

The magic word then is the *"focus"* of our intent on the desired result. Since it is thought that determines whatever manifests itself in our life, the only important thing for the success of any initiative is to focus with all your being on the desired result.

The mistake we commonly make is to think instead of all the obstacles that we might encounter, thus ending up diverting our attention from the solution, to focus exclusively on the problem.

Someone at this point might argue that analyzing possible problems is important to avoid making mistakes, and that sitting there thinking only of the final solution would lead us nowhere.

On the surface this reasoning might seem right, but it is important to understand the way things really happen. First of all, let's keep in mind that by thinking about possible problems, we do nothing but obtain the materialization of those problems.

The other important aspect to consider is that the Universe immediately fulfills our wish, indeed that wish has already been fulfilled somewhere in spacetime. The Universe immediately sets in motion to lead us to that result, exactly as a GPS navigator would do. And just like a GPS navigator does, it constantly gives us directions to bring us to the desired result. How? Certainly not with a sweet little voice that indicates all the decisions to be made, it would be too good (but perhaps also too boring).

The Universe shows us the way through what we call "coincidences". It can do this at any time and in completely unexpected ways, such as a sentence that is said to us by an acquaintance, or a sudden and unexpected phone call, or an intuition that suddenly leaps into our mind.

So, action is indeed necessary, but it becomes truly effective only if it is guided by the signals we receive and that we are able to recognize. In short, we have all the tools to succeed in any business, and the most interesting thing is that we can do it regardless of the path we choose to take.

The only really important thing is **to stay focused on the final solution**, and pay close attention to all the signals the Universe sends to put us on the right path. Don't worry, because even if we "miss" some indications, the Universe immediately recalculates the path, and will still lead us where we wish to go, as long as we remain focused on the final goal.

In other words, for those who know how to do it, **it is impossible to go wrong**.

Like the Flutter of Butterfly Wings

Like the flutter of butterfly wings, every thought or word has an effect on our reality. We need to be aware of this in order to rule our world.

Surely you have heard of the butterfly effect[6], according to which every slight disturbance, created even by the slightest flapping of a butterfly's wings, creates an effect on the world. It is the theory of chaos, according to which it is practically impossible to predict the evolution of a system, except for very short periods of time.

This is true in any chaotic system, such as weather forecasts or financial markets, and this is why any long-term forecast can never be trusted.

From the point of view of **quantum physics**, the butterfly effect derives from a fundamental quantum principle, called the *Heisenberg's Uncertainty Principle*, according to which it is impossible to measure with absolute precision both the speed and the position of any particle. The more accurately you measure the velocity, the less you can determine the exact position of the particle, and vice versa. And since the evolution of a system depends strongly on its initial condition, it follows that it is equally impossible to calculate the long-term effects of any disturbance.

Any disturbance. Let's think about this term. What can be considered a disturbance? Don't make the mistake of thinking only of physical actions, such as the flapping of a butterfly's wings. Matter interacts with energy, and you know very well that thought is a form of energy, so even a thought can be considered a disturbance of the environment in which we live.

---

[6] http://en.wikipedia.org/wiki/Butterfly_effect

How many times have we had a negative thought, but then we have thrown it back into the "oblivion", thinking that this would have no effect on our life? It is a very serious mistake every time we think something negative about some person or situation.

We are actually triggering the butterfly effect, the result of which cannot in any way be overlooked. Sometimes only hours pass, sometimes days, other times months or even years, but rest assured, that thought will come back materializing in some event, which will follow the nature of the initial thought. And since it can take a long time, we usually do not recognize the event of the initial thought, placing the blame on "chance" or bad luck.

According to the Law of Attraction, then, you know very well that every thought attracts other similar thoughts to itself, therefore that initial thought, which we may have considered insignificant, grows over time, becoming something very significant.

And finally, another very important thing must be taken into consideration: **every thought never leaves the mind that generated it**. This means that we are absolutely responsible for everything that happens to us, because any event, whether good or bad, **is always the result of our previous thoughts**. Don't believe that your life can be influenced by others.

I felt the need to write this chapter because I realized that too often, indeed always, people ignore the effect their thoughts and words have on reality.

So, what can you do? Take control of your thoughts. As suggested over and over in this book, eliminate that inner voice that talks to you incessantly telling you how difficult the world is, or how impossible it is to succeed in that undertaking, how unfortunate you are, etc. Stop telling yourself all those lies that cause nothing but pain. You must know that those thoughts will come back exactly as they were thought.

But since fortunately the same law also applies to positive thoughts, let's use them to our advantage by placing the utmost confidence in the infinite abundance of the Universe, and feed our minds only with **the highest idea** we have about ourselves and the world.

In short, **there are no neutral thoughts**. Every Conscious Creator knows very well this law of the Universe and respects it.

"Actuators" of a Divine Design?

I can perfectly imagine the emotion of that scientist who, at the beginning of the twentieth century, in a small photographic laboratory, extracted the two large plates of photosensitive material from the developing bath to verify which image had remained imprinted after exposure for several hours to the bombardment of electrons passed through a panel with two slits, as predicted by the famous experiment conceived about a century earlier by Thomas Young.

The first of the two plates had been impressed after placing a sensor near one of the two slits to reveal which and how many electrons passed through that slot. The second plate, on the other hand, was imprinted with the sensor turned off. The dim light of a candle shielded by a red glass that illuminated that small photographic laboratory made the atmosphere unreal, and highlighted the numerous wrinkles on the frowning forehead of the young researcher, an evident sign that he was no longer in his skin as he looked at the image which slowly appeared on the two damp slabs hung to dry.

That young researcher knew that if only two lighter bands appeared on the first plate, he would have the proof he was looking for. Finally, the moment arrived, and the dim light of that small laboratory did not prevent him from noticing that on the first plate there were in fact only two lighter stripes appearing, unlike the other, where instead there were at least a dozen.

That was the proof that the observation made with that sensor changed the behavior of the electrons, which stopped behaving like waves to "collapse" and became particles, the only ones able to justify the two clear bands that that scientist, with eyes full of emotion, was observing on that photographic plate. The world, or rather the vision of the world that emerged from that experiment was never the same again. Somehow that was the irrefutable demonstration that observation changed the observed reality, making matter appear out of nowhere, just where the observer's attention rested.

The presence of numerous light bands on the second plate showed that matter, when not observed, appears as an impalpable wave. A wave instead of a solid particle. But what does this mean? Upon closer analysis, it was found that the wave simply represents the probability of finding the particle at a certain point in spacetime. Nothing physical or tangible, therefore, only a probability.

But where does that particle go when it is not observed? We could say everywhere, and at the same time nowhere, this is the only sensible answer that can be given to this question. In fact, that particle does not exist when not observed, because in its place there is something totally immaterial, without borders, which permeates the entire space. There is only a probability, something that does not exist in this material world, except as an idea, or concept, expressed through a series of mathematical formulas. There is only "the information" of the potential existence of a particle.

A two-level reality

The double-slit experiment showed us that a particle can only appear as the result of the "collapse" of the wave that describes it. We speak of "collapse" because the boundless wave that permeates the entire space instantly concentrates in a single point, transforming itself into the observed particle.

Quantum physics has finally lifted the veil on the reality of things, revealing a strange world composed of two different levels. There is a first level, which we could define as "immaterial", where there is neither time nor space, made up only of "probability waves", a level where anything exists in "potential" and "unexpressed" form. The second level, on the other hand, is the one to which "material" things belong, the world that we can experience with the five senses, where time and space are the masters.

The waves of the first level express the concept, or idea, of things which then appear on the second level. We could call them *thought-forms*, because they are composed of intangible *thoughts* that *shape* the material things that we can experience on the second level. Only ideas, or concepts expressed, which when *expressed through observation*, are nothing more than the material objects that we experience with the five senses, the physical expression of those concepts.

It is clear to everyone that, in order for a particle to appear, a wave that describes it must necessarily exist beforehand. Nothing can therefore exist on the second level, the material one, without its "idea" or thought-form being conceived on the first level.

But how does a wave collapse and manifest a particle on the second level? In other words, how does this creation mechanism materialize? Well, if you have been careful, you will have guessed that, since it is the observation that works this "magic", it probably has to do with the observer, that is, with ourselves, beings with a conscience. The totality of all thought-forms, that can be considered as "potential" energy, need to be "observed" in order to express themselves in the real world.

But what exactly does "observe" mean? Here we are not talking about observations made with the eyes, of course, because we are referring to a wave which, as an expression of an idea or concept, can only be observed by a mind. It is therefore a choice, nothing more than a process of "choice" or "extraction" made among all the infinite thoughts that a mind can conceive.

The creation of reality is in the end nothing more than a choice, a deliberate choice, which we can compare to a mechanism of "implementation" of a Primary Idea, existing in principle only in a potential and unexpressed form. It expresses itself in the exact way we allow it to express itself. As conscious beings, we make choices constantly, whenever we can focus our attention on an idea or on a concept.

The mind as an instrument of "implementation" of reality

Our role in this magical process of creation has finally been revealed. In fact, we represent the connecting bridge between the two levels, a sort of "actuators" of the infinite potential existing on the first level, which by its nature, as we have seen, needs to be "recognized" and therefore "chosen" in order to express itself in the so-called "real" world.

A fantastic mechanism designed to allow a "divine" mind to experience itself and enjoy the possibility of creating a world in its image and likeness? Who knows, no one can say for sure. Everyone is free to draw their own conclusions.

The Mind as a Means of Expressing the Divine Idea

If you want to know the true purpose of your incarnation, read this chapter and you will discover your true nature.

Let's start this chapter by talking about spirit and matter. Have you ever wondered what really distinguishes these two concepts? Let's try to find out together with some reasoning. Before going on, however, I would like to answer the question that many will ask about the purpose of such a "philosophical" chapter within this book.

The answer is simple. A Conscious Creator, in my opinion, is a student of the laws of nature who wants to become aware of how reality works, in order to be able to exploit the laws to his own advantage. It is a necessity, and those who are not willing to learn cannot claim to acquire the "awareness" necessary to become masters of their own destiny. This chapter is by no means easy to digest, and many will abandon reading. Do you feel like you are among the few who will go all the way?

So, let's see what can be said about **matter**. Surely, we will all agree that it is something characterized by a shape. Having a shape means occupying a well-defined space, having some consistency (solid, liquid, gaseous, etc.), and other characteristics such as color, smell, temperature, etc. But what does it mean to occupy a space? It means that different parts of the same material object are separated by physical space, and in order to travel the distance from one point to another time is involved. The concepts of time and space are therefore indivisible from that of matter. We could say that matter needs space and time in order to be defined, and therefore to exist.

Well. Let's now turn to the **spirit**. To clear up any doubt, by spirit I mean the essence, understood as the idea or concept that underlies any being, living or not. As an essence, idea or concept, spirit surely has no form, and consequently does not occupy any physical space. So, it goes without saying that it does not even make sense to talk about time, because since it does not take up any space, there is no travel time to bridge any distance. We can then say that the spirit lives outside of time and space.

So far, we have remained very adherent to what we can read in any text of physics, as far as the subject is concerned, and of theology, as regards the spirit.

But let's take a closer look at the implications. To say that the spirit exists in a reality that is independent of time and space, also means that the spirit must necessarily be everywhere, both in time and in space. Everywhere means that it is something infinite and eternal. But this also means that it has no direct relationship with other parties. That is, it exists independently of any previous condition (it makes no sense to speak of previous in the absence of time) and of any bond with other entities external to it (it makes no sense to speak of something "external" in the absence of space).

You will have no trouble understanding this last step by referring to the properties of thought. We can in fact imagine anything (for example owning a villa with a swimming pool or knowing how to fly), without any relationship with real things or events.

The sum of thoughts constitutes the Whole

If all thoughts have the property of being infinite and eternal, we can then say that the sum of all possible concepts or ideas represent the Whole, or the Universe, or God for those who are believers. We can think of this Whole as the sum of any concept, **impersonal** by its nature (because it is not referred to and cannot be referred to any particular thing) and **unexpressed**, because it exists only in a "potential" form.

In fact, a concept is *expressed* as nothing more than a material object, the physical expression of that concept. This then explains the relationship between spirit and matter. First of all, there must be an idea, or concept, which is then expressed in physical form in the real world, through matter.

Every material object must be based on an idea shaped in space and time. (I don't know why, but this thing reminds me a lot of the Law of Attraction).

Our mind is the instrument through which Divine thought is "implemented"

But here we come to the central topic of this chapter, expressed in its title, discovering the purpose of the mind as a means of expressing the Divine Idea. Here we come into play, living beings with a thinking mind. Thinking means that we are able to give life to the concepts and ideas that underlie any object or event in our material reality.

Here then is our purpose revealed. We are "actuators" of the Infinite Consciousness, which by its nature, as we have seen, is impersonal and therefore unexpressed. Infinite Consciousness is "potential" energy that needs to be thought and recognized in order to express itself in the real world. It will express itself exactly as we allow it to express itself.

Finally, we come to explain the concept of Conscious Creator: if our level of awareness makes us believe in a random reality dictated by chaos, then our reality reflects that belief, since we only allow it to be "chaos".

Reality expresses itself through us, and this expression obeys the idea we have of the reality we are going to create.

At the base of everything therefore is the Initial Idea, and thanks to the desire to express it in the real world, and therefore to experience it, that the physical Universe was created.

Infinite Consciousness, impersonal by its nature, needs our "personal" mind to find its expression, and all the power to **control**

this process is given in response **only to those** who recognize the existence of the Primordial Idea and respect its principles.

Awareness is power, never forget it.

The Universe Has No Will of Its Own

We are constantly alarmed by the thought that something unpleasant might happen at any moment. But if we knew that the Universe has no will, then we would no longer be afraid of anything.

I decided to write this chapter because I have been receiving emails from people who, starting to study the mechanisms with which we create our reality, discover that everything is centered on the concept that our mind governs the world in which we live, indeed more exactly creates it.

These emails mostly contain questions on how it is possible to attract positive events to oneself, if our life has to deal with a harsh reality and in many ways full of difficulty and suffering. The underlying fear is not believing that you can have control over your own reality, convinced that the world out there is something external and uncontrollable.

In reading these emails I realized that many people are unable to take control of their mind, and therefore of their life, due to the lack of understanding of a basic concept. A concept that, if fully learned, can really make the difference between those who suffer in their own lives and those who manage to govern their life at will.

But let's go in order.

Consciousness is only One

Whenever we think of the real world, we conceive it as an entity external to us that can do anything to us at any time. In fact, we think that the danger is around the corner, and we could suffer accidents, violence, scams (and so on and so forth), at any time, without us being able to do anything to control these "accidents".

Well, I want to reveal to you the true nature of the world that you see and conceive as "outside you". You already know, if you have read the other chapters of this book, that the world is actually within us. There is nothing out there. But I want to go a little further and deepen this very important concept. We have already seen that everything is Consciousness. But let's pause to consider what this Consciousness is. Consciousness is all that remains of our being, once we remove thoughts from our mind. It is our True Self, it is Who It Is. Consciousness is that state of being that simply waits for a thought to occupy it and "use" it to shape some concept or idea. It is there to be used at our will, by conscious thinking.

It is therefore the white screen on which all our thoughts are projected. And since thoughts create reality, Consciousness is consequently the "substance" (pass me the term) through which all reality takes shape and materializes.

However, with this definition, even if shocking, we have not yet come to understand the true essence of Consciousness. Perhaps it will surprise you that saying that every living being, every plant and every inanimate object has a Consciousness. Indeed, it is made of pure Consciousness. What differentiates a stone from a plant from an animal is only the level of Consciousness, which in living organisms is of a higher or evolved form. But now comes the fun. You must know that Consciousness is One. Yes, only one.

Consciousness is in fact all that exists in the Universe. Think of it as a substance that permeates all existing space. Indeed, it is all the existing space. We are almost at the end, so don't give up.

The Universe Has No Will of Its Own

Now we have come to the core of this chapter. If Consciousness is only one, guess what Consciousness is? Of course, it is the Consciousness of the Universe (if you are agnostic), or it is the

Consciousness of God (if you are a believer). But the term used doesn't matter. What matters is the concept.

But since Consciousness is only one, then our Consciousness is also one with the Universal Consciousness. This is why it is said in many writings that we are One with our Creator. The reality is that the Universe (or God if you prefer) expresses itself through us. It does this through our thinking which, by shaping Cosmic Consciousness, creates the reality we observe. Do you understand what this means? It means that Consciousness is all that exists in the Universe, and since it is one, **it cannot be different from ours**.

This explains why the Universe has no will of its own.

All things existing in the Universe have our own Consciousness within them, and therefore they must necessarily respond to our thinking. But since we and only we govern our thinking by our will, then the Universe has no will of its own, because that will is one with ours. Read this sentence more than once if necessary.

This is the reason for the functioning of the Law of Attraction. We must finally understand that when we govern our thinking, the Universe must necessarily give us the things we ask for. It cannot do otherwise. It cannot act independently of our will. It is a physical law. I will repeat: the Universe has no will of its own, whether you accept it or not.

But what is the problem at this point? The problem is that most of us are unable to control our thoughts. And then consequently unable to control our own reality. Hence the illusion that the world is something separate from us that can harm us at any moment. Let's abandon this illusion and take back our Divine Right to rule the world. But to do this **we must train ourselves** to regain control of our mind to think only the things we wish to think.

Responsibility as a Means to Create Reality

This time we will talk about Responsibility and how it plays a crucial role in creating your own reality.

Surely, you have read a lot about the Law of Attraction and you have gotten a good idea of the power that our thoughts exert in creating reality.

Also, in this book you can read about how things and events in our lives can be somehow 'drawn' to us through our thoughts, whether conscious or unconscious.

Well, I have **good** news and **bad** news for you:

The good news is that based on what we have said, we can have or become anything in our lives, and so far, nothing new. The bad news is that we are solely responsible for everything that happens, good or bad.

Why would the second piece of news be bad? Because the concept of having total responsibility for every event in our lives scares the hell out of us, so many run from this uncomfortable truth.

The news is not pleasant also because there is no way out: if you want the Law of Attraction to work for you, you must necessarily be aware and take charge of this responsibility.

Unconsciously we are in fact led to escape from this burden by always trying to blame what happens to us on something or someone out there.

The crisis, the thieving government, our boss who does not value us, the partner who doesn't understand us, the annoying neighbor... and I could go on for several pages.

We are locked into our comfort zone, and we do everything we can to stay there as long as possible. It is convenient to always blame someone else, but we do not realize that through victimism we unknowingly lock ourselves in a cage of fear and resentment. We are our own jailers.

Now let's see how things **really** are instead.

Believe it or not, the world around us is solely a reflection of what we think or believe. The people and places we associate with are nothing more than the material representation of how we are made inside. As I have already had occasion to say, there is nothing out there. In fact, there is no one out there (the outside world) separate from our mind.

Quantum physics has proven, beyond a shadow of a doubt, that we create our reality moment by moment, simply through conscious and unconscious thought.

Reality is within you, and it changes as a result of the change in your inner state. Of your being.

Do you really want to take charge of your own destiny? The answer is in the title of this chapter: **take full responsibility for what happens to you**.

Stop complaining about the world around you. If you created it, why are you complaining about it?

If you complain about it, you are giving the outside world the power it does not have, and you are giving up your Sovereignty altogether. We all create based on our innermost beliefs, so if you believe there is a dangerous world out there over which you have no control, guess what kind of reality will you create?

The problem is that we do everything we can to feel victimized by circumstances, so that we can have an alibi that allows us to complain and shift responsibility to the outside world. This makes us feel good, because, as I said earlier, responsibility is scary, and most people react strongly against this truth in order to safeguard their right to complain.

How do you think you can successfully apply the Law of Attraction if you do not believe you are solely responsible for the events in your life?

How do you claim to be able to consciously create the future if you do not believe you have created your present at all?

If you really want to change your life, start by accepting your current situation, good or bad. Love yourself and be thankful each day for all that you have. Stop complaining and become aware of your full responsibility.

Claim your place on your throne. Feel that you are the undisputed **Sovereign** of your world, and only then will the world begin to treat you as a Sovereign…

You Wrote This Chapter

Everything that exists was created by you, including therefore anything you encounter along your path of personal growth, and this chapter, of course.

The title of this chapter might sound absurd, but what I want to deal with is really the fact that we are the sole creators of everything we experience in our reality, and everything, but everything, has been purposely put there to facilitate our journey of growth.

This may be one of the *'toughest to digest'* chapters I have ever written, but those who have the patience to read all the way through will surely be rewarded for the effort.

A hidden direction

I don't know about you, but it happens to me that books, articles or seminars that I come in contact with are almost always perfect for that moment. I have realized that it is as if there is an occult direction that determines at any given moment which texts are suitable according to my level of personal growth, and organizes events so that I come into contact with them in one way or another.

Actually, this happens for any event in our lives, because everything always happens at the right time, but to stay true to the title, in this chapter we will focus only on books or articles that come into our sphere of awareness.

Before I spoke of an 'occult direction', but in reality, the one who organizes all the events of our life is none other than our True Self, that is ourselves, or rather the divine part of us that lives outside of space and time, and that knows perfectly well what the purpose of our incarnation is.

This chapter has always existed

As you may have read elsewhere in this book, time and space are just fictitious constructions created by our mind. All events, both past and future, exist simultaneously in the here and now and based on our thoughts and beliefs or expectations we experience the corresponding events, which are nothing more than the materialization of our primary vibration.

What does this mean, and what does it have to do with the title of this chapter?

The consequence of the fact that time does not exist is that all the books or articles we will read, as well as all the seminars or lectures we will attend, already exist somewhere in *spacetime*. They have always existed. But we also know that there is nothing and no one out there, *spacetime* exists only in our minds, and therefore **we are the ones who create** whatever events, books or seminars we encounter in our life journey. We put them there, along our way, even before we come into the world, so that one day we can take advantage of them.

In short, we are the creators of everything we need for our growth, creating both the *'educational program'*, i.e., the path of growth, and the *'educational material'*, i.e., the books, articles and seminars we come into contact with.

Does it seem absurd? If we recognize that we are the only creators of our reality, it can only be so, otherwise we should assume that there is the existence of something or someone outside of us. However, this would violate the principle that we are the only creators of the world we experience, but also violate the principle that we are One and only One with the entire Universe.

And so maybe it is clear to you why I say that you wrote this chapter, and you put it on your growth path so that you can read it at the right time.

We could end here, but if you feel like following me for a while longer, I would like to talk to you about an even more important concept, which stems from what has been said so far.

The True Nature of Time and Space

To say that time and space do not exist and that they are therefore only illusions of our mind does not tell us much, because probably none of us understands what this really means. After all, we have direct experience of both time and space. If we want to go somewhere far away from us, in fact, we must necessarily travel through space, and it will necessarily take time to do so.

So where is the illusion? Let's start from the conclusion: time and space exist only as a consequence of the fact that we are not aware of our being divine, and that we do not recognize that we are One with the whole Universe.

Well, let's start with **space**. As I am sure you already know, we are constantly creating reality based on our innermost beliefs. Consequently, as long as we believe that we are separate from each other, we will necessarily create a world in which things are separated by space. Physics, through the principle of quantum entanglement, has shown that two particles, even if separated and placed at enormous distance between them, always behave as if they were a single particle. From a physical point of view, therefore, the space that apparently separates those particles does not exist.

Space is just our own creation to justify our mistaken belief that we are separate from the rest of the Universe.

What about **time**? We have said that our true nature is not the body we inhabit, but rather our True Self, which is the divine being that lives outside of space and time, and therefore knows the true Reality and is not being affected by the illusion of the apparent world we live in. Well, the fact that we do not believe that we are already aware of the true Reality, forces us to create a temporal separation between us and the hypothetical moment of our enlightenment. In reality **we are already enlightened beings now**, we have always been, but we do not believe it, and so we think it takes 'time' to reach that enlightenment.

Time is only our creation to justify the mistaken belief that we are not enlightened beings already aware of the true Reality.

So that is why you wrote all those books, including this chapter, and you are reading them a little bit at a time, during your *'long'* journey of growth, with the sole purpose of *remembering* all these things.

Karma and the Law of Attraction

If it is true that we create our own reality and are potentially capable of manifesting our desires, how does this reconcile with the fact that Karma also exists, according to which our destiny is in part conditioned by what has happened in the past?

We have all heard of Karma, and I think everyone has an idea of this "law" of the Universe. According to the principle of Karma, every thought, word or action of ours has in some way an influence in what will happen to us in the future. This mechanism of action-reaction can act independently from time and space, because its effects, according to some, can occur at any time and in ways that cannot be predicted.

But as stated several times, I first urge everyone to consider themselves the sole creators of their own reality. We are divine beings, as I have said many times, and having been created in the "image and likeness" of our Creator, we in turn have inherited the ability to create.

How then does this freedom of ours to create our own destiny fit in with the laws of Karma that we described at the beginning of this chapter? How is it possible, in other words, to think that we can make the Law of Attraction work, when at the same time we are at the mercy of the action-reaction mechanism determined by our previous actions?

It is simpler than you might imagine.

We live in a dual Universe, in which there is everything and the opposite of everything. In fact, we will all agree that we can experience darkness and light, beauty and ugliness, joy and sadness, ... and I could continue with another ten pages of examples. Well, these two aspects are in constant balance. How do I know this? Just look around you. If our universe was not balanced, the preponderance of any one aspect, if not counterbalanced, would eventually grow out of all proportion and destroy the universe. It is like a pendulum: the more we push towards one of the two extremities, the more the weight will come back with force towards the opposite extremity, and then at the end it will rest at the center once the initial force that broke the balance is exhausted.

So, the universe we live in works this way. Any "disturbance" is sooner or later counterbalanced by an equal and opposite force that brings everything back into balance. Simplifying, this is Karma.

What if it is just a manifestation of Karma?

What if the Law of Attraction is nothing more than another manifestation of Karma? Um... let's try to analyze this idea.

You may remember one of the 7 laws of Hermes Trismegistus:

> "As above - so below,
> as below - so above.
> **As within - so without,**
> **as without - so within.**
> As in big - so in small."

It is no coincidence that I highlighted the words *"As within, so without..."*. This, if you think about it, is the very law upon which what we call the **Law of Attraction** is based, according to which what we "are" on the inside will always manifest on the outside. It is the concept of "being" for "becoming".

If I think I am lame, the Universe will go out of its way to prove it to me, but the reverse is also true, of course.

How does this principle act? Any "imbalance" between what we "feel" to be, and what we "are" in reality, will be somehow canceled, so that the outside world will be uniformed sooner or later to what we think we are. If you reread this last sentence, you will probably find exactly the mechanism through which Karma works. If I change my "feeling" about who I am, the external reality can only remedy the inequality that has been created between "inside" and "outside", making sure that this difference is canceled. How? If we keep our thoughts still without being conditioned by external events, the universe will not be able to do anything but modify the external reality bringing back the correct balance between things.

It can only be so, because what we call "outside" is nothing but the projection of what we are "inside". Indeed, to put it better, both the inside and the outside are in our mind. We are the ones who contain the Universe, not the other way around, so everything must necessarily conform to our beliefs about how things should manifest.

And the law of Karma is there precisely to make sure that this always happens, without exception.

The True Nature of the Law of Attraction

We have always been led to believe that we can only attract what we somehow 'deserve'. Instead, there is no such thing as a limit, and this chapter will explain why.

With this chapter I wish to continue the series of chapters in which I explain that there is no physical limit to what we can achieve. As I have said several times in this book, in fact, we are Divine beings endowed with free will who have decided to incarnate and experience their divinity, passing through a state of non-divinity.

This means that, even if we do not know it, we actually possess all the powers to have or become anything. The problem is that we are not aware of our powers, and because of the illusion of being separated from a Universe that appears external to us and hostile, we do not believe we can really see any of our desires come true.

In fact, we all have the feeling that there is some force outside of us that decides what desire we deserve to fulfill. We have inherited this common thought from all the conditioning we received as children.

We have always been led to think that not everything can be achieved in life, that we have to earn with sweat any achievement, and certain religious teachings have made us believe in the existence of a God outside of us who judges and decides whether or not to listen to our pleas.

That is not how it works. It is hard to change beliefs that have been imposed on us from the outside since we were children, when we did not have the tools to decide whether what we were told was really the truth. The problem is that everything we have accepted as the truth has now heavily conditioned our existence.

In this chapter I would like to show you an aspect of the issue related to the functioning of the Law of Attraction that you may not have considered.

The Universe is Unconditional Love

Let's assume that the wrathful God who judges our actions does not exist at all. It is a pure invention of the various religions, which have used the image of a judgmental and vengeful God for their exclusive use and consumption. Judgment is an exclusive characteristic of man, and so it is logical that we have projected this aspect of ourselves into the God of almost all religions.

God is everything that exists, visible and invisible. You can call it One, or Universe, you choose, but as I have said many times in this book, I will not dwell on the terms used, since the really important thing are the concepts. We ourselves are part of that One, representing one of its many expressions.

The idea that I want to show in this chapter comes from a reflection read in a book by Ramtha. His enlightenment in fact took place while observing the Sun, which every morning, inexorably, rises on the horizon. It does so always and in any case, regardless of what may have happened on Earth. And the same goes for the Moon and the stars, but also for the air, the wind, the birds and any other beautiful expression of the Universe.

Ramtha then realized that nature is the perfect expression of the God it represents, because everything that exists is simply given to us, always and everywhere, regardless of what we might have done. The Sun asks nothing of us in return. It does not ask if we deserve its light before rising, and so does the Moon with all the stars. This is when we realize that the Universe is the expression of God's **Unconditional Love** towards His Creations.

Love gives and unites

To complete our reasoning let's see in detail what Unconditional Love is. You all know that Love is the opposite of fear, and while fear divides and distances, true Love is a force that simply gives and unites all things, and it does so unconditionally, without judging or asking for anything in return. But let's think for a moment about the words *gives and unites*.

The central theme of this chapter is the Law of Attraction, and you all know that this law exists because we actually live in an attractive Universe, where similar things attract. In fact, we all know that according to the Law of Attraction, thought, which is a form of energy, is able to attract by resonating other similar thoughts. Just as the Sun does not ask itself if we deserve its light, so the Law of Attraction **unites** similar things and unconditionally **gives** us the materialization of our thoughts.

So here we come to explain the title of this chapter. Perhaps you had never thought about it, but in fact the Law of Attraction and Unconditional Love are **two aspects of the same thing**. We can say without a shadow of a doubt that the Law of Attraction, based on its ability to give and unite, **"is"** Unconditional Love. So, let's stop thinking about something or someone judging our requests, and realize that the only obstacle in obtaining our desires is only us, with our miserable thoughts of fear, scarcity and inadequacy.

The Law of Attraction and Unconditional Love are the same thing, and I want to reiterate this once again through Ramtha's beautiful words:

> *"For the Love of God called Life, has always been given to*
> *You. Despite all Your miserable experiences, the sun still*
> *comes out and dances in the heavens. The seasons still come*
> *and go.*
> *The sylvan birds still fly to the northern sky.*
> *And the night bird still protests publicly in the night as You*
> *close the doors of Your room. It is in the continuity of All these*

things that, if You look, You will realize the forgiveness and eternity that Life has always granted You."

Be Careful What You Ask For, Because It Will Be Given to You

We have to be very careful about what we ask for, because the Universe always responds to us with the utmost precision.

I wanted to write this chapter to highlight an aspect of the Law of Attraction that perhaps not everyone has considered in its full meaning. In fact, many people express their desires without really paying attention to the content of what they are asking for. You have to consider that every thought we have is an order that is always executed 'to the letter'. When I say 'to the letter' I mean that any detail must be expressed with the utmost precision, leaving nothing to chance.

I want to tell you about a couple of episodes that happened to me in the past, when this concept of precision was not yet so clear to me.

Living in a residential hotel

A few years ago, having just discovered the existence of the Law of Attraction, caught up in the enthusiasm of being able to ask the Universe for anything, I immediately thought that I could become rich in a short time (original, don't you think?). Since I had heard that you should never ask for money (a few years later I discovered that this is only partially true), I began to wonder what rich people usually did, so I could ask for the same thing, instead of the vile money.

It occurred to me that many rich people live in hotels, so I began, every night before falling asleep, to close my eyes and imagine myself in a hotel room. Since I could ask for anything, I thought that perhaps it would be more useful to ask the Universe to live in a residential hotel, so I would also have all the comforts of a small apartment, such as a small kitchen, a small living room to receive friends, etc.

In my visualizations I imagined myself coming home in the evening and being greeted by the receptionist, taking the key and going up to my apartment, finding it perfectly clean and tidy each time, feeling the satisfaction of finally being able to live the life of my dreams.

I did these visualizations for at least 5-6 months, almost every night, and then almost forgot about them (I realized later that *'forgetting'* is really important).

About a year and a half later, the company I work for offered me a job for a period of about two years in Paris, to supervise an important project.

Guess where I lived for those two years? That's right, in a residential hotel, in the center of Paris, in an apartment with a kitchenette and a small living room. And just like in my visualizations. Every evening when I returned from my office I was greeted by the receptionist, who by now knew me and handed me the room key without me having to remember the number.

Everything as I had visualized, down to the smallest detail, with disconcerting precision. The problem was that I had not become rich, because the room was paid for by my company, and I continued to receive my normal salary. Where did I make a mistake?

I had simply *'forgotten'* to feel rich in those visualizations. That's what the mistake had been. The Universe reproduces everything to the letter, including our emotions. So, the Universe brought me everything I had asked for, while also making sure that in reality, in that residential hotel, I felt like the same person I had always been, just as I was during the visualizations.

My penthouse of 140 sqm

If you are still not convinced, listen to this other episode. About a year ago, tired of living in my house in Fiumicino, I decided that the time had come to change and return to live in Rome, my beloved hometown. In the meantime, regardless of this need, I also began to draw up the 101 wishes with the technique described by Igor Sibaldi. Since Sibaldi invites you to exaggerate when expressing your desires, I wrote down as one of the 101 wishes that of wanting a beautiful 140 sqm penthouse near the area of Rome where I work (for those who know Rome, near Villa Pamphili).

Since I could not afford a penthouse of that size in that area of Rome, I did not connect that desire to the house search I was doing, so much so that I was not looking for a penthouse at all. For the Universe, that was an expressed desire, therefore a precise order to be fulfilled, on which I was also operating through precise actions, such as the fact that I started scanning all the ads for apartments in that area (the action that follows a desire is of fundamental importance, don't forget that).

At some point, for the sake of brevity I will not explain how (but there is some magic in the way it came about), I was offered a penthouse with a view of Villa Pamphili, more or less at the price I intended to spend. Guess what? The penthouse consisted of a 40 sqm apartment plus a huge and beautiful 100 sqm terrace.

Yes, the Universe had brought me a penthouse with a total area of 140 square meters, exactly as I had asked. In this case, when I wrote my wish, I had not indicated the size of the covered area, so the Universe did what it thought best for me. And since I lived alone, I would not have known what to do with an apartment of 140 square meters. Amazing, isn't it?

Always make the right request

You will have understood, therefore, that it is very important to ask precisely what you want, trying to imagine all the details, without neglecting any of them. Very important is the emotion you feel while visualizing your desire.

God's perfection is reflected in the perfection of the entire Creation, so never forget to be accurate when you ask for something, because then **it will be given to you with staggering precision**.

Your Defense Is Your Real Danger

Perhaps you have never realized that it is your own fear of being attacked that attracts the one you are defending yourself against.

I felt the need to write this chapter because I am becoming increasingly aware of the difficulty people are having in understanding the enormous influence our thoughts and words have on the reality we create moment by moment.

We are usually led to believe that our thoughts have no influence, but, as we already know, every thought sooner or later returns and affects our lives with an event that faithfully reflects that thought or belief.

In this chapter, I want to focus on the fact that it is our very attitude of defensiveness that creates the things or people from which we think we must defend ourselves.

By now we know very well that we are the ones who attract in our life any event or person that is in correspondence with the primary vibration of the thoughts that crowd our mind. Well, perhaps few realize that this is a law of the Universe, and as such it always works, regardless of our will or awareness.

Every time we are *"against"* something, we do nothing but attract the very thing we are fighting against. This is why Mother Teresa always responded to those who asked her why she never participated in anti-war demonstrations:

When you organize a pro-peace demonstration, give me a call.

Mother Teresa had certainly foreseen the mechanisms by which the Universe works.

You must always consider that we live in an *'attractive'* Universe, not a *'repulsive'* one. This means that words like *'not'* or *'against'* simply have no meaning.

I would like to tell you about an article I read some time ago in a local newspaper, which may make you think about what I am saying. The headline told of a girl who had been hit by a train at an unguarded level crossing, fortunately escaping with only a few broken bones. Intrigued by the headline, I read the whole story, discovering that the girl's father had long been fighting a personal battle against the railways to make that level crossing safe. In the body of the article, it was written that the father, before the accident, had written **over 100 letters of protest** asking that the case be considered.

Think about how much energy, bolstered by feelings of anger, that father had focused on the possibility of someone being hit by a train. And perhaps who knows how many times he had also visualized the scene of a train running over some unfortunate passerby. All that energy could not remain unexpressed, and that unsuspecting man could not even begin to imagine that he was creating the conditions for the very event he wanted to prevent.

Of course, this mechanism works for any danger we want to escape. In the book "A Course in Miracles", in fact, this concept is expressed in several places. Believe it or not, we are precisely the ones who create our enemies through our attitude of fear and subsequent defense.

What we really need to understand is that all the reality that we see separate and outside of us exists only in our minds. As I have had occasion to say many times, there is nothing out there beyond the projections of our innermost beliefs and fears.

We will have nothing left to defend ourselves from when we finally understand that we are the sole architects of our own destiny.

This is unfortunately still a taboo subject for many. In fact, every time I address this issue, I am harshly attacked by someone who protests by saying that victims of crimes cannot be held responsible for their misfortunes. It is obvious that those people *did not consciously draw* their problems to themselves, it is so obvious that I consider it **completely stupid** to think that I mean something different.

It is our *unawareness* our true enemy.

It is our constant *falling asleep* that causes thoughts of all sorts (mostly negative) to crowd our minds, thus creating the reality we are then going to experience. We must finally realize that the enemies we see out there are only the projections of our deepest fears, and as such can be eliminated simply by recognizing their ephemeral reality. We are only the true enemies of ourselves, and we are so every time we ignore what the true laws of the Universe are, and every time we refuse to believe in the immense power of our mind.

I leave you with the wonderful words of Master Teacher, one of the most famous and trained teachers of "A Course in Miracles":

You have heard him say, "An eye for an eye", I will defend myself because I am attacked. I say no. You must forgive your enemy.
Why must you forgive your enemy?
...I didn't hear you.
Did you say "I am my own enemy"?

Ladies and Gentlemen, Make Your Choice

You must choose what you wish to be, and as a result life will respond bringing you what you desire. It is all about choices, there is no middle ground.

We all know the phrase from the Gospel:

Ask and it will be given to you, seek and you will find, knock and the door will be opened to you.
The one who asks will always receive; the one who is searching will always find, and the door is opened to the man who knocks.
(Luke 11, 9-10)

It has become even more famous thanks to the fact that Mr. and Mrs. Hicks used it as the title to one of their most important works. But have you ever really analyzed what this phrase means? What did Jesus mean by *"Ask and it will be given to you"*?

Those who do not understand the deeper meaning of this phrase cannot even use it for their own purposes, and perhaps this is one of the main reasons why the Law of Attraction most of the time does not seem to work.

First, let's look at the concept that underlies all of our reasoning: **you can only ask after you have chosen what you want**. That's why in the title of this chapter I wrote 'make your choice'. Sometimes the most obvious things are precisely those that escape superficial analysis.

Mind you, I am not saying that we do not know what to ask for, because I am convinced that each of you knows more or less what you would like to have from the Universe. The problem is that **we do not choose**.

Choosing means something else far more profound, which we will now explore.

Like the whims of a child

Choosing means **making an unequivocal decision** about what we want. It means considering one outcome - just one - and discarding any other assumptions about any alternative that does not fully satisfy our primary choice.

You know when a child is said to be "having a tantrum"? If a child wants something, he puts forth all his energy to manifest his choice, and it is difficult to divert him from what he wants, if not by accepting, he complains and manifests his disappointment by having a tantrum.

This means to choose, and children, not yet contaminated by the wrong idea that something can be impossible to obtain, know very well that to obtain something you have to be absolutely categorical and firm on your decision, aligning your whole being towards the satisfaction of that desire. We must learn from children, because they know very well how the Universe works, much better than our obtuse rationality would have us believe.

Well, this is what it means to choose. It does not mean wishing for something and then hoping that it will come true, based on some supernatural force or divine intervention. That's not how things work. We are in possession of immense power, but we must claim that power, manifesting it with all our strength.

The problem is that we have misrepresented the concept of *asking in order to get*. We think that there is some force outside of us that receives our request, and then somehow, provided we are worthy enough, provides us to have it. After reading the books on the Law of Attraction, in fact, we do some visualizations and then we spend our time 'hoping' that something will happen, believing in a Universe separate from us in which there is a strange law that brings us (if we have been good) the things we ask for.

No, ladies and gentlemen, this is not how the Universe works.

The child does not just ask, because at the same time he is **absolutely convinced** that it is possible to have what he is asking for, more importantly, **he focuses with his whole being** on that thing and acts in such a way as to obtain it, at all costs.

For us adults, who of course cannot have tantrums, all this translates into the absolute focus and certainty, on a mental level, that what we are asking for can be ours, and at the same time any thought, word or action of ours must be aimed at supporting that idea. There can be no such thing as *'we hope that...'*, or *'who knows if...'*, or worse *'it will be difficult that...'*.

Hope is the virtue of losers.

Every thought we have is a very specific order, and doubting it is **a very clear command** we give to the Universe to **cancel our request**. There is no force or divine entity out there that has to bring us what we asked for. The concept is very simple: we do not have to ask, we have to choose:

If we ask, we assume that there is something or someone separate from us to whom we are asking.

If we choose, we are simply taking what already exists and is already ours, without any intermediary.

Did you grasp the concept?

That's what it means **to choose**, which then, in case you did not notice, is nothing more than a **synonym to create**.

Perseverance and Willpower Are the Keys to Wealth

Being good or prepared in life is not enough. Perseverance and willpower are the real keys to wealth.

Several years ago, I purchased and read the book "Think and grow rich" by Napoleon Hill. This is one of the most famous books which, in the first half of the last century, brought to the attention of the general public the principles underlying the Law of Attraction, revealing for the first time, and in a way accessible to all, what the real keys to wealth are.

Anyone who strives to succeed should read this invaluable book. Hill was the first to realize that the keys to wealth and success are hidden in our minds. Don't look for them anywhere else, for you will search in vain.

In flipping through it again in search for some inspirational thoughts in which I wanted to devote precisely to the keys to wealth, I focused on the first chapter, where Napoleon Hill addresses the concept of perseverance through an interesting anecdote.

Perseverance: one of the keys to wealth

In the 1800s, during the gold rush, an American prospector, heedless of the fact that it was generally believed that finding a gold vein was an almost impossible task, armed himself with a shovel and pickaxe and, having found promising ground, began to dig incessantly, day and night.

Finally, after several weeks of hard work, his perseverance was rewarded, because he found a gold vein, which foretold the presence of a large quantity of the precious metal in that land. He then began to extract the gold with great enthusiasm, but after just a few meters from the first discovery, suddenly the vein seemed to be exhausted. The man dug again, but after days and days of incessant work without getting any results, he surrendered to the evidence that the gold vein unfortunately did not exist.

He then gave up, and resold all the material for a few dollars to a local junk dealer. The junk dealer, however, did not give up and asked a mining engineer to make calculations on the land. The engineer came to the conclusion that the gold vein should be only one meter lower than where the previous prospector had stopped digging. And so, the junk dealer reopened the dig and extracted millions of dollars' worth of gold from the ground, becoming extremely wealthy.

Many people stop just a step away from success. The **key to wealth** will only be handed to those who persevere in their intentions and never give up.

Willpower: another indispensable key to success

In the same chapter there is another beautiful story that shows us how even iron will is one of the indispensable keys to wealth.

We find ourselves in an old mill in colonial America, where a boy and his uncle were grinding wheat. Suddenly a little black girl, the daughter of a sharecropper, came in and shyly said to her uncle, "My mama says she must have fifty cents from you." "Not a chance," said the man. "Now go home at once."

The girl said "Yes sir", but did not move. The man looked at her sternly, and said threateningly "I told you to go home! Go or I'll give you a whipping." Again, the girl replied "Yes sir", but she did not move an inch. At this point the man took a stick and approached the child with a threatening air. The nephew watched the scene terrified, knowing the angry nature of his uncle. At this point the little girl took a step forward and, with all the breath she had in her throat, she screamed at the man, "Mommy must have those fifty cents! The man stopped, dropped the stick, and astonishingly took 50 cents from his pocket and gave them to the girl. After that he sat down with his eyes lost in the void, thinking about the 'whipping' he had just received from that little girl.

Sometimes we do not realize the enormous strength we have inside, that if expressed at the right time and in the right way allows us to achieve any goal. That little girl had shown that she had an iron and immovable will, that no obstacle, not even a man 3 times bigger than her could have even dented. Her enormous determination to go back home with the 50 cents made her far stronger than that man.

The one great truth and lesson to be learned is that the keys to wealth and success are handed to those who demonstrate perseverance and will to achieve their goals. But if you think about it for a moment, in both episodes the keys to wealth were hidden in the minds of the protagonists, regardless of the apparent external adversity. How many would have resumed digging in that ground, and how many in place of the little girl would not have fled in the face of that man's threats?

Our mind can turn any adversity in our favor, we just need to believe in it and show the Universe that we have perseverance and unwavering will.

Then the Universe can only help us to find the solution to our problems.

The Role of the Will in the Creation of Reality

Everyone tells us that you have to have an iron will to achieve your goals. But no one has ever explained to us the true role of the will in the conscious creation of reality.

We all believe, because that is what we have always been told, that the will is the tool to achieve any goal in life. True, but the role of the will in creating reality is not what you have always believed it to be.

Let's start with a little experiment. Try closing your eyes and imagining yourself driving a car down a highway. Imagine your hands on the steering wheel, the road in front of you, and the sound of the wheels on the asphalt. Try to do this by imagining that you are driving at least 2 kilometers, and that you are checking the distance travelled by means of the markers placed every 100 meters that you see running along the side of the roadway.

Well, try it now and do not open your eyes again until you have covered at least 2 kilometers (equivalent to 20 markers).

Done? How many of you have managed to keep your focus on visualization without digressing or stopping to imagine highway driving? I think very few people.

This is the very first reason why we cannot get what we desire through the application of the Law of Attraction. We are talking about the will. In fact, the lack of will.

We are discovering a very important truth, which almost no one has ever told us, and which you will not find written in almost any book about the Law of Attraction.

The true role of will in the creation process

Let's start by saying right away that the will is not creative, in the sense that it is not enough to strongly desire something to obtain it. By now we should have understood that the necessary ingredients are many, such as Faith, Gratitude, Positive Thinking, etc.

But all these ingredients are useless if we do not also consider the very important role of willpower.

The will is not to be used in the way we have all been told since childhood. We already know that the action resulting from the will to obtain something in most cases will not bring any result if not accompanied by **a work of visualization of the final result**, combined with an unshakable faith that we can get what we want.

This is precisely the point. The Law of Attraction brings us what corresponds to our primary vibration, which can be controlled and directed deliberately through a work of visualization in which we must 'feel' that we have already achieved the final result.

Here then is where the will comes into play. If we want to achieve something, the main thing is to have the iron will to reach that goal, otherwise it is not even worth trying. But the most important thing is **to keep one's thoughts on the desired end result constant over time**. To do this we must have an iron will, otherwise, as in the experiment of driving on the highway, it will be very difficult, if not impossible, to keep the focus on the object of desire long enough.

Willpower is the controlling power in your mind that keeps your thinking going in a given direction until the result is achieved.

Here at last **is the true role of the will** revealed. And this is why we have been endowed with will from birth. It is one of the main ingredients for us to be able to create the desired reality.

It is the will that leads the thought towards a specific purpose until it is fulfilled, or that keeps an idea in a specific place in the mind until it is given a shape.

We can think of the will as a thought-stabilizer, in the sense that it is the only force in our mind capable of holding a focused thought stable in order to achieve its materialization.

Using the words of Thomas Troward in The Edinburgh Lectures of Mental Science,

"If, using the word in its widest sense, we may say that the imagination is the creative function, we may call the will the centralizing principle. Its function is to keep the imagination centered in the right direction."

In other words, success or failure is dependent on only one thing: mental control, and the role of the will is precisely to represent that controlling factor.

Willpower must be trained constantly

Now that you know the role of willpower, you will surely know how to use it in the best way, but remember that willpower is not a gift we get for free. It must be trained through specific exercises because without training we will always be at the mercy of our mind, which will wander preventing us from focusing our thoughts long enough on the desired image.

I will leave you with another thought by Thomas Troward, one of the pioneers of the Law of Attraction theory, which brilliantly sums up what I have said so far:

"The business of the will is always the same, that of keeping your mental faculties where they will do the work you intend them to do."

We Use Free Will to Control Our Lives

In this chapter we will talk about a fundamental concept in creating our reality, but which is often underestimated: Free Will. Let's find out what it is and how it should be best used.

If you think you possess free will, raise your hand.

I can see a forest of raised hands, and rightly so. In fact, we are all endowed since birth with free will, but the real problem is another: the truth is that *we do not exercise it*.

Don't you believe it? Okay, then answer this question honestly: how many of you would be able to smile and thank the one who is hurting you?

Or rather: which one of you can **choose** to smile and say thank you in the face of a serious wrong?

I can't see any hands raised....

I intentionally used the word **choose**. How can we think we possess free will if we are not in a position to choose how to deal with the situations in our lives?

Reality, unfortunately, is that we do not act, we react to situations that come our way.

If something good happens, we are happy, if something unpleasant happens we are sad or angry.

It is as if there are buttons in our brains with "RAGE", "FEAR", "JOY", "TREASURE", etc. written on them.

The people we meet or the events that happen to us do nothing but *"press"* one of these buttons, and we automatically perceive the corresponding emotion, reacting accordingly.

Now you may ask: what the hell does free will have to do with creating your own reality? It does, it does.

We must understand that we are not our body or our mind.

In reality, we are so much more. We are spiritual beings inhabiting a physical body with a mind. Our body is a perfect biological machine. Perfect and beautiful, but still a machine.

And as such, if left to its own devices, it can do nothing but "work" according to a preset program, built up over the years through the experiences it has lived and the education it has received.

These biological mechanisms operate undisturbed because we identify with them, even believing that it is normal and right to get angry for something wrong done to us. We are not aware of the enormous power we have, and so we react to the outside world not believing we can influence it.

The reality is that we are asleep, even when we are not in our bed. Our minds are constantly being invaded by compulsive thoughts of which we have no control, and this makes us *less present*.

What does *less present* mean? It means that our true Being, the Master of the House, is usually absent, and the mind, as a biological machine, works without any control.

Think about it for a moment: you are in the car, and you think: "...I should call Marta... the last time I heard from her was on her birthday... by the way, today is Mario's birthday, I have to go to the bookstore to buy a book... who knows if I manage to find a parking space near the bookstore... I also have to remember to pay the parking ticket I got last week..." ...and so on and so forth.

In a complete lack of control, and for no reason at all, hundreds of thoughts crowd our mind.

Although we possess it, we do not use the free will that has been given to us since birth to consciously control what thoughts **we want** to think.

But remember. The mind, and therefore our thoughts create our reality.

The formula is simple:

Random and uncontrolled thoughts => Random and uncontrolled reality

So, if we do not have control of our thoughts, our emotions, and our reactions, how do we think we can control our reality?

Let's exercise **Free Will** and let our **True Self** regain control of the biological machine. And let's enjoy the results....

In the following chapters, we will delve more deeply into the consequences of this *chronic falling asleep* that we are all unknowingly afflicted with.

A Gateway to Conscious Creation

We are very powerful Creators, but we do not know we are. So, let's learn how the unconscious can be used as a way to access Conscious Creation.

I have already spoken in this book about the role of the unconscious in creating our reality, but few, I think, have really understood the mechanism by which it works, and how to use it fully to their advantage.

The title of this chapter is very clear on the fact that the unconscious is the way to access the Conscious Creation. Indeed, it is the only way available to us, and only the knowledge of this very important aspect can allow us to become truly Conscious Creators of our reality. I have already spoken several times about these concepts, but in this chapter, I want to emphasize some mechanisms that are important for you to know. In fact, as I have said many times, only through the knowledge of the true mechanisms that underlie the Law of Attraction can we become Conscious Creators.

Let's start by explaining what differentiates the conscious mind from the unconscious one. Well, you must know that the unconscious mind can only reason deductively, while the conscious mind can process both deductive and inductive reasoning. **Deductive reasoning** is able to determine the consequences of facts or predetermined assumptions, but it is not absolutely able to determine whether the initial assumptions are true or false. The latter task is delegated to **inductive reasoning** which, starting from objective observations of reality, can reach conclusions.

Too complicated? I will try to explain it in another way. Through inductive reasoning, a property possessed only by the conscious mind, we look at the world around us, and on the basis of observations made previously, we draw conclusions about which facts we can consider as really true. Inductive reasoning is consequently linked to previous situations, or to the experience about a particular phenomenon, which is then used to draw conclusions. This fact makes inductive reasoning strongly linked to the concepts of time and space.

Deductive reasoning, instead, typical of the unconscious mind, is not able to make autonomous assumptions on the basis of past experiences, but is limited exclusively to take for good the assumptions that are suggested from the outside, in our case from the conscious mind. The unconscious mind lives outside of time and space, not being influenced in any way.

The most careful will have already understood what the power behind what has been said is. The unconscious mind has no way of determining whether what is said by the conscious mind is true or false. It does not concern itself in any way. **For it, everything that the conscious mind conveys is true by definition.**

The pathway to Conscious Creation is unveiled

At this point we should consider that the unconscious mind is directly connected with our True Self, which represents our creative part. I will not dwell here on the true nature of the unconscious mind, but know that its function is precisely to transmit the assumptions coming from our conscious part to the creative power of our True Self, which in turn represents a part of the Universal Mind that permeates the whole Universe.

The result is that our unconscious is able to activate the Law of Attraction bringing to us everything that the conscious mind has determined to be true.

Okay, but how can we use this knowledge? Simple: **by visualizing the desired things, and assuming with absolute certainty that they are already ours**. Visualization must totally disregard current circumstances, places, people or past experiences. Remember that the unconscious takes for granted the things that are suggested to it by the conscious mind, without questioning them. It really does, because the mechanism I have described is one of the most important laws governing the functioning of nature. If you can imprint a desired thought in your mind long enough, sooner or later that image will **necessarily** become your reality. Not believing is one of the main reasons why the mechanism described above is jammed, thus failing to access the infinite creative power of the Universe.

Those who do not know or refuse to believe this fundamental mechanism live at the mercy of their uncontrolled thoughts. People who know and accept this truth, on the other hand, use it to their advantage by exercising constant control over their conscious mind, in order to imprint in their unconscious mind only the desired facts they wish to materialize in their lives.

Becoming Conscious Creators cannot be separated from the knowledge and application of this fundamental principle. Now you know it. So, stop complaining and use your will to become a Conscious Creator and finally change your life.

The Unconscious Does Not See with Our Eyes

It may seem strange, but what we see is not what is taken into account by the deepest part of ourselves. In short, the unconscious does not see with our eyes.

Almost certainly you have seen the movie "The Secret", and read numerous other books dealing with the Law of Attraction. However, it is unlikely that these texts have revealed to you one of the most important things to know in order to successfully apply the Law of Attraction.

What I want to talk about in this chapter is the actual mechanism by which we manage to create our reality, and if you have the persistence to read all the way through, you will also understand the reason why I chose this title.

It is of paramount importance to understand that the Law of Attraction works on the principle that we attract to ourselves objects, people and events that are perfectly attuned to the primary vibration we emit. This vibration is the energetic expression of who we feel we are. Pay attention to the words I am using. I wrote "what we feel we are", not what we think, or imagine we are. We have to "feel" we are something in order to become it or attract it into our actual experience.

You may have read countless times the following concept:

If you want to become rich, you must first be rich within yourself.

The truth is that the external world is only a reflection of the internal world. If we do not truly feel that we are, or have something, we can never experience it directly. It is the Law.

Well, but how exactly does this mechanism work? It is important to know, in order to deliberately use it for our own purposes. The title of this chapter surprisingly is not about the unconscious. Why?

Simple, because it is precisely the unconscious that emits the vibration related to our being, which attracts to us corresponding things and events. All our convictions, beliefs, ways of being, etc. are rooted in our unconscious, whose main task is precisely to vibrate at the frequency corresponding to what we have transmitted to it with our thoughts and emotions, in order to experience them sooner or later in real life.

The Big Secret

Okay, but what does it have to do with the fact that the unconscious does not see with our eyes? It really does. In answer to this question lies one of the greatest secrets behind the Law of Attraction, and knowing it inside out means being able to consciously take control of your life. You need to know two fundamental aspects of how our unconscious works in order to truly understand what I mean when I say that the unconscious does not see with our eyes.

The **first aspect** to consider is that the unconscious does not receive our thoughts, but only the vibrations corresponding to our emotions and feelings. In fact, if you simply think about any event, but you do not feel emotionally involved, that is you do not actually feel you are living it directly as if it were happening here and now, then the unconscious will not receive any information. If, for example, you think you are going to win a large sum of money in the lottery, but you do not experience the corresponding emotion, then you will barely be able to attract to you the experience of winning.

The **second very important aspect** is that the unconscious does not judge or evaluate the information that reaches it. The task of filtering and applying logical reasoning is entrusted exclusively to our conscious part, which in fact has the role of controller or 'guardian of the door' of everything that is transmitted to our unconscious. From some experiments carried out in the laboratory, for example, it has emerged that an athlete, who imagines to participate in a race, emits brain signals (detected with special instruments) exactly identical to those emitted by the same athlete while participating in a real race. In other words, the unconscious *does not distinguish in any way* between a lived experience and one imagined.

These two aspects should now have clarified what I mean by 'the unconscious does not see with our eyes'. The unconscious **is in the dark within our being**, and cannot in any way become aware of our real situation. It follows then that it is only and exclusively what we send to it on an emotional level that is taken into account by our unconscious. The unconscious does not see and does not know, for example, that we do not really own that villa with a swimming pool.

If we are good then, we can visualize the **feeling** to be in possession of it, for the unconscious that is the reality, and it will then do everything to bring that experience into our real life. You will also have understood why a chaotic and uncontrolled mind generates an equally chaotic and uncontrolled reality.

Now that we know that the unconscious does not see with our eyes, we have added another important piece to the knowledge needed to become true masters of the Law of Attraction. We now know that our current situation has no effect on our real chances of getting what we want, and woe betide if we pay too much attention to it.

Success is based only on our ability to control the conscious mind so that we transmit to the unconscious mind only and exclusively the emotions corresponding to what we want to achieve in our lives.

Easy? Not by a long shot, but with commitment and the right techniques, anyone can do it.

Learning to Dialogue with the Unconscious

Only if we learn to dialogue with the unconscious, can we discover the most intimate part of ourselves and use it to our own advantage.

Dialoguing with the unconscious is important, but we do not know why or how to do it. So, let's delve into this concept and discover the importance of learning to dialogue with the unconscious.

We have now learned that our thoughts and beliefs create the reality that surrounds us. We have already given in the pages of this book several scientific explanations of how it happens, through the analysis of the most modern theories of quantum physics.

But while quantum physics explains in an indisputable way what particles of matter are made of and how they are influenced by our thoughts, it cannot explain what the mechanism inside us is, that develops this creative influence on matter itself.

The title of this chapter gives us a precise indication: we all exert our influence on the world through the unconscious. This is why it is essential to learn how to **dialogue with the unconscious**, so that we can consciously create our own reality.

Let's first look at how all this works. We already know that we are in fact made up of three interacting parts: **the conscious mind**, which receives all impulses from the outside world and processes thoughts by the brain, which is the seat of our mind, **the unconscious mind**, which oversees the functioning of all our vital activities (such as the beating of the heart or the functioning of the glands) and the so-called **Superconscious**, which is none other than our True Self, the spiritual part of our being.

The importance of learning to dialogue with the unconscious

Although the title of this chapter is "Learning to Dialogue with the Unconscious," we actually already do this, all the time, simply because through this dialogue we give continuous orders to our unconscious. Our conscious mind is the part of us that processes thoughts and beliefs through our idea of the world. Our unconscious mind, however, does not process any logical reasoning, but has the task of accepting everything that comes from the conscious mind and transmitting it in the form of energy vibrations to the Universe (of which our True Self is part), in order to manifest in reality everything that the conscious mind has processed.

Do you understand what the problem is? In this area, in fact, for an unawakened mind, the countless false beliefs that we have learned from our parents, school, our acquaintances, etc. are the masters.

What is the problem? Simple, the problem is that because we are unaware of how the mechanism of creation works, we are not able to dialogue with the unconscious in a proper way, and we let these beliefs give 'wrong commands' to the unconscious, which cannot do anything but obey, thus influencing our reality in a chaotic way.

It is then of fundamental importance that we take control of our mind and our thoughts, in order to be able to dialogue with the unconscious in a correct way.

This is why I have written in several chapters that a chaotic, uncontrolled mind inevitably leads to a chaotic reality, making us seemingly succumb to external events.

Our internal 'executor', which is our unconscious part, will not argue and will take for granted all the elaborated beliefs sent to him by the conscious mind. And since it is in close communication with our True Self, which is endowed with infinite power, it will make these beliefs manifest in reality.

An examination of your conscious thoughts will tell you a great deal about the state of your inner mind, intentions and expectations.

In fact, your thoughts, once examined, will allow you to see where you are going. **What exists in the world is first and foremost in thoughts and emotions**. There is no other rule.

So, let's learn to dialogue with the unconscious in order to take control of our lives. Only if we are able, through the knowledge of the underlying mechanisms (in which this book is trying to contribute), and especially through constant practice, we can really take the reins of our life and guide it towards what really pleases us, making us finally escape the prison in which we have chained ourselves.

Choose Who to Be and Become It

We only become who we are. We need to remember this every time we wish to achieve some goal.

William Shakespeare in his famous *Hamlet* wrote:

"To be, or not to be, that is the question."

Exactly, that is the question, which many people forget or ignore whenever they wonder why on earth the Law of Attraction does not work for them.

In this chapter I wish to bring to your attention a fundamental concept, perhaps the most important one, which cannot be ignored by those who aspire to become Conscious Creators:

You can only become what you are.

Perhaps this statement may seem a little strange, but I will try to illustrate my thinking.

The concept is quite simple, and probably many of you have heard it before: in order to obtain something, you must first feel that you have already have it. Well, nothing new there, and we have already talked about it several times in this book. What I want to emphasize is another aspect of the same statement, which perhaps few have ever pondered upon in depth.

We must start with the consideration that **being and having** are in fact the same thing. Yes, you read that correctly. Usually when we ask the Universe, we think of something to *obtain*. More money, a love affair, a new job, a villa with a pool, etc. Well, if you think about it, "having something" can be translated into "**I am** the one who has that something".

The difference is subtle, but this simple shift in perspective opens the door to a number of very important considerations.

The real desire is to be, not to have

The basic concept that needs to be emphasized is that we are all Divine beings who have come down to Earth to experience this world, and the gift of being able to create our reality we received from God so that He could also experience earthly things through us. I hope by now you have formed your own thoughts that we are one with our Creator, and that therefore our experiences are also His.

Well, no one will object if I say that a divine being has no desire to possess, because as Almighty, he can get everything he wants. The real desire is to experience Himself as God. This is the main mission of our existence: to obtain the real knowledge of what it means **to be God**. To enable us to achieve this goal, God made us 'forget' our divine nature, so that we could rediscover it through experience, starting from a condition (only apparent) of non-Divinity.

Here is the key to everything. In our lives we do not have to discover who we are, but rather **choose who to be** from time to time, according to our deepest desires, in order gain experience. We are the protagonists of a continuous process of creation, in which we decide first of all **who to be**, and then, feeling as such, allow the Universe to help us become it. This is not a play on words, read them again if you have not grasped the concept.

To be is the heart of the problem. Every experience, whether positive or negative, is there to allow us to reaffirm who we are. How? By simply giving us the opportunity to ask the question, "Does this experience reflect who I wish to be?" If the answer is no, we simply need to move beyond it, and react to that experience in the way that the person we want to be would.

Our thoughts, words and actions determine Who we really are.

An example: do we wish to become Conscious Creators of our reality? Well, when some negative events happen to us, we should think and react exactly as a true creator would. That is, we should roll up our sleeves and firmly believe in the abundance of the Universe and in our ability to create reality. In this way, we would firmly reaffirm to the Universe our choice **to be absolute masters** of our destiny.

On the contrary, a passive reaction of discouragement or concern, or worse, of complaint, would only reaffirm to the Universe that **we are victims** of circumstances and **powerless** in the face of adversities. This attitude is received as an order from the Universe, which gives us back in the form of experience all that we "feel" to be.

Do you understand the importance of our attitude in front of any event in our life? *We become what we are*: each time, through our reaction, we decide Who we Are, and consequently what we become.

In short, returning to the title of this chapter, **pay attention to your thoughts and attitudes** before life's circumstances, for it is your responsibility alone to *decide Who to be and then become it*.

I Will Only Be Happy When...

Many people think that you can only be happy when something good happens. Let's explore in this chapter why this way of thinking is absolutely wrong.

How many times have we said, or heard, that...?

When I find a job, I will feel accomplished...
If I had someone to love, I would be really happy...
With that money problem solved, he will finally be free...

We tend to think that in order for a desired effect to occur (feeling fulfilled or happy) there must necessarily be a cause to trigger or justify it.

Normally, we are used to this from an early age, as we have heard our relatives or acquaintances talk this way thousands of times. We have even been led to base our entire lives on this pre-constructed association between cause and effect. What parent has not told his children at least once *"study to get a job"* meaning that happiness and fulfillment in life is subordinate to an antecedent event, such as studying and getting a degree. I am not saying that you do not have to study or work hard in life to reach a goal, but the huge number of unemployed or underemployed graduates shows us the illusory nature of the (apparent) chain of cause and effect:

study → work → achievement → happiness.

We are basing our entire lives on the absolute illusion that the effect needs a cause, without which it can never manifest. Nothing could be more wrong, and if you follow my reasoning, I will show you why.

We are the masters of our emotions

The problem stems from the fact that we think we are separate from the world around us, and that any event is completely independent from us. In fact, even worse, we think that we are the ones who are dependent on external events.

We think that it is normal to be happy when something pleasant happens, and to be sad when something undesirable happens. This makes us **robots dependent** on what happens outside of us. As I have already written in a previous chapter, it is as if we had buttons with written "Joy", "Anger", "Sadness", etc. Each event just pushes one of those buttons, and we re-act accordingly.

I do not know about you, but I really do not like re-acting as if I were a mechanical robot.

The truth that we often forget is that **we are the masters of our emotions**. As I have written many times, there are no good events or bad events. An event is an event. It is enjoyable or not, depending on how we react to that event. This is the only truth to remember.

The world does not work the way we have always been taught to believe. There is no world out there that can do anything to us at any time. The truth is something else: we can (and should) decide how we feel about any event in life. This is what allows us to take control.

Be happy, and the lover will come

Says Osho:

If your lover comes along, you're happy. Happiness is the effect, and the lover is the cause. The wise man says, be happy, and the lover will come. Create the effect, and the cause will follow.

This is the secret of Conscious Creation. It is not possible to wait for the cause to arrive in order to feel happy, because it is obvious that the cause depends on a thousand factors, almost all of which are beyond our control.

The trick is to understand that **what we have full control of is the effect**, which is none other than **our emotions**. So, let's feel happy, and the Universe will necessarily have to find a reason to make us happy.

Let's begin to feel that we already have the things we desire, let's feel the corresponding emotion. Are you wondering how? Don't tell me it is hard, because there is a surefire way to do it, a way that has always been right under our noses, but we have never seen it: **gratitude**.

Let's practice every day to be grateful and appreciate whatever is part of our lives. The Universe will only bring us more things to be grateful for. This is the law, the only law in nature.

A Song to Make Our Wishes Come True

An almost forgotten song by Lucio Battisti reveals one of the greatest secrets of the Law of Attraction. Let's rediscover this magical text together...

A few days ago, I was listening to some songs by Lucio Battisti, when at a certain point, listening to *"Dove arriva quel cespuglio" (Where that bush is)*, I almost jumped on the chair when I realized that the lyrics written by that genius Mogol contained a real 'lesson' on one of the main techniques to follow to materialize your dreams.

The song, contained in the album "La batteria, il contrabbasso, eccetera" (in my opinion one of the most beautiful ever written by Battisti-Mogol), is about an engaged couple who imagine their new house built in the middle of a field, *'Where that bush is'*, precisely.

Surely you know that it is not enough to visualize something to achieve it, but that it is absolutely essential to feel the corresponding emotions as well, trying to involve all the senses as much as possible.

Well, take a look at what the lyrics of this beautiful song say:

Where that bush is, the kitchen
will have morning sun. Where my
cap is, there the bedroom will be,
and in the direction of the pond we
will build our bathroom.

The protagonist of the song begins by describing to his companion the various rooms of the house, associating a detail to make it as real as possible, such as *"the kitchen will have the morning sun"*, or *"where my cap is, there the bedroom will be"*.

The house does not exist yet, but in the eyes of the two lovers it is slowly materializing, through Mogol's fantastic words. But let's continue...

Come on in, it's your
home, your home among
the roses.
As soon as I get paid,
the first wall, your house I
swear to you.

Here is another great lesson through two important concepts. First, it is important to **visualize a movement**, a gesture, anything in short that makes us 'feel' that we already possess the object of desire: *"Come on in, it's your home, your home among the roses"* is the action described in this case. Imagining it among the roses inserts a very important **emotional element**, which can make the visualization even more pleasant and powerful.

The other element is **the action that must always be taken** to declare to the Universe that you really intend to obtain what you want. In this case the phrase is *"As soon as I get paid, the first wall, your house I swear to you"*. This promise also has the purpose of breaking down the resistance of the rational mind, declaring as feasible that dream, because you will be able to build it one piece at a time, with the salary received at the end of each month. As many people know, the unconscious is not able to evaluate whether a statement is true or false, so it considers as real everything that the rational mind accepts as possible. Here, then, is the importance of **having unwavering faith** that the wish can be fulfilled. That final *"I swear"* is a reinforcer containing incalculable creative energy.

Simply fantastic. The two lovers can already see their dream come true and feel that the house is theirs, even if in front of their eyes at that moment there is only a barren and uncultivated field.

But now the real stroke of genius:

*Now sit here where the fireplace will be
and think about when all those people
going by they won't see anything. That
door is not a dream, it's sturdy, it's
made of wood.*

The two lovers are already imagining their house made of solid walls, but most importantly surrounded by people walking by it. Basically, the two are visualizing not only the house, but also an entire neighborhood full of people. Placing your dream **within a real context** is one of the indispensable ingredients to make it so.

And then *"that door is not a dream, it's sturdy, it's made of wood"* gives a further boost to the feeling of the real existence of that house, not only by describing the door, but especially by 'perceiving' its solidity.

I don't know if Mogol was aware of the Law of Attraction, but certainly in this song he described with incredible precision a large number of techniques that should always be applied to see one's dreams come true. Ah, I was forgetting perhaps the most important thing... the fact that **there were two of them imagining** the house, and that one of them was describing aloud their common dream, this greatly strengthens his creative energy. For you will remember the words of the Gospel, *"Where two or three are gathered in my name, there am I in the midst of them..."*

Emotion Is a Place

We mistakenly believe that emotions are only states of being characterized by particular sensations, positive or negative, and that these have no effect on our reality. Emotions are more than just feelings, and we will discover this in the following pages.

Until now we have considered emotions in a completely incomplete way. Here is how the Treccani Italian encyclopedia defines the word "emotion"[7]:

"Inner process elicited by an event-stimulus relevant to the interests of the individual. The presence of an emotion is accompanied by subjective experiences (feelings), physiological changes (peripheral responses regulated by the autonomic nervous system, hormonal and electrocortical reactions), and 'expressive' behaviors (body posture and movements, vocal emissions)."

As the title of this chapter states, I would like to draw your attention to the fact that although this definition is correct, at least apparently, it actually describes only part of the truth. Emotions are far more than what official science believes, they are one of the most important tools in the act of consciously creating our reality.

The two sides of the coin

As I said, the official definition of emotions represents only part of the truth. In fact, it describes emotions as a process *"...elicited by an event-stimulus relevant to the interests of the individual"*.

---

[7] http://www.treccani.it/enciclopedia/emozione/

Correct, but there are actually **two different forms** of emotion:

The first form is the one just described in the dictionary, which attributes the cause of an emotion to some external event-stimulus. This is the type of emotion to which we have always been accustomed, and that we believe is the only one that exists. In reality, this is the way in which an unawakened being relates to reality, feeling the emotions caused by external events, on which he has, or thinks he has, no control.

Being subjected to our emotions, **mechanically** re-acting in response to external events, is the worst use we can make of emotions. In this way we are not only subject to our emotions, but also and above all of the outside world, because any event or person makes us its prisoners, determining at any time our mood, without any possibility of control on our part.

It is a way of life that does not differ much from that of a mechanical robot, capable of responding to external stimuli only according to a preset program.

The second form is certainly more interesting, and describing its importance is why I decided to write this chapter. Although no one ever tells us, you should know that we can evoke emotions at will, without having to wait for some external event to trigger them. It is clear that in this case, since they are deliberately evoked by us, we are specifically interested only in positive emotions.

Why should we do this? Before answering this question, it is a good idea to make a quick review of how reality works, focusing on the concept of time, to see how future events unfold within our lives.

One thing that should be emphasized is that time is not linear, but there are infinite pasts and infinite futures, and the specific future we are going to live is always determined by our thoughts, beliefs and **emotions**.

Yes, also and above all by emotions. If we want to have an experience, it is important to try to reproduce in our mind the same emotions that event would make us live. Ok, you may say, but what does this have to do with the concept of 'place'? Don't worry, we are about to find out.

When we focus on an image of a hypothetical future, and we feel the same emotions that we would feel in experiencing it in reality, we are in fact 'moving' physically, within the **realm of infinite possibilities**, towards the event we wish to experience. Who or what makes this 'shift' effective? Emotions, of course. This is why they are so important. An aseptic visualization, without any emotion, does not produce any effective displacement, resulting in a simple mental exercise that brings no results.

Therefore, I hope you understand the importance of anticipating events through emotions. If we behave actively, and not reactively to life events, we can make sure that **emotions determine the events we are going to experience**, and not the other way around. So, emotions are a place. Let's get used to 'travel' with the mind to those **'emotional places'** in the realm of infinite possibilities, so as to choose and go to the event we wish to experience.

I leave you with a beautiful quote from Abraham, channeled by Ester Hicks:

Take your time to align energy first, and the action becomes irrelevant. ***If you don't*** *take your time to align the energy,* ***if you don't find the emotional place*** *of what you are looking for, there will be no action in the world that will make any difference.*

The Factory of Emotions

Emotions are the fuel of the creative process. Let's find out how to induce any emotion we desire at will.

Several times in this book I have stressed the importance of emotions in the process of creating our reality. We can consider emotions as the real fuel that allows our desires to express themselves in reality.

As I have already written in a previous chapter, we can define emotions as a real **place** to which we move our attention, in order to materialize it in our here and now. Even if we are not aware of it, we move physically, within the realm of infinite quantum possibilities, to the emotional place corresponding to the emotion we can feel. Thanks to this shift, the Universe brings us an event that corresponds to the emotion felt.

How does this happen? We must always remember that in nature the law of cause-effect does not work as we have always imagined it. In reality **the effect precedes its cause**, indeed it is the cause itself. Strange? Maybe, but if we think about the fact that thought is the first and only cause of everything that happens in our lives, all this becomes more understandable.

Our thought, fueled by emotion, instantly creates the object of desire in our future timeline. The Universe at that point will create all the intermediate events that will allow us to reach the materialization of our desire. Each preceding event will appear to us as one of the causes of the final effect, representing only the trick that the Universe had to find to bring us where we wanted. The final effect then produced its apparent causes.

This is how the conscious creation of reality works, or at least this is one of the main mechanisms through which the Law of Attraction can be successfully applied.

The Factory of Emotions

Okay, you will say, but how do we create at will the emotions of happiness or fulfillment before we have actually gotten what we ask for?

There is a method, and it has always been before our eyes: **music**. Well yes. We all know that some pieces of music can induce particular emotional states, so why not use them as a **factory of emotions**, able to produce the *"emotional food"* we need for our creations?

Where to find the right music? We have an infinite number of sources through which we can access any song without spending a single cent. Today we have YouTube, or SoundCloud, which provide us with music of any genre.

How to choose the right genre? It depends on the emotion we wish to feel, of course, but perhaps the most useful genre is the one related to motivational music, which inspires feelings of triumph, joy, achievement, satisfaction, etc.

For example, go to SoundCloud.com and search for tracks by AudioMachine, a group that produces epic, emotionally charged music. Any song will do, as this group plays music that evokes feelings of strength and victory.

How to use music? Here are the main rules:

- Get into a comfortable position, sitting or lying down

- Use headphones for maximum sound output and to isolate yourself from the world around you

- Focus on the desire you want to achieve (e.g., pass a very difficult exam)

- Calm your mind as much as possible by focusing on your breath or parts of your body

- Start the music and imagine the scene of the wish already obtained. In the case of the exam, imagine the professor shaking your hand and congratulating you, or yourself telling your family and friends that you have passed the exam.

- Experience the scene firsthand, as if you were actually there, and let yourself be emotionally dragged along by the music, trying as much as possible to feel the emotions corresponding to the desire. In short, if you could cry with joy, that would be the best.

- Repeat the scene every night, more than once a night

Audio Machine's music is ideal for any desire that involves passing a test, or achieving a specific result.

Of course, you can use other songs that particularly inspire you, the ones suggested here are just an example. It will not be difficult to find them by searching the two sites given and using keywords such as *epic, triumph, motivational*, etc.

Or, if you want to find your soulmate, look for very sweet songs that inspire feelings of love, and imagine happily walking hand in hand with your partner on a beach at sunset, or having dinner with him/her by candlelight in an intimate atmosphere.

In short, you have at your disposal an immense **factory of emotions** to be able to induce any emotional state you want, all of which you can use with extreme ease and free of charge.

Music is the toolbox of every Conscious Creator. Now you know it too, make good use of it.

Inside Out, the Other Side of Emotions

There is a lot of talk about the emotions described in the movie Inside Out by Pixar©, but few have really analyzed the message conveyed by this cartoon. Let's analyze it together.

Let's continue the series of chapters devoted to the importance of emotions with an analysis of a very popular film, which was a great success and whose message will long remain etched in the minds of the people who saw it.

Let's talk about "Inside Out", a cartoon film by Pixar©, which stages the various emotions that 'govern' everyday lives. For those who have not seen the film I recommend at least reading the plot on Wikipedia[8] before continuing to read this chapter.

I have to say that I really enjoyed the movie. It is really well made, it has a great story that keeps you breathless until the end, and certainly it is one of the best animated films produced in recent years. What I say, therefore, should not be considered as a critic to the film, which indeed I highly recommend, but simply a proposal for reflection on some issues that I usually deal with in these pages.

Several times I have written in this book that nothing should ever be taken for granted, and that a person who is on a **true path** of personal growth **must always ask the right questions**. The idea of writing this chapter came to me when I read many interpretations given to the contents of the film, some of which perhaps exaggeratedly enthusiastic, arriving, in the most extreme cases, to consider this film an *'ideal model'* of the real mechanisms that would act within our minds.

---

[8] https://en.wikipedia.org/wiki/Inside_Out_(2015_film)

I then asked myself the question: but is this really the case? Does the film really represent the model of how to interpret the emotions that act in the human mind? To tell you the truth, some doubts had come to me even before seeing the film, and its subsequent viewing fully confirmed my first impressions.

A eulogy to mechanicalness

The first remark I would like to make about the film is that the emotions are described only and exclusively as a reaction to the situations and events that happen in the life of the little protagonist. I absolutely agree that this is really what happens to 99.9% of the human population, but those who regularly read these pages know very well that this is not the 'natural' way with which we should approach the events of life, and certainly not the 'ideal' way to teach our children.

Emotions have a very specific role, because as I have said they are the working material with which any person can operate the work of inner transformation and personal growth.

Emotions are the *'fuel'* that we must use as a unique and irreplaceable source of elevation to higher states of consciousness. Re-acting to events is not the way to approach life, because, as I wrote earlier, this passive way of responding to events makes us more and more subject to external events, making us behave like **automatic machines** at the mercy of the whims of the world.

The film is a true *'eulogy to mechanicalness'*, where it is completely normal to be sad when something goes wrong, or happy when something pleasant happens in our lives.

To show in the film only the (limited) use that most people make of emotions, I do not think is correct, especially considering the fact that some *"motivational coaches"* have taken it as an absolute and indisputable model of their teachings.

Emotion as a cause, not an effect

I would like to emphasize how important it is to use emotions correctly. We must use them as an *'instrument of creation'* of our reality, because **they are such**. Emotions can (and must) be used as a trigger of the events that we want to live, not as a passive reaction to past events. This implies a non-trivial upheaval in the approach we have towards life.

If you want to experience positive situations, you must first align yourself with those situations emotionally. You must, in short, experience the emotions of joy and fulfillment **before the desired event occurs**. The Universe at that point can only bring us events and situations that will induce such emotions again.

Emotions are a **cause**, not a consequence, of events.

The problem is that no one explains it to us, and this film is unfortunately no exception, missing the precious opportunity to use its huge success to convey constructive messages of **real change**, and show us the other side of emotions, the real ones.

As a final thought, I would also like to remind you that, with regard to one of the main emotions described in the film - anger - it is absolutely harmful and inadvisable to experience this emotion uncontrollably in response to negative life events. There are studies that show in detail **the harmful effects** that negative emotions such as anger have, on a cellular and physiological level, **on our health**.

The fact remains that this is a really well-made and entertaining film, so let's watch it with joy with our children, but do not load it with meanings it does not have, and consider it for what it is: just a great opportunity to spend two hours carefree.

The Power of Imagination

We are constantly absorbed by the images of the world that we define as 'real', believing that it is all that exists. Instead, we do not realize how far this idea is from reality.

From the moment we open our eyes in the morning we begin to interact with the world around us, believing that what we perceive with our five senses represents the truest we can experience. We are deeply convinced that we live constantly surrounded by 'things' that are external and separate from us, and we base any thought or action on this belief. We are blindly loyal to the paradigm that thought, or imagination, plays a 'secondary' role within this reality, and that their influence is limited solely to any emotion produced by those thoughts.

Nothing could be more wrong.

We are lost within a deep hallucination made of lights and sounds that have no real consistency, if not as a mere reflection of what we are internally. And do not tell me that you know everything about the Law of Attraction, and that you know very well that thought has an influence on what we experience.

Bullshit. Those are also simple illusions, because we are constantly absorbed by what we hear and see, and we get angry at the annoying neighbor, the rude person who tries to pass us in line at the post office, or we engage in 'virtual' fights on the Internet when we read posts or comments that disagree with what we believe or think. Simple machines that react to what their biological sensors perceive. Nothing more than mechanical behaviors, belonging to a predetermined program over which, despite all the beautiful books on personal growth that we have read, we do not have the slightest control. Don't be offended, but this is exactly how we conceive and face this world, convinced that we are dealing with 'others' that sometimes we like, sometimes we are annoyed, and sometimes we are even afraid.

The reality is that - but you already know this – you are creating the world moment by moment based on how you think or imagine that world should manifest. But admit it, you just cannot bring yourself to embrace a new way of thinking. I cannot help you except by explaining how the world really works. It is up to you to change your attitude and habits of mind, if you really want to turn your life around, and finally abandon the big error you constantly fall into.

That wave of probability

As anyone who has read my books knows, the world is composed of two different levels, and as I explain in depth in the first chapter of that book, this concept comes from what the double-slit experiment showed us, where a particle appears only as a consequence of an observation, which makes the wave describing the infinite possibilities collapse and make matter appear.

These two levels must be understood for the meaning they really have. The first level, that of the wave of probability, which we can call the infinite unexpressed possibilities, is the origin and primary cause of any event that occurs on the second level, what we call 'reality' and that we can perceive with the five senses.

Nothing can exist if it is not first conceived on the first level. Absolutely nothing.

Read this sentence several times before moving on with your reading.

It must be understood that the so-called 'unreal' world of thoughts and imagination is of **primary importance**, because it absolutely determines what we can experience in what we call 'reality'.

But all of us unfortunately give extreme importance to that second level, ignoring that it is only a mere reflection of something more 'fundamental' and decisive in the definition of what can be part of our lives.

Make this basic concept your own: if you live with your attention constantly turned **outward**, you are actually living in a consolidated past, in the already collapsed wave, where nothing can change from what it was. If instead you turn your attention **inward**, choosing with your mind to live where you actually would like to live, you are drawing from the world of infinite possibilities, where the wave has not yet collapsed, where therefore everything is always possible and where you can really **make choices**. There is no choice possible in the world of the second level, the world of 'crystallized' thoughts.

Neville Goddard wrote:

Your belief in powers outside of you is a tree that needs to be uprooted from your mind.

Get into the perspective that everything you are perceiving with your senses is nothing more than past stuff, it is the crystallization of your past thoughts, and as such have no importance. You give it importance by worrying about what you see, and giving to it a power that it does not have. You are constantly living in the result of your past thoughts. This should make you understand something fundamental: your imagination is the most real thing that can exist. It is the realm of infinite possibilities, of which you are the sole Ruler, and where you have the power to choose, from an infinite reservoir, whatever you wish to experience. It is not just a 'new-age' belief, it is about how the world really works, whether you believe it or not.

Move your mental habits into the realm of imagination, and live as much as you can in the world you would like to live in.

Reserve moments in the day when you can devote yourself to imagining that you already find yourself in the fulfilled desire, enjoying the sensations. Living in the imagination of your dreams as already fulfilled does not mean escaping reality; it is living **in the only**

place where you can build that reality. Again, in the words of Goddard:

What you want, you already have. If you recognize as a true and real fact that you are already what you wish to be and you do not let yourself be diverted or distracted by any external element, no power in the world will be able to prevent you from manifesting your desire.

Dream then, dream and imagine as many times as you can that you are the person you wish to be, with the assurance that a certain situation already exists. Move away from constant worries about the world you perceive, to the feeling that you are already who you wish to be. This is the only rule you must make your own.

Do not value the world you already see, but devote yourself to building the one you want. I want to put it to you in another way, hoping you will make this thought your own:

you see, dear reader, creation is finite, and you can become aware of larger and larger portions of it. What are you waiting for?

Instill Life into Your Desire

You have surely read countless books on the Law of Attraction, but maybe you still do not understand how you can obtain something from this strange law of the Universe. Maybe, without any tangible result, you even thought that they were all American extravagances invented to make money damaging gullible people. Well, it is not like that, so much so that the ways to see your desires realized have been written for thousands of years in the Holy Scriptures, but no one has ever given us the correct key to reading them. Let's try to do it, with the help of modern quantum physics.

Let's try to read what the Holy Scriptures say about the creation of man, starting with what the Holy Scriptures say was the first cause of everything:

*"In the beginning was the Word,
and the Word was with God, and
the Word was God" (John 1:1).*

In the beginning was the **Word**. Now, in the original version written in ancient Greek, Verb is the translation of the word Logos, which can have different meanings. From a fragment of Leucippus, a Greek philosopher who lived in the fifth century B.C., it seems that Heraclitus can be attributed a meaning of Logos[9] as a "universal law" that regulates all things according to reason and necessity:

"Nothing happens by chance but everything according to logos and necessity."
(Leucippus, fr.2)

---

[9] https://en.wikipedia.org/wiki/Heraclitus#Logos

Those who have read latest books know very well that, according to Thomas Troward, the origin or primary cause of anything that materializes is represented by thought. This thesis, as I explain extensively in the book, is confirmed on a physical level by the concept of *syntropy*, enunciated by the Italian mathematician Luigi Fantappié.

We can therefore affirm that the Logos, or Word, can be traced back to divine thought, the Primary Cause of all things, as John himself explains to us in his Gospel:

"all things were made through him, and without him nothing was made of all that exists" (John, 1:3)

In the above-mentioned extract, with the pronoun "him" John refers to the Logos, according to the original Greek version.

Logos, or thought, then, is an indispensable element in bringing to life whatever we may experience in our lives. This is the first important step to take in the process of creating our reality.

Step 1: Make your wish, in other words, make your choice from the field of infinite possibilities.

Just as in quantum physics a particle cannot exist without a wave describing it, so no event can happen in the world without a corresponding thought being conceived. Don't expect anything if you don't express a wish first.

But a desire is only a thought, something not palpable or perceptible with the five senses. How can we bring a desire to life? Here the Old Testament comes to our aid, in the second chapter of Genesis:

"Then the Lord God molded man with dust from the ground and breathed into his nostrils the breath of life, and man became a living being." (Genesis 2:7)

I believe that no explanation could be more effective than this one in detailing on how the creation of reality takes place. I believe the first and most important book on the Law of Attraction, and therefore how reality really works, is the Holy Scriptures, but no one has ever told us that.

Any thought or desire is like dust on the ground. It has no vital energy to make it come alive and manifest itself. It is like the design of a house drawn on a sheet of paper: the design is not a house, because it only describes it. To have a real house you have to bring that drawing to life.

The same thing happens with our desires: they are just designs, nothing else, and they need the *breath of life* to manifest themselves. But what is this *breath of life*?

Here is the most important point, and it has to do with the fact that Genesis itself teaches us that God made us in his *image and likeness*. Of course, this phrase does not mean that we have the same appearance as God, because God does not have a body and therefore has no form to resemble. Being created in his image and likeness means that he gave us the same faculties he had, and therefore we are in turn divine beings capable of creation.

But if you think about it, creating means *giving life* to something that did not exist before. Well, to give life means literally **'to give one's life'**, in the sense of becoming the means by which a potential thought can become something tangible and manifest. How? Simply by giving life to it, that is, by living it.

To give life = to give one's life = to live it within oneself

Giving life to something means living that something, that is, making it live within itself.

Yes, that divine breath is nothing other than *life given* through the possibility we have of making our desire *live within us*. How? The whole world exists only in our mind, so it is clear that I am talking about **visualization**, in which the only thing we have to do is to live that desire in the here and now, feeling it 'alive'.

Step 2: Give life to your desire, in other words give it your own life by making it live within you.

This is the secret hidden in the words of the Holy Scriptures, which have been revealed to us for thousands of years, but few have had the ability to see this immense truth.

But there are some among you who do not believe (John 6:64)

And only those who can see are given the ability to use their immense power:

He (the Logos) was in the world, and though the world was made through Him, the world did not recognize Him. He came to His own, and His own did not receive Him. But to all who did receive Him, to those who believed in His name, He gave the right to become children of God, children born not of blood, nor of the desire or will of man, but born of God. (John 1:10-12)

Have Faith. Here Is the Secret Ingredient

The Law of Attraction works, but only if you follow certain rules. In this chapter we will talk about how important it is to have faith.

Let's continue our series dedicated to the different methods in making the Law of Attraction work. I am convinced that there is a large group of people who have approached this very interesting topic, but despite all the attempts made, few or none of their desires have become true.

In these pages we are going to talk about perhaps the most important ingredient. **Faith.** What does it mean to **have faith**?

Perhaps there can be no better explanation than these wonderful verses by Apollinaire:

"Come to the edge," he said.
"We can't, we're afraid!" they responded.
"Come to the edge," he said.
"We can't, we will fall!" they responded.
"Come to the edge," he said.
And so they came.
And he pushed them.
And they flew.

Wonderful. Therein lies the essence of what having faith means. They hesitated at first, and it was only because of their faith that they eventually came close to the edge. And their faith was rewarded.

It is no coincidence that Jesus often speaks of Faith in the Gospels, explaining that having faith is the only way to reach the Kingdom of Heaven (which is a state of mind, not a place).

"Have faith in God," Jesus said to them. "Truly I tell you that if anyone says to this mountain, 'Be lifted up and thrown into the sea,' and has no doubt in his heart but believes that it will happen, it will be done for him. Therefore I tell you, whatever you ask for in prayer, believe that you have received it, and it will be yours." (Mk. 11:22-24)

I believe that the Gospels are the most important and authoritative text on the Law of Attraction. If you read them carefully, you would not need to read any other book on the subject. Jesus explained to us in a thousand ways how to apply the Law of Attraction in our lives, too bad that the true meaning of those words arrived (more or less intentionally) distorted to our ears.

How to have faith

The fundamental point to always keep in mind when asking the Universe for something is that our request has been granted "even before it is spoken" (other words from the Gospel).

This is what it means to have faith: to be sure and to feel in one's heart that what we are asking for is already ours, without any doubt or hesitation.

But therein lies the difficulty. We cannot fool ourselves. We now know very well that we only get what we really believe in, and what we really believe is carved into our unconscious. This is why we have to manifest that we have faith by starting with the simplest thing we can do: the words we use to ask the Universe and the emotion we feel as we speak the words.

As I have already said in other chapters, we use different words, so our prayer should not be a request, but **a thanksgiving**, felt with all our heart, for what we are asking. And what do we give thanks for, if not for something we have already obtained? This is having faith and influencing the unconscious in a simple way.

Why you must have faith

You must know that the Law of Attraction is at work, constantly. Even at this moment you are unconsciously asking the Universe, and the Universe is answering. The Law of Attraction **is a physical law**, which will surely be taught in the universities of the future. It is like the law of gravity. Would you doubt that an object thrown in the air would fall to the ground? You wouldn't. Then why do you doubt the Law of Attraction?

This physical law states that every prayer, every statement, every thought, is composed of energy and is creative. Depending on the level of energy, the level of faith with which the request is considered true and with the same level that request will be granted.

Then begin to have faith that your life can be changed. How do you do it? Simple, just have faith.

The Art of Asking the Universe

We think we know everything about the Law of Attraction, but do we know how to ask the Universe for our desires? Let's find out together.

This chapter takes up the discourse already begun regarding the importance of faith in the act of **asking the Universe** for the object of our desire.

In the previous chapter, one of the most important concepts has only been mentioned, and perhaps has not received the attention it deserved. So, I would like to resume the discussion to deepen what I think is one of the indispensable ingredients on how to ask the Universe effectively.

In "Conversations with God," Neal Donald Walsch explains, through the words of God, that we cannot have what we desire. The concept behind this statement is that if we desire something, we are in fact denouncing its lack of. And what does the Universe do? Simple, it obeys our affirmation, sending us more...lack.

If this seems strange to you, it should be clarified right away what the main mechanism is by which we create reality, and then we can ask the Universe with maximum effectiveness.

To ask the Universe for something means to vibrate with the same energy.

Everything in the Universe is energy. Everything, even the book you have in your hands, your body or the chair you are sitting on. Energy is manifested through force fields (I am simplifying, and some physics graduate will forgive me for that) that vibrate at a certain frequency. Our thoughts vibrate as well, since thought is itself a form of energy. Well, the vibrations of our thoughts, through our subconscious, are radiated outward, and thus attract other energies (i.e., objects or events) that vibrate at the same frequency.

In other words, in order to ask the Universe for a villa with a swimming pool you have to emit a corresponding vibration. But beware! You do not have to emit the vibration of the villa with a swimming pool, but (take note) **the vibration of owning** a villa with a swimming pool.

See the difference? That's the whole trick. In other words, if you try to ask the Universe simply by thinking and imagining a villa with a swimming pool, you will hardly get it. Instead, you have to imagine, indeed **feel, that you own** a villa with a swimming pool. It is the vibration of possession that makes you become the owner of that property.

You must become rich inside before you can become rich materially, but you have heard this a thousand times before. Now you also know why.

In the previous chapter I said that such vibration can be obtained only with the faith of having already obtained that good, and I also said that it is very difficult to feel inside such faith every time we are going to ask the Universe.

The solution exists, and it is precisely described by God in N. Donald Walsch's book. God suggests that the author use prayer in a different way. Prayer should not be the act of asking the Universe for something, but should instead be a time of thanksgiving for having already received that something. Those who understand this difference hold the keys to their lives in their hands. We forget what we have always been taught, that prayer must be an act of pleading to the Lord.

The true meaning of prayer has been lost over the centuries, but now we are able to regain awareness about how to use this very useful tool.

Therefore, prayer must never be an act of pleading, but an act of thanksgiving. Those who know our true power and our indissoluble union with the whole Universe, know that any prayer is answered without any mistake. Remember that with prayer we address the power that is able to create entire Worlds. Do you think it is not possible to materialize an ordinary villa with a swimming pool?

So instead of asking the Universe, thank that enormous Power that is always at your service for having already granted your wish. Everything is already there, always has been, you just have to go and get it.

Then make a statement of gratitude to the Universe for **what is as it is**.

Impersonate the Role of the Conscious Creator

The most powerful way to create your own reality is to be in full control of your mind. Stepping into your role without being absorbed by it is one of the most effective techniques for accomplishing this.

Several times in this book I have written that a chaotic mind can only generate a chaotic reality, in which each of us is at the mercy of events without any possibility of controlling our own destiny.

This truth stems from the fact that our thoughts create reality at all times, even as you are reading this chapter, but for most people this creation occurs mostly unconsciously, because not possessing mastery of the mind, the resulting reality is necessarily out of your control.

We are in fact led to consider the world as something external and uncontrollable, and we mistakenly believe in the absolute validity of the law of cause and effect. For this reason, we tend to think about the future as a logical consequence of past events, and whenever we are not aware of our thoughts, they automatically wander towards mostly pessimistic predictions of life. In fact, you may have noticed that we often find ourselves immersed in negative thoughts about the outcome of some future event.

These thoughts, according to the Law of Attraction, constantly create the reality we are going to experience, consequently we self-condemn ourselves to constantly reliving the past, or variations of it.

Letting your mind wander uncontrolled is one of the most dangerous things of all and to be avoided at all costs.

Have you ever thought about what *to let your mind wander uncontrolled* really means? In fact, some might argue that thoughts, being generated by our own brain, must necessarily be under our control. Nothing could be more wrong.

The brain is a biological machine. Beautiful, complex and perfect, but still a machine, and as such it cannot do anything but blindly execute the program that has been set. This program is something that we have learned from the outside since childhood through the conditioning received at school, in the family, by religion, etc.

The thoughts we think, for the most part, are not our thoughts, but simple 'programs' that have been imposed on us from the outside and in which we have believed without offering the slightest resistance.

We think, but when thoughts are left to themselves, we are literally *running a program that is not ours*, implanted from the outside. The problem is that such program is running our lives without our knowledge.

The importance of impersonating a role

We are getting to the core of the problem, or rather, its solution. How can we control our minds to think thoughts of our own, and consequently create the life we desire?

Through roles. Yes, that's right, through a **conscious impersonation** of the different roles we are called to play in our lives. What does that mean? It is much simpler than it sounds.

You may have noticed that when we first introduce ourselves to someone, we tend to say 'I'm an engineer' or 'a doctor,' etc. Basically, we totally identify with the role we play in life, even to the point of saying we *are* that role. This is one of the results of the conditioning received from the outside. In fact, we can say with difficulty 'I *work as* an engineer' or 'I *practice* medicine'.

Here is the thing. Just as we identify with our profession, to the exact same degree we totally identify with any other role in our lives. When we are with our children, in fact, we **are** the parent, or at the restaurant we **are** the customer, and so on.

What is wrong with that? Nothing, if we could do it without totally, unconsciously identifying with the respective role. When we get into each of these characters, in fact, we completely forget that **we are Divine beings** who are experiencing the fact of being an engineer, a doctor, a parent or a customer. And the consequence of all this is that we lose control of our reactions and emotions. In fact, if our child does something we do not like, we immediately re-act automatically, based on the stereotype of parenting learned from others.

We automatically execute the program that has been implanted in us, and that we have unconsciously accepted, believing it to be ours.

Now, as Divine beings, we are constantly creating our reality based on how we react to any event. We attract the events of our lives with the sole purpose of experiencing them and choosing, by our attitude towards those events, what to become, to have a new experience, ...and so on.

Life is a continuous process of creation, and from time to time we can choose what to become and therefore what experiences to have.

All this **is precluded to those who identify themselves in their role**, because in that state of total and unconscious identification, our reaction is automatically managed according to stereotypes learned from outside. And since we create our reality according to the attitude we have in the face of life events, an uncontrolled reaction will create an equally uncontrolled reality. By worrying about some event that we consider critical, for example, we reaffirm to the Universe that we are not able to control our lives, and consequently we choose to experience an uncontrollable reality. The Universe can do nothing but obey our will.

The conscious interpretation of one's role

What is the solution? Simple, taking control of your mind through the interpretation of different roles, while maintaining a conscious detachment from that role.

In every situation in your life, you play the role of employee, manager, parent or customer from time to time, but **never identify with that character**.

Georges Ivanovic Gurdjieff said:

A typical trait of the refined man is his ability to play to perfection whatever part he wants in his eternal life, while inwardly he keeps himself free.

Here is the key to it all: **keeping yourself inwardly free**, and you can only do that by always maintaining the presence and constant reminder of Who We Really Are.

Avoid re-acting automatically at all costs, and state to yourself at all times that you are in control of your mind and consequently of your destiny.

In other words, live life well aware that you are only experiencing the various roles you have chosen to impersonate.

Reality is not created by speech, but exclusively through the conscious choice of how to react to different situations, which results in conscious attitudes and actions.

In this way you will not be dominated by destiny, because the Universe can only respond in accordance with your *way of being*. Become Sovereign, and a Kingdom will be given to you.

I Am Not Getting up This Morning Until...

Let's learn how to properly set up each new day by performing a small ritual to create the day we desire.

We have at our disposal ideal moments during the day, in which we can decide our future, holding in our hands all the power to choose, and therefore create, what the events that we will experience in our lives will be. These moments are available to us almost all the time, but unfortunately, not being aware of them, we are not able to use them properly to create the future we desire.

One of the best times to create your day is **in the morning as soon as you wake up.** In this chapter, I want to show you that we are so unaware of the importance of the first moments after waking, that not only do we not use them to our advantage, but we even do things that are detrimental to the continuation of the day.

The 'traditional' awakening

You surely know the scene: you open your eyes in the morning, perhaps awakened by the deafening sound of your alarm clock, and even before you realize where you are, your mind immediately races to the thought that there is another hard day's work ahead, and that you would have gladly slept a little longer.

You get up with your eyes still half-closed, and as you go to the bathroom you start thinking about everything that is waiting for you: the crazy morning traffic, the parking that is always hard to find, the paperwork that you have to turn in by the end of the day, your boss who is probably in a bad mood, etc.

What we normally do is wake up from a night sleep to… immediately fall back into a deep 'daytime sleep'.

In fact, we believe we are awake, but in reality, we are constantly slumbering in a 'daytime sleep' with our eyes open, mistakenly believing we are awake. Are you arguing that during the day you have your eyes open, you move around and do things, and therefore you must necessarily be awake? Wishful thinking.

Being truly awake is a state of mind that few people on this planet have had the opportunity to experience.

What we believe is a state of wakefulness, in reality is a state of deep sleep, in which we have no control over our mind, leaving it wandering in a chaotic way among thousands of thoughts, mostly negative, about life, our past, what we believe awaits us in the future, etc.

To be truly awake means to have total control over your thoughts in order to choose which thoughts to think of in order to create the desired future.

Now you know that we create reality through our innermost thoughts and beliefs. Just to give a trivial example, how do you think you will be able to find a parking space for your car, if you leave your house already with the belief that finding a place will be very difficult?

Our mind wanders restlessly immersed in negative thoughts, hypothesizing what the events that we will experience in the day may be, obtusely believing that what has occurred in previous days and months will necessarily occur again. We do not realize that our brain is running an automatic program, which makes sure that the only possible outcome of future events can be the one already experienced in the past.

Like it or not, the truth is that we are sleeping, at the mercy of an uncontrolled dream that generates an equally uncontrolled reality. How can we get out of all this? Keep on reading and you will find out that you can do it very easily.

I'm not getting up until…

Let's start to take control of our mind, and above all let's try to do it from the first moments of the day, which are surely the most profitable as they are not yet 'contaminated' by any past thought.

The first moments after waking up, in fact, are characterized by the fact that the conscious mind has not yet completely taken control, therefore in that moment any image we fix in our mind can reach our unconscious very easily, not finding any resistance represented by the rational mind, which in those first moments after waking is still partially asleep. Since reality is constantly created by the beliefs imprinted in our unconscious, this means that we can easily plan the day we wish to live.

From the very first moments after waking, start striving to be what you want to become during the day. Attention, I said that you must try *'to be'*, not just imagine or visualize. *To be* is to 'feel' the emotion corresponding to what we wish to experience.

Say to yourself:

This morning I won't get out of bed until I really feel like what I want to experience during my day.

Do you want to find a good atmosphere in your work environment? Imagine the smiling faces of your colleagues and your boss and feel happiness and fulfillment inside you. To be in order to become, this is the main concept that you must always keep in mind.

Another very important thing we need to remember to do in the morning is to **be grateful**. Grateful for what? For all the beautiful things that are part of our lives, and which we no longer notice, taking them for granted: let's remember to be thankful for our beautiful home, for the hot water that comes out of the shower, for the aroma of coffee that we sip, for the sun that rises every morning, for the singing of the birds, etc.

In short, once again *to be in order to become*. Be thankful every morning and be happy, and the Universe will be forced, before evening comes, to give you something to be thankful for and feel happy about.

"The morning breeze has secrets to tell you.
Don't go back to sleep."
- Rumi

Your Wish Is Granted Instantly

It is not a matter of probability that something happens. You make things happen, and I will show you that in this chapter.

You have surely heard about the fact that time does not exist, and that it is just an illusion of our mind. Have you ever thought about what this means? Simple, it means that events happen at this instant, in the here and now.

In the here and now? So why don't I see the Templar army on the street, and why have I never met a real dinosaur? I mean, if everything happens in this very moment, why am I experiencing this one reality? Where are the inhabitants of other ages?

It is all about vibration

We are made of pure energy, and what we see around us is only what vibrates at our own frequency. The wall in my room, this computer and all the people who live in my city vibrate at exactly the same frequency as me, so that is why I can interact with them. Everything else vibrates at completely different frequencies, and so even if they exist, I cannot experience them.

Nice and interesting, you may say, but what does it have to do with the title of this chapter? It does, and if you have the perseverance to read all the way through, you will understand what I mean.

If everything exists in the here and now, then this applies not only to the past, but also to the future. In fact, it makes no sense to talk about the past and future in a Universe where time is only an illusion. This means that future events also exist in the here and now.

Mind you, I am not saying that our destiny is predetermined, because that future of which I speak is composed of the potential of possible futures, all of which exist in the here and now.

What future will we live in then? I just told you, **it is all about vibration**. We will therefore live the future that corresponds to our vibration. That future you desire is already there. It has always been there, and all you have to do is to allow that future to reach you.

This time I will not just talk about theoretical things, but I will give you some real examples of a couple of episodes that happened to me.

The 9A seat

I often travel by plane for work, and since I have a frequent flyer card I have the possibility, if I book well in advance, to reserve my favorite seat at no extra charge, it is the one in row 9, the one that is in correspondence with the emergency exits, and therefore has ample space available to stretch your legs and get up without disturbing your neighbor.

One day a few months ago, I failed to check in on time, so I was reserved seat 28A, at the back of the plane. But I did not lose heart, and I accepted the situation thinking that it would go as it should. I entered the plane in calmly mood and made my way to my assigned seat. To my surprise, I found the seat already occupied by a child, and the lady next to him saying "Excuse me, but they have assigned me and my son two seats far apart. Could you be so kind to exchange seat?". I accepted without objecting, after all, it didn't change anything for me. I look at the lady's ticket and what do I read? Seat 10A. Wow, it's not row 9 but it's a big step forward.

I sat down in my new seat, right behind my beloved 9A. It wasn't over, because at one point the girl who was sitting in front of me turned around and asked me in English laced with an elegant French accent, "I would like to be next to my friend who is sitting next to you, would you mind if we switched seats?"

Bingo! A minute later I was sitting in 9A, on a day I had checked in just 30 minutes before departure, with a plane filled to the brim.

A fluke? Maybe, and then why did that lady specifically have the 10A seat and not, say, 12A? Read on and I will tell you.

That book I could not write

A fluke? Maybe, but listen to this other episode. I had been wanting to write a book for a few months now. I had tried several times to get something down, but it wasn't like writing a blog article. Punctually I would get stuck without being able to move forward. I had a list of topics to cover, many of them unpublished and never addressed, and I was very clear on what I wanted to write about. But there was no way I could write more than 3-4 pages.

I then asked myself whether I could write a book using a technique similar to the one I use for my blog, but for months I received no response. Until, one fine day, when I had almost given up on my idea, **Sandra Lussu** contacted me in a chat room to ask me if I wanted to write a book together with her and her friend **Sabrina Cau**, in the form of a conversation in which we exchange opinions on various topics related to **Conscious Creation**.

Bingo! It was just what I needed, because that way I could make short speeches, exactly in the style of my blog, which I definitely do better.

The result is our book "The Way of Conscious Creation", and given the result I thank Sandra immensely for contacting me that day.

I had made a specific request to the Universe, and it could not be any other way. It was the Universe itself that found the ideal solution to fulfill my desire to write a book. A solution that I could never have thought of on my own.

What happened in all these cases? That future already existed, and my desire brought the Universe to me, through completely unpredictable paths.

As I have written several times in this book, cause and effect are reversed. First comes the final effect, which is literally created by our thoughts, and the apparent cause that leads us to that effect is just the ploy that the Universe invents to bring us to the desired effect.

I did not get seat 9A because that lady had 10A, but that lady had 10A so that I **could occupy** the desired seat 9A. Seen this way, it is clear that chance does not exist. You are chance. Learn to look at the world with different eyes, and the world will look different to you.

If we can accept the present as it is, and maintain the certainty that what we desire already exists, then the Universe will be forced to invent something to bring us to that desired future. It is just a matter of frequency, exactly.

Appreciation as a Powerful Means to Create

To desire something is not to reject what we already have. The possibility of creating one's own reality comes precisely through appreciation of the present moment.

Several times I have stressed the importance of knowing how to appreciate the things you already have. I have explained many times, in fact, why, from a physical point of view this statement is true, and how foolish it is, if not downright stupid, to reject the present moment with attitudes of anger, dissatisfaction, complaint, etc.

The basic concept is that whatever situation we are experiencing right now, it is nothing more than the 'crystallization' or materialization of past thoughts. By now you should know that quantum physics teaches us that nothing can exist without first being conceived through a thought.

And so, if we created the current situation (consciously or unconsciously), what is the point of rejecting it and resisting it through dissatisfaction and complaining?

In this chapter I want to go beyond this concept, to bring you to think about an important aspect of the creation process.

In fact, you must always keep in mind that we live in an *attractive* Universe, not a *repulsive* one. This means that it is **physically impossible** to remove something from your life by complaining about it. Complaining is only a means by which we focus our attention on the unwanted thing, and as a result of the attraction operated by our thoughts, we do nothing but repeat to the Universe that we want more. The Universe, as you may already know, does not argue.

It executes just about every request we make.

Basically, we continually create our own reality through focusing on our thoughts, and we draw to us the things which we rest our attention on for long enough.

This is why controlling your thoughts and words is of fundamental importance. It is physically impossible to attract joy to oneself starting from a situation of unhappiness.

Whenever we complain about something, all we do is 'vibrate' at a frequency that prevents desired things from entering our lives. It is like inviting someone into your home and then not opening the door when they arrive.

Appreciation is the key

The solution can only be one: we use appreciation as a powerful tool for creation. Let's remember to **always appreciate** everything that is part of our life, with **gratitude** for the things we have, even the most obvious, and **living with joy** in the present moment. Joy attracts more joy, that is how the world works.

Appreciation is therefore a powerful tool that, once understood, can be used to change our lives and get out of the prison in which we have locked ourselves, through the incorrect and unconscious use of thoughts and words.

The fundamental concept to understand is that the world is perfect just as it is. Although few will agree with this statement, remember what I said at the beginning of this chapter. Whatever happens, insofar as it is demanded by us, it is still a mirror of who we are inside, in other words it is the material representation of our thoughts and beliefs.

This is why it is perfect. We cannot reject our own creation, as this would mean denying our faculty to create reality, with the only consequence of not being able to exercise our will and not using in an active way our free will, keeping us in a condition of subjection to the world around us. It is a different way of conceiving things, but if you do not believe these truths, please stop reading this chapter, you are wasting your time. Those who want to grow and become masters of their own destiny must make an effort to get out of the usual way the masses think.

The entire Universe is made of pure energy, so it is all about vibration.

Appreciation allows us to vibrate in tune with our desires.

Now it should be clear to you why we need to consider appreciation as a powerful tool for creation. This is the key that allows desired things to come into our lives. To appreciate the present moment is to reaffirm to the Universe that we recognize our power to create reality. As I wrote in the book "The Way of Conscious Creation", a Conscious Creator is aware that he or she has created the reality around him or her, and strongly claims responsibility for it by observing and appreciating the result of his or her creation. This is how one earns the right to create the desired reality.

A Conscious Creator knows that the power to create reality must be claimed, not delegated.

The Trampoline to Materialize Our Dreams

Let's discover the true meaning of acceptance, and how to use the present moment to build the future of our dreams.

Often when I speak or write about the importance of accepting the present moment, I receive several complaints from people who point out that **resignation** to what we do not like was not, in their opinion, a good approach to changing negative situations.

Evidently this problem stems from a misinterpretation of what I mean, so I decided to write this chapter to hopefully put things back where they belong.

The acceptance of which I speak has nothing to do with resignation. On the contrary, it is an absolutely positive approach, the only one with which we can build the future of our dreams. Let's see why.

The trampoline

Imagine having to jump. Would you choose to do it on a muddy and soft ground, or on solid and resistant ground, such as marble or concrete? Or, even better, would you choose a trampoline, which with its elasticity would launch you far with minimal effort? Surely you would opt for the second or third option. Why? Well, in the case of jumping, it is easy to understand: a soft and yielding ground would not allow us to give the necessary push to take the jump we would like to make.

The same thing happens with the creation of reality. If you want to *make a decisive leap* in your life, you obviously could not make it starting from a negative situation, in which you complain about what happens to you or what you already have.

The mechanism is very simple: as I have said many times in this book, *it is not possible to build a joyful future starting from a situation that is not one of joy and fulfillment.* If you are complaining, you are in fact denying your ability to create, because since everything that happens to you is the result of your creation, by complaining you are denying your creative power.

But not only that. Since we attract to us things and events that are in tune with our primary vibration, it stands to reason that in a state of disapproval and constant complaining we could never attract to us what vibrates in disagreement with our primary state of mind.

That is why appreciation and gratitude for everything you have **now** is not an attitude of resignation, but on the contrary, it represents the only solid and stable point from which we can make the leap into the future of our dreams.

We must learn to take charge of everything that happens to us, for better or for worse. Whenever we complain about something, we are in fact empowering that thing, giving it our power, and causing the Universe to bring more of it into our lives. It is a physical law, and as such it is completely impossible to ignore it and hope to get away from it.

The dirty trick of the ego

The problem is that too often we identify with our ego, and we do everything we can to make it the absolute master of our lives. Complacency is a trick of the ego, which does everything to maintain its supremacy, keeping us where we are. The ego knows very well that it can only succeed by making us deny our power to create reality. And complaining is one of the most effective ways to do this. Blaming something or someone else for our troubles is one of the most damaging things we can do, but unfortunately this is considered completely normal by most people.

Every now and then I post on my Facebook page "Campo Quantico" some aphorisms that highlight the fact that we must always forgive whatever wrong we think we have suffered. And every now and then someone comments that they would never forgive, that it is their right to resent those who have wronged them, that only God can forgive... and so on and so forth.

It is incredible how most people claim **the right to feel bad**. If you look carefully at these attitudes, you will recognize very clearly the action of the ego, which in order to keep on dominating is willing to do anything, making the unsuspecting victim believe that it is his sacred right to hold a grudge and feel bad as a result, brooding day and night on the wrong suffered.

If people really understood how damaging this stupid attitude is, national healthcare would save a lot of money because the average person's health status would undergo an incredible improvement.

Let's not fall into the trap, then. Let's stop complaining and blaming someone else for our problems. We have done it up to now, and nothing has changed. Why persist in this harmful habit?

Let's take back the power to be Conscious Creators of our lives through total appreciation of what we have already created, and let's strive to no longer believe that little voice that would like to keep us always enslaved and victimized by external circumstances.

Gratitude Strengthens Our Power over the World

In this chapter we will talk about gratitude, even towards those we think do not deserve it, and we will discover how important this feeling is to reaffirm who we really are and take control of our lives.

I will ask you a question, but you must answer truthfully: would you be able to love your enemies **unconditionally**? If your answer is no, by the end of this chapter you will understand why you are wrong.

We have already seen that we are solely responsible for everything that happens to us. In order to understand what I am about to tell you, it is of fundamental importance to realize and firmly believe in this important concept.

So, let's see how it all works.

The vibrations we emit in every moment, coming from both conscious and unconscious thoughts, thanks to the *Law of Attraction* (and the laws of quantum mechanics), *attract* the events and the people that are part of our lives.

It is important to know that our reality is created mostly on an unconscious level. We do not know anything about our most hidden thoughts and beliefs, which is why it seems to us that we apparently did not create those events.

In other words, our unconscious continuously *projects* outwards all that dwells within it, and this causes events related to that state of mind to occur sooner or later in our lives.

It is as if we lived in the center of a sphere whose inside walls are covered with mirrors. We look around, but everything we see is nothing more than a reflection of some aspect that dwells within us.

As we look at the world around us, we literally observe ourselves.

This is one of the reasons why it is absolutely useless to try to force events by acting only outwardly, without first trying to solve the problem within ourselves.

I am not saying that we should not act outwardly, but that before we do so, we necessarily need to be aligned with our **True Self** and resolve any internal conflicts that caused the problem we are about to solve.

Don't hope for success if you don't take this important step. Acting only outwardly is like realizing we are disheveled, and trying to comb our reflection in the mirror (!)

A few examples? You change jobs, but after a while you find yourself in the same frustrating situation you were in at your previous job. You change partners, but after the initial period of euphoria, the same defects of the previous partner reappear!

It is impossible to escape from oneself. It is like running trying to escape from your own shadow.

I have discussed broadly the concept of gratitude, which is the central topic of this chapter, but it was essential to clarify the concepts on which what I am about to say is based.

Now, if we accept the fact that the external world is nothing more than a reflection of who we are internally, someone will ask: but what is the point of all this? Why do I have to constantly observe the projection of my unconscious thoughts?

The question partly contains the answer.

We continually project ourselves in order to *observe* ourselves, and consequently be able to evolve by removing the blocks and false beliefs that exist within us.

How could we resolve the emotional blocks hidden within if we did not see them materializing as outward projections?

Let's come to the point. Everything that happens to us, whether positive or negative, is created by ourselves to allow us to observe the problem that is within us, and thus give us the possibility to solve it.

Think about it: we called that guy who pissed us off, and he offered to play the part we asked him to play.

The universe is constantly plotting in our favor so that we can evolve into higher states of consciousness. All the people in our lives **are there to help us** to do this very important work successfully.

So, how can we not express infinite **Gratitude** towards them and love them with all our heart?

Train Your Gratitude

Several times on these pages we have stressed the importance of gratitude in the process of creating one's own reality. Let's see in this chapter how to develop the notion of gratitude.

By now the importance of gratitude should be clear in order to attract the things you want in your life. The reason is that the first and fundamental mechanism through which we attract things and events into our lives is to use *the power of attention*. Everything we place our attention on, in fact, is materialized into some event that we will necessarily experience sooner or later.

The mechanism of attention needs an indispensable ingredient in order to function: **emotion**. You have surely read many times that simple focus has no creative power, if not accompanied by some emotion. Emotion is highly effective in the process of creation because it makes us experience the feeling that the object of our attention is already part of our life in some way.

This is a double-edged sword, because depending on the emotion we feel, we can obtain more or less the results desired. For example, when we 'fear' something bad might happen to us, we are attracted to the very object of that fear. On the contrary, feeling an emotion of fulfillment and joy for something we desire, being able to feel that we already possess it, makes that thing materialize sooner or later in our reality.

Here, then, is the immense importance of always keeping our thoughts and emotions under control, *choosing* which ones to keep in our minds, and which ones to let go. As I have repeatedly stated in these pages our **free will** translates precisely into the ability to choose our thoughts, avoiding dwelling on those related to unwanted things.

Easier than it sounds

Okay, nice words, but how do we do that? How do we experience the positive emotion before we even own the things we desire?

The answer is simple: through training. Could you lift an 80Kg weight without working out in the gym first? Definitely not, but I am sure that after a period of training, more or less, anyone could do it.

Well, the same thing applies to the emotions we wish to feel. Okay, but the next question is: how do we train ourselves to feel positive emotions? What are the 'tools' to use?

Again, the answer is really simple: we use the things we already have, for which it is not difficult to feel the 'joy' and 'satisfaction'.

Let's start with the little things

You can practice every day by starting to look around and notice all the beautiful things around you. Train your gratitude by learning to enjoy the small moments of each day. Give thanks for everything that is part of your life, but that you may not notice because it seems obvious to you. And, very importantly, feel **immense gratitude** as you do so.

Give thanks for the things that make your life enjoyable, such as the warm bed that greets you at night, the hot shower in the morning, the aroma of coffee, your home, your family, ... strive to always feel immense gratitude. In short, put your attention as much as you can on the good things in life that you already have. And I assure you, you really do have a lot of them, if you just pay attention.

This way you will not have a hard time getting your mind used to feeling emotions of joy and gratitude, because by using things you already have, you will easily eliminate the problem of having to force yourself to feel for things that are not part of your life.

The mind is like a muscle. If you train it to be grateful, you will see that it will become natural to do so after a while, and since it has been proven that the mind cannot hold two different thoughts at the same time, I assure you that you will feel better and better, because a mind committed to being grateful for the good things in life cannot focus on any negative thought.

If you do this with commitment and perseverance, you will see that your mood will slowly improve, and having replaced the bad thoughts with gratitude will ensure that the outside world will reflect your joy in time, bringing you more and more things to be grateful for.

But the most important thing is that after a while, once your mind gets used to feeling gratitude, you will be able to do it very easily even for the things you want that you do not have yet. **It is the exact same emotion.** Once you are able to recall it in your mind, you will be able to do it pretty much *'on command'* for anything.

You will discover the enormous power of knowing how to combine and use the mix of *attention and gratitude* to your liking, which will allow you to bring everything you want in your life.

Forgiveness as a Means to Heal Oneself

Everyone thinks that forgiveness is a gesture of kindness towards another person. Let's learn to see beyond this common way of thinking to truly change our lives.

As I wrote in the subtitle, forgiveness is often conceived of as an act of 'mercy' towards a person or people we believe have harmed us. At least that is the most common meaning of this word. This is why we generally tend not to grant **forgiveness** whenever we are convinced that we have been wronged in a way that is too great to be forgiven, and in doing so we feel totally at ease, since the other does not deserve our mercy.

Nothing could be more wrong. We do not realize that by doing so we are literally closing ourselves inside a virtual prison, in which we lock ourselves up together with the supposed 'enemy' who wronged us.

One of the reasons why we should grant forgiveness regardless of the wrong suffered has been explained in the previous two chapters, which I invite you to read again, if you wish. I have in fact amply highlighted how the people we see as 'enemies' are actually there to help us grow, highlighting with their behavior an aspect of our subconscious that we must bring to light and overcome.

But that's not all. So far, I have talked about gratitude for the help received. In this chapter, however, I want you to reflect on another aspect of forgiveness that is just as important.

Forgiveness as a concession we make to ourselves

Yes, the title of this paragraph clearly states why we should always use forgiveness towards our neighbor. In order to understand it, we need to start from a basic concept, repeatedly stated within this book.

The world we see is nothing more than a projection of our being. In fact, we live inside a sphere whose inside walls are mirrored, and wherever we look we see an aspect of ourselves. All the people we meet are nothing but our projections, created to allow us (if we are awake and evolved enough to do so) to rise a little more in the evolutionary path that our soul is making in this life.

It follows then, as stated by various spiritual doctrines, that our neighbor represents a piece of ourselves. In fact, we are all part of a One, with no real separation.

Bearing a grudge against any other person, then, by denying forgiveness, only binds us even more to that person and the unpleasant event caused by them. We do not realize it, but our hatred brings even more hatred, proving to the Universe that we did not want to learn the lesson that person had come to teach us.

But know that we can only decide **when** to learn the lesson, **not whether** to learn it. This second option is not contemplated. Sooner or later that same person, or another in similar circumstances will necessarily come into our lives and will come again to present us with the bill, and our dull persistence in not wanting to grasp the lesson will doom us to put off that lesson yet again. One more time again.

Remember, our soul is eternal, and the Universe has plenty of time to teach us a lesson. Our free will allows us to choose each time what to do with that lesson, but it will be our destiny to learn it sooner or later.

So, let's stop choosing to be continually put off.

Forgiving others is actually forgiving ourselves.

Yes, you read that correctly. By granting forgiveness you are not doing any act of mercy to the one or ones who have wronged you. You are forgiving yourself, and by forgiving, you are giving yourself **an enormous gift**, and the reward you will get for understanding the lesson will be infinitely greater than any expectation.

I will close with a statement to ponder....

Forgive the world for the mistakes you have made

The Whole Universe Was Created for You

Don't you think that the whole Universe was created for you? Well, read this chapter and I am convinced you will change your mind...

The title of this chapter may seem a bit excessive. To think that the Universe was created for you is really hard to believe. In fact, we have a whole series of beliefs that have always been imparted on us, which make it extremely difficult for us to assimilate this concept.

Firstly, we are convinced that the Universe has existed for billions of years, and therefore long before we were born. Secondly, we are also convinced that compared to the entire Universe we are an insignificant particle on a tiny planet at the edge of a galaxy, placed among billions of other galaxies. How could the whole Universe care about us? Last but not least, we are convinced that the Universe is something 'external' to us, and therefore exists apart from us.

Nothing could be more wrong. I want to start with a little anecdote, which happened to me some time ago while I was driving my car in the streets of Rome. At one point another car almost hit me coming out of a road without a right of way. The guy on the other side, heedless of the fact that he was wrong, started to swear with words that cannot be repeated in this book. Assailed by anger, which in the eyes of most could be justified, I turned away, cursing the guy, wondering how he could feel right, having violated so blatantly traffic rules.

That is normal, you might say. In a city like Rome, you see dozens of these 'little theatrics' every day. True, it was not the first time something like this had happened to me, but that was the first time I was finally ready to realize that there was a lesson to be learned.

There is always a lesson to be learned

With the anger gone, I started thinking about what the odds were of running into that guy. All I had to do was leave the house 1 minute earlier or 1 minute later, or stop for an extra 30 seconds at a traffic light, and I would have never run into that guy. I thought about the infinite sequence of events, all related, that had to happen since the day I was born, to bring me to that point, at that time, and to cross that guy who would not respect a stop sign. Very little chance, practically close to zero. Then I remembered that I am a personal growth writer, and that I write all the time that apparent reality exists only in my head. That is when a thought crept into me, giving me so much joy that if I had met that guy again, I would have hugged him and thanked him.

Don't worry, I haven't gone crazy. I just realized, in a very clear way, that that guy had come (without his conscious knowledge, of course), or rather had been sent by my True Self to meet me at that point and at that moment just to give me an important lesson. The lesson was represented by the opportunity to be able to 'wake up' and see beyond the veil.

If anyone is wondering what lesson I have learned, it should be made clear that lessons are always related to the moment in life and the state of personal growth. At that moment, I clearly had not yet fully processed the fact that all events are created by me to allow me to make a choice about what attitude to have in response to those events. I needed a strong event in which it was seemingly obvious that I was on the right side, and that this guy was dead wrong. It had to be hard to make the right decision, or it wouldn't have been a lesson.

In fact, I could have chosen the (easy) path of getting angry, and then feeling righteous in resenting that guy. Instead, I chose (though not immediately) another path, which is to look beyond the veil and recognize the Angel hidden behind that hit-and-run mask.

At that point I realized that not only in that episode, but in every moment of my life, the Universe is constantly acting in my favor, always giving me what I need to allow myself to awaken from the deep sleep in which I, along with all the inhabitants of this planet, have been immersed since birth.

The guy was an Angel dressed as a hit-and-run driver. And that 'disguise' was the only one possible, at that moment, to allow him to open my eyes and make me understand what the true reality was. Just think, every person who enters the sphere of our perception, for a moment, a day, or a lifetime, is there to help us grow. And rest assured that each one of them will 'disguise' and impersonate the most suitable role to facilitate our path to be awakened.

No more railing against those who are ostensibly enemies. As I have had occasion to write more than once, no one loves you more than your enemy, because he agrees to let you hate him in order to help you grow.

Get it now? The whole Universe is continually putting all its infinite means at your disposal to help you. Every person you meet is there for you. Only to help you. Does that seem little to you? You have an entire Universe at your disposal, which is constantly 'moving' to meet you and facilitate your growth path.

There is no point in starting any path of awakening without realizing this important truth. Stop complaining and seeing the people around you as potential enemies. Prove to yourself and to the Universe that you no longer belong to the ranks of the sleeping complainers, and that you are able to see beyond the veil. Give thanks every time you receive a visit from an Angel in a suitable disguise for you. If you do not recognize him, he will be so patient as to come back again, perhaps in a slightly different disguise, but he will never tire of supporting your decision to be awakened in every way. In short, it should be clear to you now that **the whole Universe was created for you**.

Become a Conscious Creator

Do you really want to change your life? Then you must strive to become a Conscious Creator. How? Read and you will learn how.

In this chapter I would like to set the record straight about the act of creation. Don't get me wrong, not the Divine Creation, the one that according to the Bible was done in 6 days.... (the seventh resting) etc., but instead the creation **made by us**.

By us? Of course! If you believe in the Law of Attraction, then you must also know that you are the one and only Creator of your reality. You do this every minute of every day. Always. The problem is that you do not know it. That's why I wrote that you must become a **Conscious Creator**. Aware that you are one, but if no one explains it to you, you can never be one.

Only knowledge leads you to become a Conscious Creator

Knowing that we know... that is the point.

Sit back, turn off your cell phone for 10 minutes, and listen carefully. I am about to explain Who You Really Are and how you can become a Conscious Creator.

Let's start in order. Every human being is One with the entire Universe, or God, or Consciousness or One (call it what you like). We were created in His 'image and likeness', and that means we have the same powers as the One who created us. Quantum physics is proving to us, without any possible error, that reality as we conceive it through the 5 senses does not exist, it is a pious illusion of our mind.

The world is inside our heads. There is nothing and no one out there.

If you have read the book this far, you are already aware of this truth.

Now, you need to know that we are born with this knowledge already. Our soul knows everything there is to know. So, we do not have to learn a damn thing, we just have to "remember". This is the first step to become a Conscious Creator.

We are on this earth to experience what our True Self already knows, but as a spiritual being, it needs a physical body to experience it. What I am about to say might sound crazy, but believe it or not, God created us to experience Himself through us. We were given the power to create so that we could experience, by creating, anything, good or bad. But the problem is that we have become immersed in our own creation, falling into a sleep from which we will eventually have to awaken. Now you may realize that becoming a Conscious Creator means much more than you can imagine.

God is Infinite Love, but without us, created specifically to reflect His unconditional Love back to Him, he could never experience it. Our sleep does not allow us to be aware of this truth, because we have created a castle of false beliefs within which we have taken refuge, convinced that out there something or someone can harm us at any time.

The sleep we have fallen into forces us to come to this Earth without any conscious knowledge of our true divine nature. We are here precisely to 'remember' that we are divine by going through the opposite experience, so that we can have real knowledge of what it means to be God. Great task, isn't it? Now you may be looking at your life with different eyes.

If you want to become a Conscious Creator you must first know, understand and accept this truth. In reality you already know everything, so you only need to remember in order to "know that you know". You can know infinite things, but if you do not have the knowledge to know, it is like not having this knowledge. All of this is to bring you out of the 'sleep' you have been living in for eons.

Nothing happens by accident. If you have come across this book, it is because your soul has decided it is time to take an evolutionary leap and finally become a Conscious Creator. You have arrived at the appointment you set with yourself at the beginning of time, when your journey began. You are now at a very important crossroad. You can refuse to believe in what you are reading, but know that your free will only allows you to choose **when to learn** the lesson, **not whether** to learn it.

Now here's the kicker. I am going to explain to you, once you have gained the awareness of Who You Really Are, how to use it to really create in a conscious way. But I am not going to do it in this chapter, because otherwise it would be too long and many would stop reading.

Keep reading, because soon you will discover the true meaning of being a Conscious Creator. Enough for now, you have enough material to meditate on your True Nature.

Become the Highest Idea of Yourself

The only way to become Conscious Creators is to imagine and embody the highest idea of Yourself.

The idea at the base of our reasoning is that we are the creators of our reality. We have already seen how quantum physics has given tangible demonstrations of this truth, bringing man to the awareness of being the only creator and protagonist of whatever happens in his life.

In the previous chapter we also revealed one of the greatest truths about our true nature, and the purpose for which are incarnate in a physical body, and why we "forgot" our divine origin. We did this in order to experience our divinity through awareness.

The keyword is **awareness**. Sooner or later, in our evolutionary journey, we are bound to come across these truths, it is a necessary step. You can choose when to get there, but not whether to or not.

At this point the question arises: why are we talking about awareness, and what is the meaning of the title of this chapter, that is, of becoming **the highest idea of oneself?**

Simple. Thought creates our reality. In other words, we are who we think we are. So, to regain the role of Creator, we must be **aware that we are**. But that's not enough. Since we are who we think we are, we must consider ourselves as we really are and aware of our greatness. In short, we must have the highest idea of ourselves well in mind in order to be able to impersonate it. Only then, can we regain control of the events we attract into our lives, making it an extraordinary experience.

What it means to have the highest idea of yourself

We are Creators, we said. Good. A Conscious Creator must then know one of the greatest secrets of Creation:

Life is a process of creation, not of discovery.

We do not need to find out what we are going to be "when we grow up," but rather decide what to be, and then become it. How? Simply by living that thought. We must understand that that our soul is only desire, and our purpose is to transform the highest concept of the Self into the greatest experience on Earth. The greatest idea of the Self must impersonate itself through us.

We all have the power we need to do this, but the condition is that first we must be able to literally become the highest idea of ourselves.

So, listen closely. Every event in our lives happens to allow us to define ourselves through that experience. There are no joyful events or sad events. There are only events.

What we decide to do with them will define our nature, thus allowing us to create ourselves through the attitude we have in response to the event. Too difficult? Let's try with an example.

A man who faces an economic problem in his life, for example the failure of his company, can decide how to react to that event. He can put himself down considering himself a victim of the circumstances, and in that case, he will only reaffirm his powerlessness in the face of events. That man, with that negative attitude, will literally "decide" to create himself a loser and a succubus of life.

Alternatively, he can understand that he brought that event into his own existence, and then react in a positive way by reaffirming his power. That man will then be creating himself as a Conscious Creator, bringing into his mind, and thus materializing, the highest idea of the Self.

We are who we think we are. Then we consciously decide to be what we actually are: divine beings with enormous power, capable of creating our own reality. We must always strive to become the highest idea of ourselves.

You have to train, study and commit yourself

Don't think it is easy. It takes years, maybe centuries and many lifetimes to get there, but the first step is to be aware of our true nature. And then we have to work hard to change the idea we have of ourselves. We must commit ourselves to seriously controlling our mind, permanently eliminating all thoughts of powerlessness or defeat. Let's continually bring to mind the highest idea of ourselves. Let's remember that we always have the ability to choose who we are. It is great power that represents great responsibility, which we must learn to administer.

We must create change in our lives not because we reject the current condition as negative, but because it no longer represents **who we have decided to be**.

We create our own failure every time we stray from the highest idea of ourselves, every time we believe we are less than what we really are. Then the Universe responds to our thoughts by bringing into our lives the events that correspond to our creation of ourselves. Do not fall into this mistake anymore. You have been doing it for too long. Now that you are aware of who you really are, train your mind to hold only and exclusively the highest idea of yourself, every minute of every day.

Life cannot show itself in any other way than the way you think it should.

A Practical Manual of Conscious Creation

So much theory is useless without the ability to put things into practice. Here is a practical manual of Conscious Creation.

In the previous chapters regarding Conscious Creation, I talked in detail about what our true nature was and how to leverage this knowledge to become true Conscious Creators.

Knowing these fundamental truths is essential in becoming aware of what mechanisms allow us to create our reality, but a proper dissertation must also provide as much practical guidance as possible.

Here then is the need for this additional chapter to enter deeper into what the rules of **Conscious Creation** are and that must be respected.

A Practical Manual of Conscious Creation: The Three Basic Laws

Let's begin with the first point, perhaps the most important. A true practical manual of Conscious Creation cannot neglect to say that **we must learn to listen to the messages that come to us from our True Self**. I will not bother here to explain who the True Self is, because we have already talked about it extensively.

But this is not easy to do, because our True Self does not speak to us with a clear, understandable voice. It speaks to us with the voice from the heart, made up of sensations, intuitions and veiled perceptions. Impossible to hear if our mind is occupied by the background noise of our inner voice.

We must silence that little voice in order to be able to "listen" to the subtle and imperceptible messages of our True Self, which really knows how things are and which lives outside of our 'illusion', in a world without time and space. How do we recognize the messages of our True Self from all the others that our inner voice artfully creates to keep us captive to an illusion? This is a practical manual of Conscious Creation, so read on and you will know.

It is really simple, just apply a basic rule:

The true message is always the one that contains your Highest Thought, your Clearest Words, your Grandest Feelings[10]

In the previous chapter we talked about the highest idea of the Self, well that is what it is all about. We hold in our minds thoughts about ourselves that are the highest possible. We recognize them because they give us the **Joy of living**, they tell us the **Truth about ourselves** and instill **Love**, firstly towards ourselves and then towards the whole world. All the rest is useless noise, to be eliminated for good by not paying any attention to it.

Let's now come to the second basic Law.

You can be, you can do and have anything you can imagine

You have heard this many times before, but in this short practical handbook of Conscious Creation I want to point out two important things. The first is that the sentence written above is just one of the highest possible thoughts we need to hold in our minds. If you were wondering what those thoughts are, here you go. Second, this sentence tells us that we are **perfect creative machines**. We are because the One who conceived us intended it to be so. And when I say 'perfect machines', I mean without any possibility of error. We create in every moment with our thoughts. **That is the reason for the first Law**. Never forget it.

---

[10] Walsh N.D., "Conversations with God" vol.1.

It is amazing how we are careful to keep our house or our car clean, and then let everything into our minds, without realizing the serious consequences of it all.

As I told you, this practical manual of Conscious Creation contains three Laws, so here is the third one.

You attract everything that scares you.

Salvatore Brizzi, in his wonderful "Draco Daatson's Book" wrote: "The fear of being late slows down your train". Nothing could be truer. The reason is that emotions are a form of energy in motion, and as we now know, energy attracts other energy that vibrates at the same frequency. And if we set enough energy in motion, we create matter, and thus our reality. This is physics, not philosophy. We are back again to the **first law**, of which this is also a consequence. Go read it again if you have forgotten it in the meantime. So, what you strongly fear, you will experience. Don't ever forget it.

Every enlightened and conscious mind knows these laws, and respects them by being careful with his thoughts, words and actions.

Every time you complain...

every time you feel victimized by the world...every time you judge something or someone...every time you think you cannot handle it... ...you are violating these laws, remember.

And your life will reflect that choice. **Because it is a choice.**

So, choose from now on to apply the three simple rules outlined in this practical manual of Conscious Creation to your everyday life. It is worth it, believe me, because you will soon begin to see the practical effects.

You Cannot Have What You Ask For, Only What You Have

Asking for something by feeling like you miss it moves you even further away from having what you ask for. Let's see how the Law of Attraction really works.

On the surface it may seem strange what I stated in the title of this chapter, but if you follow me, you will eventually agree that it **is not possible to have what you ask for,** but only what you have.

Let's start with the Law of Attraction, and see how things really work. Surely all of you have read in the texts on the subject that, in order to get something, you have to think about that thing, and visualize it as much as possible, perhaps even enunciating phrases that help us to attract that thing to us.

Not everyone dwells on perhaps the most important part of the law. If you want to have what you ask for, you must necessarily 'feel' that that thing is already yours. Here then we find out why many times we cannot get what we want.

In fact, addressing the Universe with words such as "I want..." only distances us from the object of our desire. The concept is perfectly illustrated by Neal Donald Walsh in his beautiful book "Conversations with God", in which God himself says that...

> *"You will not have that for which you ask, nor can you have anything you want. This is because your very request is a statement of lack, and your saying you want a thing only works to produce that precise experience – wanting – in your reality. The correct prayer is therefore never a prayer of supplication, but a prayer of gratitude."*

The key to this is in the expression "...because your very request is a statement of lack."

There you have solved the mystery, and that is why you cannot get what you are asking for. But now let's move on to the second part of the question.

You cannot have what you ask for... but only what you have

In Matthew's gospel (Mt 13:12) Jesus says:

Whoever has will be given more, and they will have an abundance. Whoever does not have, even what they have will be taken from them.

If apparently this phrase might seem unfair, it is enough to interpret the terms "whoever has/does not have" in the sense of "those who know they have / do not have". Jesus of course was talking about the 'feeling' of having or not having, he did not mean actual material possession.

That is the key to the title of this chapter. You must feel that you already have something in order to have what you are asking for. Prayer then becomes no longer a moment of request, as we are mistakenly taught by almost all religions, but **an act of gratitude** for having already received what we are asking for.

Let's replace the words "I want..." or "I wish..." with the words "Thank you for...", always keeping in mind that words alone are not enough to get what you are asking for, but it is of paramount importance that you really feel within yourself the certainty that what you are asking for has already been granted.

I am well aware, before anyone points it out to me, that some authors or writers present techniques that involve asking questions that begin with "I want". I am referring in particular to Igor Sibaldi's 101 Wishes technique, but it is good to consider the purpose for which that technique was conceived. It is, as Sibaldi himself admits, a technique of inner growth, because in order to be able to formulate 150 wishes (101 initial wishes + 49 to replace those that come true, as explained by Sibaldi), we must first of all grow and become bigger than we are now, otherwise we stop after the first 15-20 wishes. The fact that some of them come true is just a pleasant side effect.

Regardless of whether or not you plan to write down 150 wishes, get your mind used to expressing gratitude all the time. This is the most powerful means for creating the life we desire.

"Feel like a king and a kingdom will be given to you." In other words, turn your supplication into a voluntary act of creation and thanksgiving for what is given to you.

The Law of Attraction Works for Everyone

Although it may seem obvious to say that the Law of Attraction works for everyone, perhaps not everyone believes it does. Let's clarify this point in detail.

The title may seem strange, because it goes without saying that, if it really exists, **the Law of Attraction works for everyone**. So, let's see what the purpose of this chapter is.

In this chapter, I would like to emphasize some concepts that, although stated several times in this book, may not be well understood, or at least it may not be well understood what I mean when I use certain terms. The title is a bit challenging, because the sense is that, regardless of the terms used, or the beliefs of each one of us, the Law of Attraction works for everyone, whether you like it or not.

Let's begin with a somewhat controversial concept, which apparently may clash with the beliefs of many of the readers of this book. The concept of God. You may have noticed that I use many different terms to refer to the same concept. Sometimes I call it the One who created us, other times the Universe, the Divine, etc. Of course, what is important here is the concept, which everyone can then translate into the most appropriate term according to their religion or belief. Apparently, this has nothing to do with the fact that the Law of Attraction works for everyone, but follow me and I will get to the point.

I use in this chapter the word Universe, so as to avoid repeating every time all the possible synonyms. What I mean is that the Universe is all that exists, visible and invisible. It is the One to which we all belong. For agnostics, it can be explained as the 'matrix' that connects all things, and that allows matter to take shape.

It is a rather strange concept to conceive, but it is what scientists are slowly discovering, whenever they realize that the observer affects the observed object. If the observer affects the result of the experiment, in the sense that his mind somehow can determine what happens, then it follows that all things are connected. It is as if the whole Universe is pervaded by some sort of 'consciousness' or intelligence that fills all the existing space and energy (you know that matter is also a form of energy, right?), taking the shape corresponding to the thought emitted by that consciousness. In practice, nothing can exist if it has not been conceived at the level of consciousness.

Our consciousness is part of this Universal Consciousness (oops... another synonym) and this makes us 'creators' of our reality. This is the physical law that underlies the Law of Attraction.

Here is why the Law of Attraction works for everyone

I say this because the Law of Attraction is a law of the Universe, and as such it works for everyone, whether they believe in it or not, whether they know about it or are unaware of it. It is like the law of gravity. If you jumped off a bridge you would still fall off, whether you studied the law of gravity or not.

The consequence of what I say is that, regardless of what religion you believe in, and therefore regardless of what name you want to give to the Universe, the Law of Attraction works for everyone, believers or not. If anyone reading my words thought that I was referring to religious concepts, they are very wrong. The fact is that modern quantum physics is discovering (or perhaps I should say rediscovering) the close connection between physics and spirituality. After centuries of separation between science and religion, we are witnessing a new era in which the two are finding more and more points of interconnection.

I felt the need to write this chapter because some readers may complain about my continuous mention of "holistic" concepts that, according to their point of view, have nothing to do with Science. I answer them that in the light of new discoveries it is impossible to talk about certain topics without bringing up metaphysical or spiritual concepts. I would like to reiterate that **I do not refer to any religion in particular**, and that my considerations arise only from carefully reading various texts, more or less scientific, which lead me to share my reflections with those who have the patience to read my words.

Anyone who disagrees with this viewpoint is free not to read me.

I would like to reiterate that nowadays, in the light of laboratory experiments, it is very difficult to distinguish between what is holistic and what is scientific. Anyone who tries to set a barrier will be inexorably destined to be contradicted sooner or later, and to revise his boundary line as science will reveal other 'oddities' of the world that we measure in our laboratories. There is no question that the observer affects the observed entity, even backwards in time. This is a fact. So, who can say if the consequences of this fact are 'holistic'? Staying only on one side of the fence would make us lose sight of the whole Design, of which we have for the moment only a partial and distorted vision. I have read a lot about quantum physics, but every scientific book in my humble opinion misses the real meaning, which is to explain how reality really works.

In my opinion, science is only able to illustrate the effects, but fails completely, or perhaps does not even try, to explain what is the cause, **the real cause** of what it observes. But maybe the concept of science itself should be revised, otherwise we will remain imprisoned in "rational" reasoning, which unfortunately shows its obvious limits in explaining the ultimate reality of things.

In short, The Law of Attraction works for everyone, and now we know that even stones have (or derive from) some form of consciousness and when I say everyone, I mean just about **everything**.

Get over it, whether you are a believer or not.

The Law of Wealth

Let's see what the rules underlying the Law of Wealth are. A useful handbook to have.

If we have read and studied the rules of the Law of Attraction, we have always focused on the mechanisms to be used in order to attract what we desire. This book has shown many of these mechanisms, but perhaps few have focused instead on what the bad habits with which we constantly violate what I call the **Law of Wealth** are.

Since birth, we have been conditioned by behaviors and clichés that over time we have accepted as our own, not realizing that we were in fact violating some of the main rules of the Law of Wealth.

It must be said that the Law of Wealth, being a direct daughter of the Law of Attraction, lays out that in order to have money in abundance we must first feel 'rich' inside, even before having accumulated actual wealth. And surely this is not easy. Imagine what can happen if we add to this difficulty all the bad habits that we express most of the time without even realizing it.

The rules of the Law of Wealth

So, let's see what these bad habits are that we need to suppress in order to make sure that the Law of Wealth is free to express itself in our lives.

Let's start with saving money. Apparently, we might be led to think that by saving money we are left with more money at our disposal. Nothing more wrong. Looking for the absolute lowest price at all costs, perhaps losing hours of our precious time, means telling the Universe "I have little money"; how do you think the Universe responds to this statement? Remember that we are Divine beings, whose word is law for the Universe. Law to be executed 'to the letter'. Alas we forget this too often. I am not saying we should squander our money, but surely saving at all costs does not help the Law of Wealth. Let's spend the right amount on what we need, with a clear head.

Now let's consider the 'vice' of many: the feeling of envy or contempt for those who are rich. This is the worst thing we can do. Contempt is a low sentiment that only makes us even poorer. The Law of Wealth wants us to get in tune with money, and how could we do that by despising it? Remember: admiration makes us similar to the object admired. And you know, like attracts like.

The sacred paladins of poverty

Another approach that is very often akin is the idea that spirituality and money are in stark contrast. This largely stems from the misinterpretation of certain passages of the Holy Scriptures, and the teachings we received at a young age, that poverty is described as the way to 'Heaven'. Get comfortable and enjoy the journey, there is no heaven to reach, and no God ever asked us to be poor. It has happened that someone has accused me of selling my books or seminars instead of donating them. According to this distorted view of reality, since I deal with spirituality, it is not correct for me to ask for money in exchange for my work.

Someone should explain to me why the time I spend writing my books and preparing my seminars should not be paid like any other job. But that is not the point; after all, I do not care about what others think of my work. I would like to remind these sacred champions of poverty that their attitude of repulsion only keeps them inexorably away from the abundance they desire. They are unwittingly falling into the trap set by those - religion and constituted authority - who have every interest in keeping people subservient and enslaved, limiting their beliefs.

What if it costs too much?

Another wrong approach is to say 'it costs too much'. The concept of "high price" does not exist. If I need something, I buy it, at the right price, but it is clear that the law of the market prevents something that costs too much in absolute terms. We must consider that everything has the correct price. And if at that moment we do not have the money to buy something, then instead of saying "it costs too much" we should start to imagine how nice it would be to own it. If the feeling of ownership is really strong, be assured that the Law of Wealth will kick in to make sure we have it somehow.

Never, ever, finally, should you think that there is not enough wealth for everyone. The Universe is abundant and has infinite resources. The Law of Wealth acts so that I will have according to my thoughts and beliefs, not according to what my neighbor has. This attitude is harmful for two reasons: first, the feeling of scarcity will bring into my life precisely the scarcity that I want to avoid. Secondly, this thought also generates induced feelings of guilt that drives money further away from us. Remember that your wealth does not bring poverty to others, and vice versa.

The problem is that behaviors and ways of thinking are sometimes even 'automatic' and are triggered without us even realizing it. Think, for example, about how many people, seeing a luxury car on the road, immediately think "who knows what the owner has stolen to be able to afford it". Those who say this are literally denying the abundance of the universe and we know that our intimate beliefs are inexorably reflected in our reality sooner or later.

We must then change our attitude and nip in the bud any negative thoughts about money. The Law of Wealth is there waiting to act for us as well. Let's help it to do its duty.

Life Is a Game. Let's Learn to Play It!

Sometimes we take ourselves too seriously, suffering even for trivial reasons. Let's learn to enjoy our existence by becoming aware that life is a game and should be lived as such.

In this chapter I want to talk to you about the fact that life is a game, and that the problem is that we do not know it, or at least we do not believe it fully.

Have you ever come across people who tell you about their vicissitudes, saying that *"life is hard"* and that they are always the ones to whom everything goes wrong, and that *"they felt that..."*, etc.? If so, you may have also noticed that when we try to tell them that, by changing their mindset about the world, they can attract positive things to them, they look at us like we are crazy and reiterate that it is all story and that nothing ever changes anyway....

If this has happened to you, you are one lucky guy. That's right, because you can say that you have had proof that the Law of Attraction works. Those people are living proof that life brings us exactly what we expect. In fact, seeing everything negative, the moment things go really wrong these people say *"See I was right?"*, thus reinforcing their beliefs.

Funny, isn't it?

I have given you an extreme (but very common) example of a person who definitely does not believe that life is a game, **but mind you**, it was a challenging example, to get you to think about the fact that we also suffer from the same limiting beliefs, albeit in a milder form.

In fact, although we believe in the existence of the Law of Attraction, we do not believe in the fact that life is a game, and we continue to make the mistake of taking things too seriously.

In fact, many of us self-limit ourselves by thinking that the really good things in life, such as great financial abundance, are things that happen "to others" more fortunate than us. We often fall into the mistake of underestimating ourselves or overestimating others. We believe that we always have to do something to deserve the good things.

In Toyland, life is a game

But if it is true that we are the ones who create reality, then we need to change our perspective. Follow my reasoning. If we create reality, then it means that we can have everything we want, without taking anything away from others. But to do this, the Universe must necessarily have an abundance of everything. So, the fact that we can have everything in abundance makes this world a **Toyland**. That's right, a Toyland. We ask, and the Universe sets in motion to give it to us. This is the way things work, and this is the law that applies in Toyland.

So, if we live in Toyland, it follows that **life is a game**. Why do we always take things so seriously?

But...wait a minute...are you perhaps thinking that this chapter is too optimistic and tells a story that does not match reality? If you thought that, remember that negative person we talked about at the beginning. Think about it, maybe you are also in the same situation?

Yes, we are all in that same situation. We do not realize that life is a game because we do not believe that life is a game... It is not a game for us. We are locked inside a vicious circle: we believe in a reality that punctually comes true, and then by watching it we strengthen our convictions by believing in that reality... that then comes true again, and again...

...Funny, isn't it?

Do you want to be living proof that the Law of Attraction works? Then try to be positive about it.

We must consider that we came into this world to enjoy life. We must eliminate all limiting thoughts. We do not have to earn or deserve anything to have what we desire. We are Divine beings who deserve all the good things in life. Life is a game, and we are here to enjoy the enormous gift that is existence, and any of our desires can be materialized, just know and believe that this is true.

Let's learn to play the game the right way

Careful. Let's not fall into the mistake of thinking it is easy. We have to toil hard by working on ourselves to change our beliefs and thus achieve such awareness. It is not enough to know it, we must also believe it deeply, carving it in our subconscious. It may take years, but it is absolutely possible, for everyone.

But we must also avoid making another mistake. While it is true that life is a game, we need to view its gifts as simple gifts to be used and to **let go** of when necessary.

Nothing is final, and nothing belongs to us. Let's enjoy the fact that life is a game, not attaching ourselves to any of the "games" that it wants to give us.

Sharing as a Powerful Tool for Creation

Convinced of the scarcity of resources, we are led to believe that sharing deprives us of the goods we share. Let's dispel this false belief by showing that sharing is the only way to create abundance.

Imagine this scene: you are walking down the street and at a corner you see a beggar. You are generous-minded, and seeing that poor man on the side of the road, badly dressed and with a beard that has not been shaved in months, makes your heart ache, thinking of your own wealth.

You then decide to give him something. You put your hands in your pockets to look for some coins, as you approach him walking slowly. You rummage through your pocket and realize that you have two euros mixed in with other coins of less value. You think that maybe giving two euros is a bit too much, so you try to separate the smaller coins in your pocket, so that you take out only the less valuable ones. But you realize that the smaller coins will amount to 20 or 30 cents at the most, maybe not enough... The ideal would be to give 50 cents, or at the most 1 euro - you think - but in the meantime you have already passed the point where the beggar lies, and then you say to yourself "ok, I will give him something next time", and you pass by without giving a single cent. You think *"it doesn't matter, after all, I couldn't donate all that money to the poor guy"*, and you think it is okay.

But you are sorely mistaken.

You do not know it, but you just became a little poorer.

How is this possible? Read on and I will explain why. Surely, you have heard the saying that **the more you give the more you get in return**, but be honest, you have never fully believed it. This is natural, because in the material world things cannot be multiplied at will.

In reality things are not like that, because for everything there is a fundamental rule, which I dare say is a real law of the Universe:

Sharing is the only means to create.

But how, you will say, if I have an apple and I share half of it with another person, I will only be left with the other half. Of course, in the immediate term this is certainly the case, but if sharing is done with sincere generosity and selflessness (i.e., without expecting anything in return), then rest assured that you will have **created abundance**, and in the long term the Universe will never let you miss the object you have donated.

Since I continue to see you as skeptical, let's take a closer look together at why I am stating this.

Having or Being are the same thing

We need to start with a basic concept: **having and being are exactly the same thing**. Yes, you got it right. In fact, *'having something'* is equivalent to saying *'being the one who owns'* that particular thing. You will agree with me that *having a Ferrari* or *being the owner of a Ferrari* makes no difference.

Moving from the concept of having to the concept of being, we get closer and closer to how things actually work in the Universe. Being is the basis of any creation, as I have already explained in other chapters of this book. You have to feel that you 'are' something in order to become it. Well, the *feeling of being* is nothing but a *thought*, and you already know that the Law of Attraction works by attracting to itself everything that is similar to that thought. What does this mean? It means that by emitting a thought (therefore sharing it) we are actually multiplying it. Here then is unveiled the mechanism that is at the base of creation.

This is accepted without reservation for a thought or an idea. In fact, if I share an idea, I will not be left without that idea, but I will have actually multiplied it, and since other people can add their ideas to mine, the result I get is that my initial idea will expand and become bigger and bigger, attracting other similar ideas. This is the concept of brain-storming, used in business meetings to find solutions to complex problems, using the union of many minds.

Perhaps it is more difficult to believe the same thing for material objects, such as apples. But if you think this you are forgetting that every material thing existing in our reality **has originated from a thought**. Nothing, and I stress nothing, can materialize in our life if it has not been thought first.

Material things are also subject to the same law. If you share something, you are actually sharing the idea of that something, and as I just said, that idea will expand and attract other similar ideas to itself. But since material things spring from thoughts and therefore ideas, this explains why we can consider sharing as a **powerful tool of creation**.

Since the world is made up of ideas, the false association between giving and losing can only fade away.

Practical advice

Of course, I am not telling you to give away and squander everything you have. What I am saying is that in order to achieve more abundance in your life, you must first create abundance through your actions, which must be aligned with the idea of abundance.

Returning to our example of the beggar, next time pull out of your pocket all the coins you have, without even counting them, and give them without reserve. But above all, while you are doing this, think that in the Universe abundance is infinite, and therefore those coins will come back to you multiplied by 1000 sooner or later. So, act in accordance with your thought. Your action in this case will be very powerful, because you will firmly reaffirm your absolute trust in the abundance of the Universe. This is the thought you emit, and since we are Divine beings, whose thought is a creator, be certain that this thought will return to you materializing in its material correspondent and, as it is written in the Gospels...

... They all ate and were satisfied, and the disciples picked up twelve basketfuls of broken pieces that were left over (Mt 14:20)

Learn to Ask the Right Question

Every time something unexpected happens to us we tend to wonder why. Well, this is not the right question to ask.

There are two main types of people: those who have not begun any path of growth, and therefore still believe in chance and bad luck, and those who have realized that chance does not exist, and therefore are convinced that any event in their lives has come to teach them something new.

If you are reading this book, you most likely belong to the second group (otherwise you would be watching the latest soap opera on TV), and as a result you have realized that nothing happens by chance, and that whatever event, good or bad, you have drawn it into your life for some particular reason.

The question then arises, "Why is this event happening to me?"

The question would seem legitimate, because if we have attracted that event to us, evidently there is some reason behind it, regardless of whether or not we are able to see it.

Instead, the question is wrong. Asking for the 'reason' of certain events happening in our lives is the worst thing we can do.

But what's the point, you will say, you have always said that we must hold ourselves responsible for everything that happens, and that any event always comes to teach us something... True, but we are only considering part of the truth. What we are missing is that the reason for that event is **not the cause of** the event itself, but **it is the consequence of it**.

The consequence? Don't worry, I am about to reveal the mystery.

Life is a process of creation

You must always keep in mind that life is not a process of discovery, but of creating our reality. In each moment we decide *what to be*, in order to *become it*, and thus create the reality that reflects that way of being, with the ultimate goal of experiencing it. Anyone who has read my books knows this concept well, and also knows how to use it to their advantage.

Fine, but how do we decide what to be? We decide it through the attitude we have in front of every event in our lives, whether good or bad. Events, if seen in this new perspective, simply represent the opportunity that life offers us in making a decision about what we want to be.

Now perhaps it is clear what I mean when I say that it is wrong to ask the reason behind every event. The reason is one and only one, and we already know it:

every event in our lives is there to offer us the unrepeatable and unmissable opportunity to **decide what we want to be**, so that we can become it.

For example, have you chosen to experience open-heartedness and unconditional love? It may happen that you are left or betrayed by your partner, so now you may have the opportunity to see beyond the veil, and demonstrate unconditional love to the person who, in the eyes of a sleeper, would appear as a despicable being undeserving of your love. Through your **subsequent reaction** to that event, you can then demonstrate to the world and to yourself that you **have become** capable of unconditional love.

Now do you understand why I said that the raison d'être of that event **is not in the cause** of the event itself, **but in its consequence**?

It is equally obvious that, since the consequence depends on our attitude in response to that event, there is an infinite number of possible consequences, and it is us who, exercising our free will, decide which one we wish to experience.

As a counter-example, if you have decided to be a victim of the events of your life, simply complain about them. You will then reiterate to the Universe that you do not feel you can be responsible for your own destiny, and that is **exactly what you will get.**

This is how we create our reality, because as Stefano D'Anna says:

The smallest change in being moves mountains in the world of events

Do you see the perfection of life? Can you perceive the beauty of everything?

The right question

At this point it is clear that we must never ask ourselves the reason why an event occurs. This question takes away our power, because of it we are affirming that there is some cause external to us, and by doing so we are dominated by events, consequently losing the faculty to consciously create our reality.

Learn to ask yourself the right question. Instead, ask yourself, *"How do I plan to react to this event?"*. In other words, what have I *decided to be*, in order to *become*, and thus *experience*?

Life continually offers us opportunities to experience new things, it is up to us to know how to take advantage of them by exercising our Divine Right to become whatever we desire.

Attention Is the Weapon of the Conscious Creator

Let's look at the role of attention in the process of Conscious Creation to understand how we can affect our reality by directing the focus of our thinking.

We know very well that thought creates our reality. This concept, although covered many times in these pages, perhaps has not been analyzed enough to fully understand its real implications.

We need to consider two important concepts.

The unconscious cannot judge whether something is true

Let's start by explaining again how we can influence our reality. At the base of everything there are our beliefs, understood as the set of rules that somehow we have been taught since birth, and that we have accepted as true, most of the times suffering because of them and not verifying their truthfulness. These beliefs are stratified within our **unconscious**, which is nothing more than a *'vibratory organ'*, which vibrates according to all the information that we have stored within it. These vibrations, extending into the Universe, attract corresponding events and people. Of course, this is a gross simplification, but that is more or less how the Law of Attraction works, and that is all you need to understand for the rest of this chapter.

Now, you must know that the unconscious does not see with our eyes, in the sense that, like any other organ in our body, it has a precise function which it blindly obeys. In fact, the unconscious has no power to decide whether a piece of information is true or not. It simply takes for granted everything that our conscious mind accepts as true, without questioning it. As you may remember, I said that the unconscious *is in the dark within us,* and therefore cannot know if that villa with the swimming pool we are thinking about is ours or not.

The cause of everything is thought

Now let's talk about the second truth. We must consider that our usual concept of time, understood as a continuum that goes from the past to the future through the present, **is just an illusion**. We are in error if we think that in the Universe there is a law of cause and effect. Each moment is brand new, and what could happen at any time does not depend in any measure on what has already happened. The cause of every phenomenon is thought. I will repeat it for those who were distracted: nothing can happen in the Universe that was not first created at the level of thought.

Well, have you ever really thought about what the real implications of these two extraordinary assertions are? We have understood that our unconscious takes for granted, and therefore attracts, all that we transmit to it, and we also know that the past does not affect in any way what we can create. How can we take advantage of all this?

The answer is simple:

Look at the world as you would like it to be, not as it really is.

This principle sums up the whole core of the matter. We must strive to imagine what we desire **as if it had already happened**, regardless of what our current reality is. Remember, the past cannot affect future events.

So, we must direct our attention as much as possible to the reality we would like to live in. We must not be conditioned by the present situation. If we can *really feel* that we are already living the desired situation, then our unconscious will take that idea for good, and will do everything to bring it into our real life. Don't ask yourself how it could happen and don't think about what your eyes see.

The Universe has infinite resources and ways to fulfill your every wish. It is up to you to know and use its extraordinary mechanisms to your advantage.

Self-Remembering to Be the Master of Your Own Life

In this chapter we will deal more deeply with Self-Remembering, a topic we have mentioned several times in the previous chapters, and which represents a fundamental exercise for personal growth.

We have repeatedly referred to the necessity of self-observation and to the importance of being constantly aware of oneself and one's thoughts. Most of the chapters of this book, in fact, revolve around the same concept, taking into consideration from time to time apparently different aspects of the same topic:

We live our lives immersed in a deep sleep, mistakenly believing we are awake.

Yes. The impact of the statement is strong, but you must convince yourself that it is the pure truth and it is the cause of all our problems.

But let's go step by step. We have already mentioned that we are much more than our bodies or minds. In reality, we are spiritual beings who inhabit a body, but, dazzled by a perfect illusion that makes us believe otherwise, we tend to identify with our body and our thoughts, blindly believing that we are one with them.

This is the *Great Deception*, which stems from the education received since childhood and which is confirmed every time something unpleasant happens that makes us fall more and more into the illusion that the world out there is a terrible monster that can determine our destiny and do with us what it wants.

The metaphor of the Carriage

A beautiful metaphor taken from the thought of the great Gurdjieff describes us as a horse-drawn carriage.

The **Carriage** represents our body, while the **Horses** can be traced back to our emotions that represent the main driving force of our lives.

Of course, the horses, as well as the emotions, must be controlled, otherwise the carriage will be dragged at random without any purpose. To do this there is the **Coachman**, who represents our rational mind, and guides the horses along the right path. But not even the coachman, though very good at driving the carriage, knows exactly where to go.

Who knows the destination? The only one who really knows where to go is the **Passenger** of the carriage, who represents our **True Self**, and is the only one who can show the way.

The metaphor fits perfectly with reality, just think of how the various elements are connected: the horses are tied to the carriage by rigid stirrups, which then make the carriage (our body) extremely sensitive to the movement of the horses (emotions).

The coachman (the mind) controls the horses with the reins, which are not rigid, so the control of emotions is not always so firm and effective. It takes a lot of familiarity and concentration to keep the horses at bay.

The main problem is that the coachman receives orders from the passenger only through the voice, which is a very tenuous connection and subject to interference. This is exactly what happens: usually our mind acts on its own without listening to its True Self (the voice of the heart), confused by the background noise represented by the metaphor of the noise caused by the wheels and hooves on the ground, and in reality, by the compulsive and uncontrolled thoughts that continuously crowd our mind.

We are like a carriage without a Passenger, left to its own devices, at the mercy of emotions and of a mind unable to control it, dazed as it is by the continuous noise of compulsive thoughts.

In fact, we are asleep, and we do not realize it.

Now let's come to the heart of the problem, the central topic of this chapter.

We have to take control of the carriage, and the only way to do that is to eliminate all the background noise that fills our mind. We have to remember who we really are. We must become aware of the fact that we are neither our body nor our mind.

We have to understand the importance of self-remembering: in some moments of the day, we have to make an effort to cancel for a few moments the thoughts in our mind, and simply remember us.

Self-remembering essentially means to become aware of our true being, and to look at ourselves in a detached way, as if the body or mind do not belong to us.

My advice is to keep a diary where we write down all the feelings we experience during the day, identifying and writing down the causes that have induced these emotions, how they arise and how they are expressed physically in our body (pain, various annoyances, lump in the throat, etc.). To do this, you must observe in a detached way what is happening inside of you, exactly as a scientist would do to study the reactions of the mind to certain stimuli.

Become the experiment and the experimenter at the same time.

You can do this exercise at any time of the day; you do not need to lock yourself in a room and meditate. It is not even meditation. Simply, at certain times of the day (in line at the counter, in the car, in the bathroom, etc.) remember yourself for a moment and observe yourself in a detached way and without judgment.

Initially it will be difficult to remember to do this, and for this reason my advice is to do it only in certain circumstances decided beforehand, which you can change on a weekly basis. Try, for example, to commit to doing it every time you get up from a chair, or enter a room, or are about to take a shower, etc.

You will see that over time it will become easier and easier to remember, and, very importantly, you will find that this act of self-observation will lead more and more to conceiving yourself as a spiritual being in full control of yourself.

Does this seem little to you? Have the perseverance to follow these suggestions, and you will discover the immense benefits of this seemingly simple exercise.

The Alchemical Work That Turns Lead into Gold

Let's learn to manage negative emotions and to transcend them, transforming them into a valuable source of positive energy.

Let's take a closer look at the concept of negative emotions by resuming the discussion we started in the chapter where we spoke about the importance of gratitude.

Do you remember? We told ourselves that we should feel immense gratitude for all the people who are part of our lives, even for those who apparently harm us.

We will extend our discussion in this chapter by talking about negative emotions in general, not only generated by the interaction with other people, but also those induced by negative events of any nature.

Whenever we experience an adverse event, we experience a great deal of negative emotion (anger, disappointment, fear, etc.), and the resulting pain leads us to believe that these emotions should be avoided at all costs, so that we can live as healthy a life as possible.

This may not be the case.

It is not possible to escape from the events of life and the corresponding emotions they cause, whether positive or negative. The goal is to transcend those emotions and use them to our advantage, not avoiding or repress them at all costs.

Repression serves no purpose; on the contrary, it is harmful. We must accept the fact that people and events in life are drawn to us and allow us to heal the wounds of our unconscious.

Transcending emotion is part of the evolution of our True Self and is the main purpose for which we are on this earth.

But how do we use negative emotions to our advantage?

Hold on tight, because I am about to reveal one of the most powerful ways to transcend negative emotions: you can do it easily through ***self-observation***.

Surely you have all heard of the Alchemists. Who were these gentlemen and what do they have to do with our discourse? They have a great deal to do with it, and now I will tell you why.

We all think of Alchemy as that medieval pseudo-science in which little bizarre chemists, in strange laboratories full of crucibles and alembics, tried to transform lead into gold.

Actually, for those who do not know, Alchemy is an exoteric doctrine much older than we think (there are traces of it already at the time of the ancient Egyptians), and the real alchemists were researchers who used techniques of introspection to transform negative emotions (symbolized by lead) in positive or superior emotions (symbolized by gold).

Over time, this initial intent was almost completely lost, and in our history books, unfortunately we only read a distorted version of this ancient doctrine.

But how did the Alchemists transform negative emotions into positive ones?

Simple: the science of the Alchemists was based on the observation of one's own emotions. One must become the Witness of everything that happens in our mind, aseptically and without applying any judgment.

The Witness observes his own emotions from the outside without judging them in any way, accepting them and living them as they are.

The key concepts here are two:

o *Acceptance*: one must welcome emotions without trying to repress them. Repression does not solve the problem, but rather aggravates it. If we reject emotions in our unconscious, sooner or later they will emerge again even more violently.

o *Non-judgment*: do not judge your emotions. Do not label them. Instead, strive to love them if you can, remembering that they are there to help you grow.

Try it to believe: the next time you experience feelings of anger or frustration, take a moment to observe your emotion, as if it did not belong to you. Detach yourself from it and do not identify with it. Just observe it, and you will see that it will disappear in a short time like snow in the sun.

You will have transcended the emotion, and this will make your True Self grow and evolve a bit more. Not only that. That emotion will appear again each time in a less powerful way, until events similar to the one that had originated that emotion will no longer provoke in you any negative feelings. You will have transcended the emotion, transforming the lead into precious and very fine Gold.

Now you understand why it is necessary to accept in a positive way even negative emotions. If you were an Alchemist capable of turning lead into gold, you would certainly be very happy to have a lot of lead available in your crucible.

Awareness as a Means to Escape Time

Let's discover together how we can use self-awareness to reach and savor that place of peace, outside of time, that has always been hidden within us.

In this chapter, I will discuss how to overcome and escape time. Yes, you heard me right. We are going to talk about how the perception of time negatively impacts our lives, and how to get out of time so that we can find infinite serenity, living in the present.

I am writing this chapter after watching a beautiful and unmissable DVD by Eckhart Tolle, *Your True Life's Purpose*, in which he explains in simple but incisive words the true meaning of living here and now.

Before this enlightening video, I had never understood exactly what the phrase "living in the here and now" meant. I had read it in many texts, pronounced by different spiritual masters, but although I had tried to understand its essence, I had never managed to grasp its true meaning.

Thanks to Tolle, this dilemma has finally been solved, and I would like to share my findings with you in this chapter. The conception is as simple as it is obvious, at least after the meaning has been grasped.

Let's start in order. In Greek mythology Kronos was the god of time, and he continuously devoured his children that he had generated.

In fact, in our perception, time devours everything, and we think of it as something that flows unstoppably, continuously devouring our present and everything it contains.

As I am used to doing in this book, I will amaze you again with a statement that will seem absurd at first glance:

Time does not exist. It is a mere illusion created and fed by our mind.

Worse, it is an illusion, therefore our own creation, of which we are continual victims. Time devours our lives, giving us the illusion that the next moment can be better than the present one, and that the purpose of our life is to achieve something - enlightenment, wealth, happiness... (everyone can choose) - in a hypothetical future moment.

This continual pursuit of the future moment leads us to live in constant dissatisfaction, always looking for something that can fill the sense of emptiness that we feel.

But unfortunately, we are also at the mercy of our past. As Tolle says, we are constantly thinking about thoughts that have already been made.

I have spoken to you often in this book about mental noise. The continual murmuring that we call the little internal voice. That little voice is constantly making us live in the past or the future, snatching away the joy of living in the present.

You must realize that the past is no longer there. It lives only in our minds. If we did not think about it, it simply would not exist, and we could get rid at once of all the problems arising from the past, such as feelings of guilt, anger at wrongs done to us, memories of unpleasant experiences, etc.

But that little voice keeps talking to us and reminding us of things that happened in the past. Old thoughts, dead thoughts, as Tolle says. But do you know what the problem is?

Every thought programs a future event in our life. This is why our little voice condemns us to continuously relive our past, projecting it into the future. That's why our life never changes, and we find ourselves always with the same problems to solve.

By continuously thinking about the past, we create the conditions to continuously reliving it.

What about the future? It is not there either, and never will be. What do I mean by 'never will be there'? There is only the present, and when the future (or what we think it is) happens, it can only happen as a present event.

All that exists therefore, is only the present. The future or the past exists only as thoughts within our mind. I will repeat: *they are only thoughts created by our mind.* Nothing real, nothing tangible that has a scientific confirmation. A pious illusion.

Whatever happens, it can only happen in the present. Are you convinced of this? It is logical and it cannot be otherwise.

So how to escape this vice? Simple, by living in the here and now. But how?

The trick is to live in constant self-awareness. Let's do a little experiment: close your eyes for a moment, and bring your full attention to the breath. Ask yourself the question: "Am I breathing?". Of course, the answer is yes, but by asking the question you will force your mind to be aware of the breath.

Do this for 10 seconds, and then answer this question: during those 10 seconds did your problems exist? No, of course not, because otherwise it would have meant that you were not really focused on your breath, but instead were still thinking about bills.

The exercise can go even deeper: close your eyes again and observe your thoughts for a while, without trying to stop or condition them in any way. Simply observe them. After a while you will see that your thoughts will slow down in both intensity and frequency. Good. Then begin to focus on the gap between the thoughts. In the absence of thought, your mind is quiet, but nevertheless you continue to have perception of yourself.

You have made a startling discovery. You are not your thoughts. If there is someone who can observe them, and who maintains awareness of himself even in their absence, who can it be?

Congratulations, you have just met your **True Self**.

The True Self is our true essence, which exists beyond time and space.

It is the white screen on which the images of our life are projected, it is the one who lives exclusively in the present because, it is existing beyond the noise of the mind and is not affected by the past or the future.

If you learn to be aware of your True Self, you will discover that there is an immense empty space within yourself, which is not empty. That Void is filled with awareness, the only true essence of which you are composed. The only essence of which, in truth, the entire Universe is composed.

In time, you will also discover that in that immense empty space there is infinite peace, which you can enjoy whenever you want, simply by cancelling every thought and paying attention to it: simply by becoming aware of your awareness.

The resulting peace and joy will be immense. You will no longer have to rely on the future to find happiness. It has always been there for you, in the here and now, silently begging you to pay attention to it.

Demanding Respect for Ourselves and from Our Inner Voice

We are going to talk about receiving respect not from others, but from ourselves. This may seem like a strange statement, but the key concept is that we do not love ourselves enough, and I will try to show you in this chapter.

Well, raise your hand if you have noticed that your mind is constantly engaged in an internal dialogue that occupies your thoughts.

I don't think I am wrong in saying that we all have an inner voice that speaks to us incessantly. It is the inner dialogue that we have already spoken about in some of the previous chapters and which tells us so many things all the time. Sometimes it reprimands us, sometimes it gives us advice, sometimes it calls us to duty, etc.

Non-stop.

We are all affected by it, without exception, which makes us think it is completely normal. In fact, the worst thing is that we think that that little voice is ourselves who, on the basis of logical reasoning, draws conclusions about the events of our lives, and then we tell ourselves about them.

We identify so much with that little voice that we even believe it! Sometimes, in this inner dialogue, we even answer it by agreeing with it, such as: "You shouldn't do that thing, it could be dangerous" - "You're right, you know? I think I'll give up..." etc.

I am about to reveal a fundamental truth that will free you forever from the slavery (because that's what it is) induced by that incessant inner dialogue:

The little voice, which constantly speaks to us, not only is not us, but it tells us an incredible amount of lies that we absolutely must not believe.

Don Miguel Ruiz, in his beautiful book "The Voice of Knowledge" speaks about the fact that within us there are two opposing figures that influence most of our lives: the **Judge** and the **Victim**.

Since our birth, we have been subjected to the constant influence from our parents, school, friends, etc. who have 'trained' us to believe an incredible amount of assumptions about what is right and what is wrong, what is good and what is bad, what to do and what not to do, and so on....

All these influences have created in us the figure of the **Judge** who judges (almost always in a severe and negative way) everything we do based on the notions that have been 'instilled' in our minds. The voice of the Judge reminds us punctually what the 'laws' commonly accepted by society are that we have violated, are violating or could violate.

The **Victim** in us listens to the Judge's accusations and, believing them to be true, feels compelled to be reprimanded or even punished for the behavior the Judge deems wrong. In the best of cases, the Judge's judgment is accepted as good advice to avoid future problems, so we self-limit our initiatives by blindly believing in the soundness of that advice.

Wake up! You are just a victim of a hallucination, which you mistake for reality.

Unfortunately, we do not realize that, as Ruiz says, we are living in a dream of our own making. We must never forget that it is we who create reality through our beliefs. If we tell ourselves, by listening to that little voice, that obtaining or doing something is difficult, and we believe it, so then obtaining that thing will be **really** difficult.

We are powerful creators who have forgotten to be powerful creators.

Get the picture?

We make something difficult the moment we believe it to be difficult.

Unlike what we think, cause and effect are inverted. We build our dream through the countless beliefs we have accepted as true over a lifetime, and the story we tell ourselves through the little voice within us becomes our reality.

Who knows how many times in personal growth texts we have read that we must love ourselves. Perhaps we never really understood what this meant. After all, we tell ourselves, no one hates themselves.

Now this phrase finally takes on a real and concrete meaning: to love oneself means to stop believing in that little voice that tells us all those stories that are not ours, but have been 'inculcated' through indoctrination endured since we were born.

We must finally understand that we live, or rather we believe, a story created by others, and on which, as long as we believe that voice, we have no influence and no control.

Words are very powerful in creating reality. Never must use them, for any reason, against yourself.

Take back control of your mind and consequently of your life. Love yourself by shutting that little voice up. Stop belittling yourself all the time and eliminate the Judge and the Victim figures that you so often identify with, inflicting unnecessary and harmful punishments on yourself that only limit your reality.

Use that little voice to your advantage, making it tell another story, a story of possibility, abundance, success and future accomplishments.

And you will finally be able to create and live a beautiful dream, the one you desire and truly deserve.

Never Use Words against Yourself

We do not realize it, but we often have the bad habit of using words inappropriately, especially against ourselves. A habit that must be absolutely eliminated.

In the previous chapter we talked about our inner voice, the one we all have in our heads, which does nothing but talk to us, every day, every minute, incessantly.

We have seen that that little voice is our worst enemy and we must be careful to listen to it. In fact, you will remember that that little voice does not come from our True Self, and even if we tend to identify ourselves with it, we **are not that little voice at all**. We will often hear it **using words of condemnation or judgment** towards ourselves or others, reminding us of rules that most often have been imposed on us by others, and we have more or less unconsciously accepted as our own.

Well, I want to return to this subject to warn you that this little voice is much more dangerous than it may seem. If it is not us speaking, who is it then? Who do we hear using the words that resonate in our heads?

In the tradition of the Toltec shamans (an indigenous Mexican tribe) the little voice is that of the *Voladores* (he who flies), dark parasitic entities that through the little voice dominate us by using our own paranoia, and transform the words into invisible prison bars. All with the sole purpose of feeding on our lower instincts and negative emotions.

Carlos Castaneda talks about it extensively in his books, in which he speaks about the teachings of Don Juan, a descendant of the Toltec shaman tribe. But there are also other distinguished writers, such as Eckhart Tolle, Deepak Chopra and Salvatore Brizzi, just to name a few.

This chapter is difficult to digest, I know, and you are free to think that this is all nonsense, the result of the twisted mind of some obsessed shaman. It may be so, but before you reject it, I invite you to read it to the end, and only then form an opinion about my words. Suspend at least for once your preconceived judgment, based solely on false beliefs that have accompanied you so far.

So, let's continue by following what Castaneda says in his books.

If you look at the effects of this "control", you will notice many similarities with the pain that afflicts man. Let's have Castaneda tell us this through the words of Don Juan:

"Predators have given us their mind which is our own. The mind of predators is baroque, contradictory, gloomy, obsessed with the fear of being unmasked. Although you have never starved, you are equally a victim of food anxiety and yours is nothing more than the anxiety of the predator, always afraid that his trick will be discovered and nourishment denied him. Through the mind that, after all, is their own, predators instill in men's lives what suits them best... Our pettiness and contradictions are the result of a transcendental conflict that afflicts us all, but of which only shamans are painfully and desperately aware: it is the conflict of our two minds. One is our true mind, the product of our life experiences, the one that rarely speaks because it has been defeated and relegated to obscurity. The other, the one we use every day, is a foreign installation.".

Let's learn to use words to our advantage

How to escape, then? First by becoming aware of it. There is only one thing the Voladores cannot do anything against: **awareness**. And awareness is achieved through constant presence, through the act of observing oneself and one's thoughts, detaching oneself from them and not identifying with the little voice that constantly speaks to us.

In this book, I will never tire of urging you to stop giving credit to that inner dialogue. The quality of your life depends on it.

We need to keep our minds clean just as we keep our house or our car clean, even more so.

We must learn to use words only to enhance our greatness. To use words only as **true positive support** for whatever action we want to undertake. The rest of the time, when it is not needed, the inner voice must be silenced.

But to do this, we need vast awareness and willpower, qualities that unfortunately are attenuated by the very inner dialogue that we wish to cancel, and of which we can regain possession only through the constant work of being present.

So, let's regain our authority and learn to use words only for our own purposes and for our own good. Whether or not you believe in the Voladores theory, let's stop using words to make ourselves prisoners of ourselves.

Beyond Mechanicalness, True Life Begins

Although we are not aware of it, our reactions to life's events are mostly mechanical. Let's see what the problems are and how to solve them.

Film production has often proposed films in which the protagonist is a robot that becomes aware of its existence and begins to behave in a way closer to humans, being able to make autonomous decisions and feelings. Examples are *"I, Robot"*, *"Autómata"* or the more recent *"Chappie"*. In all these cases, the robot abandons its 'mechanicalness', to wake up to a new way of living in the world.

Well, if anyone thinks that the way in which most human beings live and relate to the world is normal, or worse believes that it is the only way in which it is possible to live, he is very wrong.

The central theme is *'self-awareness'*. Just as robots live in a mechanical state until they become self-conscious, so we humans do not realize that there is another way of living life until we understand that for most of our time we have lived in a state of absolute mechanicalness.

Don't you believe it? Well, it is easy to prove. Would you be able not to feel anger towards a person who wronged you? In other words, would you be able to take control of your being in the face of any of life's vicissitudes, good or bad?

The answer is no, of course, at least for most people. As I have already written, it is as if we have buttons that say "Anger", "Despair", "Fear", but also "Joy", "Euphoria", etc. that are simply pressed by people or events outside of us, and we react accordingly, like simple robots that have been given a specific command.

The problem is not perceiving those feelings or having certain reactions. The problem is reacting in a complete automatic way, without the slightest possibility of exercising one's own free will and, worst of all, believing that this mechanical behavior is the only one possible.

Life begins beyond mechanicalness

There is more to life than what seems to us to be the 'normal' way of living. We can really take control of our lives by overcoming the mechanicalness that characterizes our habitual way of being.

As I have said many times, our brain is a machine, beautiful and perfect, but still a machine, and as such if left to itself, it can do nothing but execute the program that has been imparted since birth, throughout our lives.

All matter, if left to itself, can do nothing but behave mechanically. The entire Universe is a big machine, which in part conditions our existence. Whoever believes in the horoscope, that is the fact that stars can reflect our way of being and indicate our destiny is surely right, but only partially. Right in the case in which our behaviors and actions are only and exclusively mechanical. In this situation, what the Zodiac shows us reflects the mechanicalness of the Universe, where the stars and planets move according to precise physical laws, and consequently they can represent the mirror of the behavior and destiny of living beings who, being immersed in a non-conscious way, must necessarily submit to this mechanicalness.

Here is what Giordano Bruno said about it:

Whether we like it or not, we are the cause of ourselves. Born into this world, we fall into the illusion of the senses; we believe in what appears. We ignore that we are blind and deaf. Then fear assails us and we forget that we are divine, that we can change the course of events, even the Zodiac.

Self-remembering is the way out

Our destiny is not at all predetermined or predictable, because "we can change the course of events...even the Zodiac", as Giordano Bruno said, but how can we do it?

The answer is simple, and even obvious for those who habitually follow my blog or read my books. We can escape mechanicalness only and exclusively by taking control of our being through **presence** and **self-remembering**.

It's about choice, **only choice**. You can choose to live mechanically (i.e., not live) or live in presence, with full attention to the present moment and your being. Only those who have experienced the second modality can say they are *"living"*.

I am not going to dwell here on the aspects and techniques of self-remembering, because I have discussed them many times in this book, but the most important thing I wanted to emphasize in this chapter was that we must realize that the way we live **is not the only one possible**, and only by being aware of it, it is possible to access a new way of life, in which we take control of our existence, overcoming the mechanicalness of the world... even of the Zodiac.

If Doing Were Easy

Although we know that thought creates our reality, unfortunately we do little to control our minds. Let's find out what the problems with this incorrect attitude are.

I would like to begin this chapter with a phrase that Shakespeare puts into Portia's mouth in "The Merchant of Venice":

If doing good deeds were as easy as knowing how to do them, then everyone would be better off. Small chapels would be big churches, and poor men's cottages would be princes' palaces.

What did Shakespeare mean by these words? Applied to the field of personal growth, it simply means that if we all follow the instructions given by gurus, we would know what the right thing to do was, but alas, we do not do it.

We all know that the inner dialogue creates our outer world - I have written it over and over again in this book - but then we find ourselves complaining again about the noisy neighbor, the annoying mother-in-law, the dishonest politician and the rain that falls.

We know off the top of our heads everything we need to do to live the life of our dreams, but then we are unable to put it into practice, because *"If doing good deeds were as easy as knowing how to do them…"*.

That little voice that speaks to us constantly is the one who guides, with our total permission, our lives. We have given it complete authority to control our existence, and it certainly never misses an opportunity to take control of our mind and lead us to 'enjoy' complaining, self-pity, judgment, until we think that it is right to do so, after all, it is others who behave badly, what has it got to do with us... and, as I once read in a comment on my FB page, written in response to a sentence of mine that invited forgiveness: *"I prefer to get angry and take revenge on those who have offended me, so then I feel great"*.

Poor thing, she doesn't know what harm she is doing to herself. She is right in saying that then she feels great, but that pleasure we feel in having thoughts of revenge is only the effect of a drug to which we are addicted, and which conditions our mind, because we are addicted to it on a physical level. That pleasure comes at a huge price, in terms of physical health and quality of life. A price that must be paid in the end, because sooner or later we will be presented with the bill.

The Two Gifts

Neville Goddard, one of the fathers of the Law of Attraction, reminds us that since birth, we have received two immense gifts - the **Mind** and the **Word** - of which we do not realize its immense potential, and therefore do not use as we should. The Word in this case is not only the spoken Word, but also and above all the thought Word. Our inner voice, in fact.

That little voice creates our world and, as Goddard says, our world:

is the inner dialogue that is crystallized in the world around us.

If we could control our thoughts in every moment of the day, choosing only those thoughts that are aligned with our desires, we would see everything materialize in the external world. So, the question that I ask is, **"What are you creating right now?"**.

It is not only the thought that you have in your mind right now that you have to look at, or rather your voice and your **dominant thought**. What attitude do you have towards life? **Be aware of it** if you really want to change your existence for the better.

But reading it here is of no use if you do not commit yourself to modifying something within yourself, abandoning what you have been until now and embracing a new thought, a new way of being, which will necessarily result in a new world around you.

You surely already know all this, but maybe you have never put it into practice. You have heard about it and memorized it, but answer this question honestly: have you ever made it your main rule of life?

Nothing will change if you internally entertain the same old conversations you have always had, and as Goddard says:

Don't think for a second that knowing what to do will do anything for you. It is the doing that counts. So, if in every moment of time you know what to do, then do it. If you carry on a negative inner dialogue, stop it, even if it gives you pleasure, as it happens to many people who find it so amusing to criticize.

If you think they are just thoughts, and that no one is therefore listening to you, know that you are very wrong. Those thoughts are **explicit orders** you give to the Universe. They are **waves of energy** that radiate in space, attracting and materializing things that are in tune with those thoughts, and that will become sooner or later the reality you will experience.

It is the whole Universe listening to you in every moment of your life, and bringing you what you ask for. Does that seem little to you?

Free Your Mind to Free Your Life

Having control of your mind is equivalent to having control over your reality. Let's discover together a very effective technique to do this.

By now, you already know how I have insisted on the importance of controlling our mind in order to eliminate all the noise that normally occupies our thoughts. I'm referring, as you already know, to the inner voice that speaks to us incessantly, and whose danger has been highlighted several times in this book. If it is true that our thoughts create our reality, then it follows that a chaotic mind can only create a chaotic reality, in which we feel victims of circumstances that we believe we cannot control.

Our brain is a biological machine, and even if perfect, it is still a machine. As such, if left to its own devices, it will work according to a preset program, a program that we have assimilated little by little, year by year since our birth. Never having questioned it, and therefore having accepted it as true, it dominates *"without our knowledge"* our mind, and consequently our life, creating all the problems that we have experienced and that we will experience in the future if we continue to let it control our brain.

The problem is that we think we are thinking, but in reality, we are not thinking at all. We are constantly 'executing' an automatic program.

Salvatore Brizzi writes in his wonderful Draco Daatson's Book:

> *Images and phrases that appear in the mind do not represent true thought.*
> *If you can't control it, if you can't interrupt it whenever you want, then you didn't think it.*
> *It is not enough to hear a voice in your head to be a Thinker!*

As Brizzi says, without mind control we are normally asleep, similar to *'monkeys dressed up for a party'*. I am not offending anyone, because although the idea is not pleasant, it is the stark reality. It is important then to take control of our mind, freeing it from all that noise that does nothing but damage us and make us live a chaotic life at the mercy of events.

But how to do it? If any of you have ever tried to meditate, you will have found that it is very difficult to free your mind from thoughts, and even when we manage to do it, we are not able to maintain control for more than a few seconds. Almost immediately, in fact, the 'program' regains control, invading the mind again with a myriad of uncontrolled thoughts.

A technique to free the mind

So, I thought I would write this chapter to point out a very good technique that I have been using for some time now with excellent results.

Since I do not want to take credit where it is not mine, I learned this technique from a beautiful book by Andy Puddicombe entitled "Get Some Headspace" (also published as "Meditation and Mindfulness"), which of course I recommend to read to deepen the technique I am going to describe.

Let's start with a little experiment. Close your eyes and, instead of trying to repress the thoughts in your mind, **stay alert for the next thought**, like a cat waiting for the mouse out of its hole.

Done? I bet that during the time you were waiting, no thoughts (or hardly any) entered your mind. Why does this happen? Simple, because you kept a **vigilant awareness** of your mind. Waiting is just a trick to make you aware of what is going on. In fact, you have taken control of it, and as a result, no thought could peep out without your permission. Here is an important piece of information: **you are the absolute Masters of your mind**, and therefore through presence you are able to control what goes on inside it. Chaotic thoughts take over only when *you are not at home* controlling what is going on.

This technique is certainly very useful, but I want to tell you another little secret. You may have realized that resistance is useless. The energy you waste in emptying your mind turns against you, exhausting you and making all efforts futile. The secret is **to take the place of the Observer** in your mind. You know that in quantum physics it is the Observer who, through the act of observing, is able to interfere with reality by going along with its desires. But only **a vigilant awareness** can achieve the goal.

On the side of the highway

There is a beautiful analogy described in Andy Puddicombe's book: imagine you are standing on the side of a highway, watching all the cars speeding by in front of you. The road represents your mind, while the cars are your thoughts. Of course, you would never dream of standing in the middle of the road trying to block the cars with your body. You would come to an atrocious end and you would not get the desired result. The same goes for thoughts. Never try to block them with force, but simply stand on the side of the road and watch them pass by. Here then is a very effective meditation technique, which is very difficult to find in manuals that deal with this subject.

When you want to meditate, or simply stop your thoughts for a while, close your eyes and watch the thoughts come by, without trying in any way to stop them. Observe them as they come and pass in front of your awareness, and then watch them disappear into thin air, from whence they came; after that remain in watchful anticipation of the next thought. You will see that after a while fewer and fewer thoughts will come into your awareness, and their frequency will gradually decrease, until your mind is completely free of unwanted thoughts.

Do this as an exercise at least once a day, for about 10 minutes, and you will see that you will get enormous benefits. At first you will have to close your eyes to do this, but over time you will learn to do it with your eyes open, perhaps while driving or standing in line at the post office waiting for your turn. A clear mind equals greater inner peace. You will be calmer and more confident and, very importantly, you will have access to a higher level of awareness. The level of awareness that will allow you to control your reality, making you without a doubt the Conscious Creator of your life.

The Ego, Your Best Ally

The Ego is always indicated as something negative and to be eliminated. Let's debunk this misconception and discover what the Ego really is.

Ever since I started my journey of personal growth, I have always read and listened to people telling me that one of the biggest obstacles for our growth is our ego.

Our ego has always been portrayed as 'the demon' to be defeated, and described as the part of us that must be cancelled in order to finally free our True Being and thus arrive at 'awakening'.

Nothing could be more false. The main problem is that we do not know the true role of the ego, and consequently we only see its negative aspects, without considering the real purpose for which we endowed ourselves with an ego when we decided to incarnate in this earthly life. If you have been paying attention, you will have noticed that I used the words *'we have endowed ourselves with an ego'*. I did not just say that at random. Behind this statement is the concept that the ego is our deliberate choice, and since this decision was made by our True Self, it follows that there must be a good reason for it.

The True Purpose of the Ego

It must be said at once that the ego is an essential element for our survival, indeed I would say that it is the first reason why we all have one. The moment we believed we were separated from our Creator, and thus began our descent into matter, the ego was created as a logical consequence of that belief. The ego in fact represents our individuality, and its main purpose is to safeguard our being and keep it away from any potential danger. We say that the ego is the child of our instinct of self-preservation.

Unlike animals, since we are beings endowed with intellect, we have created the ego as an extension of what for every other living being is only an unconscious instinct, making it an instrument to safeguard our whole being, including our 'mental' and 'emotional' part.

Therefore, the ego is that part that allows us to feel 'unique' and 'separate' from others, and it is that part of us that reacts, even violently, to any attack (or alleged attack) to our integrity as 'individuals'.

This mechanism is essential to allow us to correctly fulfill our path of awakening within this earthly dimension. As I have said many times in this book, in order to rediscover our Divine nature, we must necessarily start from a condition of non-divinity, and the ego is the ideal tool which allows us to feel truly separate from others, and it is the main mechanism through which we 'enter' into matter until we identify with it (in fact, at the start we all believe to be just body and mind).

Without this 'penetration' and identification with matter, we would not create that healthy *resistance* without which we would have no incentive to make the path backwards towards the rediscovery of our divinity and the final identification with the One. We can consider the ego as the guardian 'guarding' our belief separate, a sentinel whose sole mandate is to keep us from crossing the threshold that separates us from awakening.

What then is the problem?

The ego itself would therefore not be a problem if we were awakened beings constantly present in ourselves. The chronic falling asleep in which we are immersed, however, means that the ego has taken total control of our mind, being able to direct our thoughts and our actions at will, with the sole purpose of ensuring its survival. In fact, you must consider the ego as a separate entity with its own self-preservation instinct, which lives within us and governs every aspect of our lives. We can say that the ego has its own **personality** and individuality, and it does everything to safeguard itself and stay alive.

The real problem is that we are all constantly asleep (no offense, because if you have read this book you know perfectly what I mean), and consequently we are 'absent' to ourselves, allowing the ego to take total control of our mind. We even identify with the ego itself, believing that its thoughts are ours. The problem then is not the ego, but our **allowing it to take total control of our being**.

Remember that the ego is a mechanical part of us, created with the sole purpose of safeguarding our individuality, therefore its mechanisms are completely 'automatic'. If we let it have total control, it will make us re-act to any external stimulus in a mechanical way, making us simply 'puppets' at the mercy of external events. There is little to be cheerful about, and above all **no one should consider themselves immune from it**, because it is the condition of 99.99% of human beings on this planet.

The true liberation from the ego

Never again believe those who tell you that the ego must be eliminated. We created it and it has a precise role in our path of personal and spiritual growth. The real problem is our falling asleep. To awaken means to become aware of the true nature of the ego and its true purpose, avoiding to become part of it, but above all preventing it from maintaining total control over our thoughts and emotions.

You must not fight it, but instead consider it your best ally for your personal and spiritual growth. The ego is not to be fought, but *transcended*.

How to do this? It is very simple, we must **learn to observe it**.

We must observe, while remaining completely detached, the emotions and automatic mechanisms that are triggered within us whenever we feel in some way 'attached'. Of course, it is impossible to do so if we are 'asleep'. Observation is only achieved through the exercise of *presence* and *self-remembering*. It is a work on oneself, more or less extensive depending on how hard we try, but the final reward is of incalculable value. In fact, detached observation removes the power from the ego, transmuting its energy and transforming it into a **precious ally** that will lead us to the full realization of our divine nature.

The Most Precious Asset You Have

We possess a very precious asset, through which we can express all our power, but the problem is that we do not use it and have it continuously stolen from us. Find out in this chapter what we are talking about.

Probably few people realize the extreme importance of one of the assets we have since birth, but no one ever taught us the best way to use it.

What am I talking about? **Attention**, of course.

Yes, attention is the most valuable asset we have, but no one gives it the necessary care, and what we constantly do is to have it stolen by others, by those who know very well its importance and know how to steal it from us for their own purposes.

You probably do not believe in what I am saying, but the ugly truth, whether you like it or not, is that we all live in a constant state of falling asleep, the result of the mental noise that is constantly expressed through that little voice with which we speak, convinced that we are the ones doing it. We are hardly able to maintain concentration on a thought or concept for more than 5-6 seconds, without something distracting us and stealing our attention that, no longer under our control, wanders randomly towards thoughts of all kinds, filling our heads with useless things.

Raise your hand if you do not often find your thoughts wandering among a thousand things, such as: "I wonder how much traffic I'll find today on my way to work... by the way, the car is dirty, maybe I should wash it... I'll do it tonight after work, hoping to get out in time... last night I had to stay until 7 p.m., but today I shouldn't have much work to do... it is difficult lately to find new clients... this crisis is claiming more and more victims..." ...and so on and so forth, in a dialogue with ourselves that has no end, but above all no sense, that 'takes us for a ride', like children dragged by the hand, through concepts that are completely unrelated to each other.

At the mercy of an automatic program

It is all normal, because that inner dialogue is nothing but the result of an automatic program preset in our brain, which, as a machine, can do nothing but function by mechanically performing what it has been programmed to do.

What is that program? It is simply the result of all the conditioning we have received since our very first day of life, and which we have accepted as true and then let into our minds, thus creating what ultimately represents the *'path of least resistance'* for our thoughts. Consider those beliefs as if they were grooves etched into the ground. If you throw water onto the ground, it will necessarily channel along those grooves, which are the paths of *least resistance*. Similarly, when we are 'absent' from ourselves (95% of the time) immersed in our state of 'sleep', our thoughts can do nothing but channel along the most common paths, endlessly repeating the same type of reasoning.

Attention, the energy source of the Observer

We must understand that all our creative energy is expressed through observation. As quantum physics teaches us, we are the Observer who creates our world through the act of observation. The creative energy goes where the attention goes, it is like a laser beam. The mechanism is very simple: when we dwell on a thought, it becomes more important, visible, familiar, and a held thought becomes a belief. The belief is a "condensed" thought, which is stratified inside us by dint of **giving it attention**, until it creates a path of *'least resistance'* inside our brain, a bit like those grooves we were talking about before in the water example.

You must always keep in mind though that our thoughts create the world we experience, as nothing can exist without being observed. In short, it is **through attention that we give permission for things to happen.**

This is why it is so important to take back control of our thoughts. The most important thing of all is to be aware of the thoughts that are going through our heads, to prevent them from going chaotic and uncontrollable, thereby creating an equally chaotic and uncontrollable world.

It does not matter what you are thinking about, the important thing is that you are aware of it.

So, stop every now and then and observe your thoughts. Focus your attention on your attention (excuse the play on words), and ask yourself the question, *"What am I paying attention to now?"* It is clear that question has no answer, because if I am asking it, that means my attention is directed to it. It is just a trick to take back control of our mind, and consequently of our attention.

This is what a conscious creator has to do if he wants to regain control of his life, preventing external forces from taking his attention away. He knows that this is the way, the only effective way, to truly become the protagonist of his own existence.

Well, now you know how to do it, you have no more excuses.

The World You See Is You

The world is nothing more than a reflection of who we are inside. In short, believe it or not, the world you see is you.

You may have read that the world we see is nothing more than a mirror of how we are made inside, of our thoughts and beliefs. Every person we meet, in fact, is there to remind us of some aspect of ourselves. Every time we notice some aspect that we do not like in someone (but the same reasoning applies to the aspects that we like), in reality that aspect is something that belongs to us. It may be something that we have repressed, or that we manifest without realizing it.

Basically, we never attract random people into our life, not even those we pass on the street and will never see again. All of them, and I stress all of them, are there to reflect some aspect of ourselves. And instead of criticizing the things we do not like in others, it would be very wise to ask ourselves why, among so many things, we noticed those very things.

But I think that what I have said so far is already known to many of the readers of this book. The law of the mirror is not new, and after the discovery and popularization of the seven Essene mirrors, the subject is certainly not new to many.

I have taken the law of the mirror as a starting point to speak about another aspect of the same theory that probably escapes many, but that I believe is of fundamental importance to become conscious creators of one's own life. The law of the mirror applies not only to what we notice in other people, good or bad it may be, but also and especially **to everything that is said or reported to us**.

Yes, everything that others tell us, whether pleasant or unpleasant, is derived **solely and exclusively** from the result of our thoughts and beliefs.

Everything that is said to us is nothing more than the reflection of some thought or belief of ours.

In other words, it is we who literally put into the mouths of others what we are told, or rather, *who ask to be told.*

Don't you believe it? Well, then perhaps it is worth remembering that we are the ones who create the world around us. Several times in this book I have written that there is nothing out there, and that quantum physics is showing us in an undeniable way that everything we see is only a reflection of what we are inside.

The world is just an illusion, in which we are lost after having created it.

Let's take an example with an analogy. Imagine that you are sleeping in your bed, and you dream that someone is talking to you and telling you things that you do not agree with at all, for example criticizing your work, or how you are dressed. Suddenly, an outside noise wakes you up and brings you back to reality. But since we usually remember the last dream we had, when we wake up, we have a good idea of what the person in the dream was saying to us.

Now I ask you a question: when you wake up, will you believe that the person in the dream really said those words to you, or will you think that they are just the result of your unconscious, which for some reason has brought that episode into your dream and made that person say those words? Of course, you would opt for the second hypothesis, since you are sure that it was only a dream, and you know, dreams are generated by the unconscious within our mind.

So, if even the reality we experience is just an illusion created by our mind, why do you find it hard to believe that criticism received in real life was 'induced' or created by yourself? I know it is not easy to accept, but if someone criticizes you for any reason, in reality **that person is only the means** that your unconscious has used to bring to light an inner belief of your own. Criticism received for a job done, for example, is actually a reflection of our negative thinking about that job. This is why successful people are also those who firmly and unconditionally believe in what they do. Because they have no negative thoughts (conscious or unconscious) about what they are doing, they simply never attract criticism about their work.

So, the next time someone says something to you that you did not want to hear, instead of getting angry or offended, consider it a gift that the unconscious is giving you to allow you to bring to light some negative beliefs or thoughts that you have about yourself. Then thank that person, because unbeknown to them, they are giving you an immense gift.

The world is a reflection of our innermost thoughts and beliefs, never forget that. This is why before starting any new activity, it is of paramount importance to align yourself with your True Self, in order to be more than convinced of the fact that we are Divine beings, and as such we can draw on unlimited knowledge and power to succeed in whatever endeavor we undertake in our lives.

The world you see is you. Never forget that.

Those Demons? Just a Dirty Trick

We are all on a path to consciousness, and the world we see around us has the sole purpose of aiding us in this quest, even when it shows us its worst sides. In this chapter we will discover how we can deal with the seemingly negative aspects of our lives using them to our advantage.

The ultimate goal, if there is a goal at all, is to rediscover our true divine nature, to realize our divinity, a divinity so powerful that it even allows us to create an entire world in which we step into a role without any semblance or memory of that divinity.

The adversities we encounter along the way are the actual resistance that allows us to grow. There would be no growth without resistance. It is only when we are uncomfortable that we begin to ask ourselves questions, and begin that healthy and indispensable work of introspection that allows us to go deep inside ourselves to unearth and illuminate the areas that are still dark.

We think we have to avoid difficulties and we spend our entire lives in the useless pursuit of a peaceful existence, locked inside our safety box, in which nothing can happen; but precisely in this dual world, in which the good and the bad have the same right to exist, and where any thing or event is always aimed at achieving the ultimate goal, we manage to reach Who we really are.

It is just a trick

The path must always be faced with our heads held high, otherwise we have no right to call ourselves Warriors of the Light. We are warriors first of all because we know that the enemy is not out there, there is no one out there, except for our demons, our creations without any real consistency, which scare us to death by becoming enemies, apparently separated from us.

Unraveling the trick is the task of the warrior, once we find the courage to face the demon, we realize it is made of nothing. It was just a trick, made of nothing, and the light of our awareness is the only means we have to wipe out that darkness in an instant, we just have to know how to recognize it.

Sometimes they disappear with the whole collection...

Sometimes they even take the form of friends, and it can happen that those you trusted turn their backs on you, as it happened to me, for example, when I had the entire earnings of one of my seminars stolen from a person I trusted. That is where the work begins, hard, painful work indeed, on the merciless hunt for the demons who try to come back stronger and stronger than before, and if you are not firm enough to recognize them, they regroup to launch the next attack.

> *"The warrior understands that the repetition of experiences has only one purpose: to teach him what he does not want to learn."*
> Paulo Coelho

Don't fight them, rather love them

Complacency and anger feed those demons, and the dumbest thing you can do is to feel like you are being bullied. Demons need to be acknowledged, not fought. Your energy must be high frequency, to illuminate dark faces. Your anger would only serve to fuel low frequency energy. The demon is just the dark side of us asking to be recognized and welcomed. It is a neglected child wanting to find the love of its parent.

You must be that loving parent. This is your job, so that you can reaffirm loudly, and firmly, that you are a Warrior.

A Different Reading of Christ's Life

In this book we couldn't help but take the opportunity to look again at the life of Christ from another point of view, a point of view that is certainly different from the so-called 'official' one.

We all have clear in our minds the life of Jesus of Nazareth, and the teachings that have been handed down to us by the official Church through the Gospels. We have been told that Jesus became incarnate and died on the cross in order to save us. But have you ever wondered to save us from what? Have you ever pondered the meaning of this statement?

First of all, we must start from the assumption that the Gospels have certainly been re-interpreted and sometimes even artfully manipulated, especially between the third and fourth century AD, when the Church became the state religion following the edict of Constantine, named after the Roman emperor who promulgated it.

The texts that have come down to us are quite far from the originals, and much of the deeply symbolic meaning of Christ's words and actions have unfortunately been lost. Igor Sibaldi in his beautiful book "The Secret Code of the Gospel" reconstructs the Gospel of John as it appeared in its original version of the second century AD. I recommend reading it to those interested in knowing the true symbolic meaning of what is contained in the New Testament.

A quantum interpretation Christ's life

In this chapter, I intend to go further. In fact, I would like to review the figure of Christ in the light of the quantum theories that we have been discussing in these pages. Let's start from the assumption that the reality we see is only an illusion generated by our mind, and that consequently time does not exist, or at least there is no linear and continuous time as perceived by our limited mind.

The little space I have available does not allow me to address these issues again, so I assume you already know them, but if you are confused, I invite you to reread the chapters of this book in which I deal extensively with these topics.

The fact that time is an illusion makes it consequential that the past does not exist anywhere, and therefore what we believe happened in the past exists only in our mind. We could go so far as to say that Christ never really existed, but perhaps the most accurate thing we can say is that there is no point in asking this question, since there is no real world in which Christ could ever have lived, except in our consciousness, which is a derivative of the collective consciousness.

Too difficult? No, if you have the perseverance to follow me to the end. If we accept the fact that reality exists only in our minds, then we must also accept the natural consequence that everything we see, including people, exist only as an effect of the projection of who we are internally. Remember the **law of the mirror?**

This is one of those Laws with a capital L, that we are not taught at school but that must be absolutely known by those who aspire to know how the world really works. According to the law of the mirror, every person we meet in our life, from those who are part of it in a stable way, up to those we meet just once, represent nothing but the projection of parts of our unconscious.

Others are nothing more than the projection of ourselves, appearing at some point in our existence with the sole purpose of helping us to recognize and bring to light parts of us that most of the time we do not know we possess.

Well, you must know that the law of the mirror always applies, even in the case of historical figures.

Here's where perhaps the salvation discourse becomes a little clearer.

If the figure of Jesus is our creation and if it is true that reality is only a reflection of part of us, then it follows that Jesus Christ represents our 'Christic' or enlightened part. What does this mean? It means that Christ is within us, in the form of our True Self, the One who knows the reality of things and lives outside of space and time, and therefore outside of illusion.

This is the true message of Christ, which no one has ever revealed to us. The message is that we are Divine Beings, and we do not have to walk along any path to enlightenment, since we are perfect beings, and enlightenment is already our natural state. If it were not so, we would never have created and 'materialized' the figure of Christ.

The meaning of Salvation

What then does the word Salvation mean? Why would Christ have saved us by dying on the Cross? At this point it should be very clear what this assumption means. Salvation, or enlightenment, is actually what is called in the Gospels the entry into the Kingdom of Heaven. And how does Jesus enter the Kingdom of Heaven? By being crucified, of course. And what does this mean for us? It means that we can reach the state of enlightenment (or salvation) only when we 'die' in order to be resurrected, but death and resurrection here have only a symbolic meaning.

To die on the Cross means to destroy one's ego, eliminating all the false beliefs that create the illusions of the world. Jesus represents our Divine part that can externalize itself and make itself visible to the world (i.e., resurrect) only after having destroyed the part of itself that belongs to matter, which for us means cancelling the ego, which is the part of us that keeps us bound to illusion. As Salvatore Brizzi says, the Gospel is a story with a happy ending, because Christ rises in the end. Everyone focuses on the episode of the crucifixion, but the real message is in the act of resurrection, through which Jesus demonstrates that Life always triumphs over death. Indeed, the true message of Christ, which no one has ever told us, is that, as divine beings, we are eternal, we were never born and we will never die, and therefore death does not exist.

On the occasion of religious feast days try to think about this interpretation, and look at the life of Jesus from this other point of view. Spend the holidays as a Conscious Creator and you will see that the world will look a little different to you. Then you will have taken your first real step toward Salvation.

Does the Soul Mate Really Exist?

There is a lot of talk about the concept of "soul mate", meaning the person who would be linked to us on a soul level, and who, once met in real life, would make our existence idyllic. Let's debunk this false myth, discussing how things really are.

This chapter will probably not please many people, because it debunks a myth which our ego clings to strongly, in the useless hope of being able to achieve the longed-for happiness through the *magical encounter* with who we believe to be our soul mate.

However, when you read it all the way through, you will discover that there is nothing to be disappointed about, because the promise of happiness can still be kept, even if not as most people believe. First of all, there is a very important concept that has already been discussed several times in these pages: we must never believe that happiness can come from anything external to us, whether it be a person, an object, an event, etc.

This fundamental truth derives from the consideration that everything we see outside of us, although it appears so real to our eyes, has no consistency in fact. Everything we see and experience is nothing more than the projection of what we have inside. As I have already written in this book, it is as if we were living inside a hollow sphere, whose inner walls are covered with mirrors. Wherever we look, we see parts of ourselves reflected.

Whether we like it or not, this is the truth.

To continue to entrust our own fulfillment to the outside world is to entrust our happiness to something totally inconsistent, which by its ephemeral nature cannot be lasting.

To explain this concept, I like to recall a story told to me by a lady who, as a child, in the immediate aftermath of World War II, was sent to a boarding school in a mountain resort. When it snowed for the first time, the little girl went out into the courtyard, and having never seen snow before, she thought it best to collect some to keep in the drawer of her bedside table, convinced that she could play with it later.

Before laughing at this story, let's realize that in our lives we do nothing but put snowballs in our drawers, convinced that we have something substantial and everlasting in our hands.

That void to fill

But back to the main topic of this chapter. Does a soul mate really exist? And if so, what is its true nature? After all, many of us will have already felt that 'thud' in our heart when we met a certain person, with whom we also shared a beautiful love story. We surely remember that beautiful sensation that went through our body, making it shiver with joy, every time we thought about or met that person.

Are those feelings proof that there is a 'special' connection between the two souls?

Certainly, but not in the way we are led to believe. Those feelings are a sign that we are literally 'recognizing' in the other person attributes that belong to us, and that are brought to light by the very person we are meeting. Every encounter, in fact, should be considered sacred, because it represents a very precious opportunity to recognize parts of ourselves that we were not aware of. Our soul responds through sensations and emotions, thus giving us the signal that we are observing some part of ourselves.

Why that joy? If those properties already belong to us, it should be completely normal for us to observe them. The reality is something else. The problem is that we are already complete beings, lacking nothing, **but we do not know it**. We believe we have 'voids', and we think we can only 'fill' them with something from the outside that can make us complete people. That's why when an important story ends, we find ourselves empty, lost, as if a part of ourselves had been taken away. The same goes, of course, for a nice car, a nice house or a prestigious job.

As a matter of fact, we "extend" our being by encompassing the external person, object or event, believing that we can complete ourselves. In reality, we are only filling an apparent absence, which in fact does not exist.

The good news

There is only one solution: let's enjoy the beautiful sensation of falling in love with another person, but let's not do it from the point of view of a 'sleeper'. Instead, let's take the opportunity **to recognize our true greatness**, extending our awareness and recognizing that the other person is there precisely to make us understand that **we are immense and complete beings**. Living a beautiful love story with awareness is exactly what is meant when people say they have to love themselves before they can love another person.

And you know what the good news is? Stories experienced with this kind of expanded awareness are based on something really real, and as a result have a very high probability of lasting a very long time, even an entire lifetime. The light of awareness gives 'eternity' to the events of our lives, because once they are understood in their true essence, they become part of the experience of our true being, so we can **never forget them again**.

True Love and Need Do Not Get Along

Love with a capital L or unconditional love cannot exist in the presence of the other person's need. Let's find out why.

The way in which many people understand love is far from the concept of unconditional love. The relationship is lived most of the time in the name of give and take, thinking that the other person must do something to make us happy.

Love can never be born from a need, of any kind.

Osho in his beautiful book "Love, freedom and aloneness" illustrates this concept with these words:

> *People are always looking for companionship. They cannot be with themselves; they want to be with others. People are looking for any form of companionship; as long as they can avoid their own company, anything will do.*

The concept is that in order to truly experience **unconditional love** we must first be comfortable with ourselves.

In fact, the search for a companion or a partner at all costs, reveals most often, the inability to be alone. This is the fundamental point. Knowing how to be with ourselves basically means loving ourselves to such an extent that we feel no need to be with someone else. We are enough.

Before we can be in companionship, we must learn how to be alone. Therefore, being 'full' of love towards ourselves, we are also in the perfect condition to be able to give this love without reserve. In fact, we are overflowing with love, and this alone is the prerequisite for being able to feel and give unconditional love.

Unconditional love is joy that overflows

Again, from Osho's:

Love is an overflowing joy. If you are bored with yourself, what joy can you ever share with another?

The concept is only one: we must first of all **love ourselves**. From the lack of this love come all the problems found in struggling couples.

Those who do not love themselves, in fact, as we have seen, are not able to be alone. You will feel the presence of the other person as a "need" that cannot be given up. But this inevitably leads to fear, the fear of losing the other person, and therefore being alone.

Have you ever thought about this? Jealousy, in whatever form it presents itself, always has only one cause: lack of self-love. Not loving ourselves, at an unconscious level, means we do not consider ourselves worthy of being loved, and consequently we live with the constant fear of being betrayed and left.

This also gives rise to the 'expectation' that the other will do something to make us happy. Sorry to say, but looking for happiness externally will inevitably lead to unhappiness. We must first of all be happy regardless of everything else, in order to feel fulfilled next to another person, without having any fear or resentment, but above all without expecting to limit the freedom of the other.

Unconditional love requires freedom, it strengthens freedom. To love oneself and feel good about oneself can have no other consequence than to give love and freedom to the other. Freedom to express oneself, without any expectation or constraint. Think about how many people believe that they will solve all their problems only when they manage to 'change' the other person. They do not realize that they are building their own unhappiness day after day, and are inexorably destined to certain failure.

*Unconditional love does not want anything, it only gives.
It gives joy, freedom, gratitude, and the more you give the more you receive. Indeed…
When unconditional love receives something, it is surprised, because it didn't expect anything in return.*

That's Who We Really Are

If you have ever wondered who we really are, you may come to understand it through enlightenment, or more simply, there is the possibility of having it explained to you by a person who has experienced it directly.

Almost all of you have heard at least once about the state of grace that could be achieved if you wanted to enter a state of enlightenment. Buddhism calls this state *Nirvana* and it corresponds to the full realization of one's own being, with the consequent extinction or dissolution of all earthly desires, thus reaching the full awareness of one's own immensity and conjunction with the One.

You may have wondered how one could feel in this state and how an awakened being would live his reality. Well, an American doctor named Jill Bolte Taylor had just such an experience. She had it as a result of a stroke in the left side of her brain, which then inhibited the functions of this hemisphere.

The two hemispheres, our duality

As you all know, the human brain is divided into two hemispheres physically separated, and connected only by a bridge of nerve fibers known as the corpus callosum. The two hemispheres have entirely different functions. **The right hemisphere** is the seat of our creativity, intuition, fantasy, sensory perceptions, etc., while **the left hemisphere** is the seat of rationality, calculations, cataloging, etc. To give an example, when we see a tree, we first perceive it with the right hemisphere, perceiving its shape, color, extension, etc. and then we give it the name 'tree' in the left hemisphere, which compares it with all the tree models already memorized, in order to rationally frame it within a well-defined category.

The right hemisphere is also the door through which we are able to connect with the higher layers of being, and thus receive a multitude of information that is outside of space and time. Insights come precisely from this hemisphere. The problem is that the left hemisphere applies a filter to all this information, in order to discard everything that cannot be catalogued within something known. Our brain receives billions of facts per second, but only a very small part arrives to our consciousness, because of the filter operated by the left hemisphere.

We could say, simplifying, that the right hemisphere is **the antenna** that picks up everything that exists in the real world, along all planes of existence, while the left is **the filter** that selects all this information in order to discard what does not have a rational meaning for us.

What happens if the filter is deactivated

Dr. Taylor, who ironically is a neuropsychiatrist, on the morning of December 10, 1996 suffered a stroke in the left hemisphere, resulting in the loss of the functions of this part of the brain.

Before continuing, I recommend you to watch the extraordinary testimony of the doctor in a video on YouTube[11].

A truly exceptional testimony. Let's reread some of the sentences pronounced in the video:

... I could not identify the position of my body in space, I felt enormous and expansive, like a genie just liberated from her bottle. And my spirit soared free like a great whale gliding through the sea of silent euphoria. Nirvana, I found Nirvana. And I remember thinking "There's no way I would ever be able to squeeze the enormousness of myself back inside this tiny little body".

---

[11] https://youtu.be/UyyjU8fzEYU

This is what it feels like when we realize our true being. The doctor had the distinct feeling that she was hovering in space, and what is really amazing is the fact that she felt really huge, so much so that she could not understand how her being could be contained within her tiny body. In another part of the video, she says at one point that she could no longer understand what the boundaries of her body were, feeling at one with the walls of the room she was in.

Once the constraints have been loosened, our whole Being comes to light, no longer restricted within the deformation operated by the filter of rationality. Remember what I have written many times in this book: **we are neither our body nor our mind**. We are actually immense beings, as large as the entire Universe. In fact, it is we who contain the Universe, and not vice versa.

The doctor had an incredible experience that made her touch this truth with her own hands. To conclude, then, who are we really? Let's Dr. Taylor's touching words tell us:

So, who are we? We are the life force power of the universe, with manual dexterity and two cognitive minds. And we have the power to choose, moment by moment, who and how we want to be in the world. Right here, right now, I can step into the consciousness of my right hemisphere, where we are. I am the life force power of the universe. I am the life force power of the 50 trillion beautiful molecular genes that make up my form, at one with all there is.

Discover the Warrior within You

You possess powers you never knew you had. If only you discover the strength of the Warrior within you, you could change your life in an instant.

I want to start this chapter with a little provocation. Do you think that a few visualizations and some sentences repeated in front of the mirror in the morning are enough to change your life and create the reality you desire?

Unfortunately, this is exactly what many books on the subject or some improvised 'guru' would have us believe, and this is precisely the reason that leads most people to get discouraged and stop trying after a while.

You have to understand that if you want to achieve results, you have to engage in a fight (because it is a fight) against the 'demons' that are within us and that keep us imprisoned in the cage that we have built for ourselves.

Demons? Struggle? But what struggle are we talking about? And against whom? It may sound absurd, but the main enemy is ourselves, that part of us that is 'asleep' and firmly believes that the world is outside of us and therefore represents a threat.

Develop your inner Warrior

If you wish to change your life, you must necessarily awaken the **Warrior within you.**

What does this mean? If you have the patience to read, it will be made very clear. However, before invoking the Warrior within you, let's try to identify who or what you must fight.

First of all, you have to fight that little voice inside you that is constantly talking to you, telling you about an illusory world that does not exist. When I talk about 'demons' I'm talking about those parts of us that act in 'our absence' taking control of our mind. Several times in this book we have mentioned the fact that our house (i.e., our mind) is almost always left to the mercy of our mechanical part, without any control.

Lack of control over the mind means lack of control over the external world.

...whether you like it or not, that's exactly how it is.

As long as you continue to hand over the keys of your mind to your inner 'demons', and as long as you let them run around freely making you think whatever they want, your life cannot change. You are at the total mercy of chance. Or rather, of chaos, the chaos that reigns supreme in the mind of those who are asleep.

That's why you must empower the Warrior within you. The Warrior is the part of you that in this book I often call the **True Self**, the one who is your true essence. The Warrior in you, however, although always present, does not take control of the situation until we allow it to do so. Our True Self absolutely respects our free will. It is in no hurry, it lives in a timeless place, so it can afford to wait forever.

But what does it mean to empower the Warrior within us? It simply means becoming aware of our True Self. It means making a daily commitment to keep a firm grip on our mind. It means to stop identifying with our body or our thoughts. A true Warrior is the one who knows perfectly well that the world is inside himself, and therefore knows that he is the only one responsible for any problems he might have. And being the one responsible, he knows that he can make the problems disappear into nothing, because problems are made of nothing and they come from nothing.

The Warrior in you knows perfectly well that everything is possible in life, and has never believed in the existence of the past or the future. He knows that time is an illusion created by the mind. The

Warrior in you lives in the here and now, knowing that this moment is the only one that exists.

But as I was saying, you must commit yourself with all your strength to repress the forces that continually throw you back into the cage of illusion. To do this you must be present, that is, you must be detached from your thoughts and emotions, well aware of their total inconsistency.

This is not easy. In fact, it is very difficult, because it takes just a moment to find yourself wandering again with your mind absorbed in all kinds of thoughts. Only the continuous exercise, supported by iron willpower, can bring to light the Warrior that is in you.

Difficult, but the reward will be great for those who succeed in the enterprise because, as Salvatore Brizzi says in his "Draco Daatson's Book", they...

> *know the art of stopping the world,*
> *their Universe is still*
> *and they dispose of it as they want.*
> *Demons fear them and become their slaves.*
> *Gods respect them.*

The Best Deal of Your Life

From an early age we were taught to be what we really are not, and we have accepted this point of view wholeheartedly and made it our own. It is a bad deal if you think about it. Let's learn to regain our true identity by rediscovering who we really are.

You have been told that you are a small being born by pure chance on a small planet that revolves around a star that in turn revolves around an immense galaxy in an infinite universe, and that your mind finds difficult to fathom.

You have been told that you were born a sinner, though you have never been told what sin you might have committed even before you came into this world. You have been told that you must be good and respect all the dictates of your religion, otherwise you would end up rotting in the eternal fires of hell forever.

At the moment of your greatest creativity, around the age of six, you were put in a classroom, together with other children of your own age, and you were made to sit at a desk with an absolute ban on speaking or moving. You had to ask permission even to go to the bathroom, hoping not to be too disruptive. They made you fill entire pages of your notebook with stupid and useless lines, telling you that they all had to be straight and lined up. You could color, of course, and you loved that, but it became less fun when you realized that you had to stay within the borders that you did not even draw, and that did not make any sense to you.

You did not understand where you ended up, considering that you were born with the belief that the whole world was yours, that anything was possible, and that you possessed the divine right to freely express your passions. You knew these things when you were born. You always knew them. You were taught, however, that you had to obey certain rules, and you were also made to understand, in some way, that it was not allowed to ask questions.

A little sinful being, who had no right to express himself, who in order to earn an imaginary paradise must stand still and shut up, obey and above all not ask any questions.

This is the identity they sold you. And **you bought it** without objecting. But it was not your fault, after all, a child cannot understand that, that is not the only way to live. If an adult told you something, you accepted it as an absolute truth, because you had not yet developed any capacity for critical analysis.

You can withdraw from that contract whenever you want

I said you bought that identity. Of course, it was not free, because **you paid dearly for it**. You paid for it by giving in return your freedom to express who you really are. You paid for it by giving up all the wonderful dreams you had as a child. It is a price you are still paying today, because that identity has entered your unconscious and forged who you are now.

A pretty bad deal, don't you think?

However, you can cancel that contract at any time. You can regain the power that they convinced you to give up for a few bucks. Now you are an adult, you have the ability to regain what you could not have when you were a child. Now you can be reborn to a new identity, your true identity, and you can do so without having to pay any price.

The new identity is not only free, but the moment you regain it, you will be rewarded with the power to determine your own life, and in the worst-case scenario you will gain the ability to deal with it better.

My first mission, through everything I write, is to make people the creators of their own reality by the acquisition of the awareness of their own immense power that comes from their own divine nature. I do my best, but it takes a small effort, also on your part to succeed.

So, abandon false beliefs about who you are, what your role in this world is, and what your limitations are. As I have stated countless times in the various things I have written and said, including in my books, **you are a divine being**, descended to earth with the sole purpose of learning to enjoy life in all its aspects and rediscovering through the love for yourself your immense beauty as a divine being.

Your role is only to rediscover who you are, and whatever mission you believe you have on this earth, you have the divine right to express it freely, in order to truly fulfill yourself and give yourself the sacred right to be happy, and consequently make the people next to you happy. This is your role, even if you have never been told.

You have no limits, get it through your head, even if there is always that little voice talking to you and reminding you that you cannot do this or that, or that it is not right, you do not deserve it, or it is not possible to obtain that thing, etc., etc. That little voice is one of those things **you bought dearly**. Return it to sender by shutting it up once and for all, and if you do not manage to shut it up, stop believing it. **It is your worst enemy**.

Start telling yourself different things instead. Teach that little voice to tell you that you can achieve anything in life. I know that right now it is rambling on about how my words are just nonsense. Watch it, realize the prison it is forcing you to stay in, and take charge of your life again by silencing it.

Be to Become

Anything you put after the words "I AM..." has infinite power, and defines who you are, and therefore who you become. Then tell yourself that you are the sole master of your destiny. Teach that little voice to praise your infinite greatness and to stop being afraid of the world because you are its only and undisputed creator.

I already know you are thinking that it would be nice to do this, but that it is difficult. Do me, and **do yourself a favor**: stop telling yourself it is hard, because that is also a limiting belief you bought at great cost. It is free, you can do it, you just have to want to.

It would be the best deal of your life, wouldn't it?

You Do Not Have to Learn Anything, Only Remember

We are convinced that we need to learn something new in order to take our growth journey. This is not so, as we will discover in this chapter.

Anyone who has started a path of personal growth will surely have felt a strong need to be informed, to read, to study, to learn more and more. The feeling is that the Truth, the one with a capital T, is written somewhere outside of us, and that our task is to assimilate as much information as possible, in order to fill this knowledge gap.

In this chapter I would like to point out that this is not true at all, at least not in the usual terms with which we approach our training regarding these topics.

Let's start right away with a very important concept: unlike what we have been made to believe since birth, **we are divine beings**, who have come here to rediscover this great Truth through earthly experience, passing through an apparent state of *non-divinity*. This means that our True Self, that is what we really are, already knows everything. In practice, we are already enlightened beings, since this is our innermost nature and essence.

The problem is that we don't know that we are. More precisely, *we do not remember* that we are. I would like to dwell for a moment on the etymology of the word *remember*, which in Italian is *ricordare* and comes from the Latin *re-* (again, back) and *cor, cordis* (heart), meaning **to bring back to the heart**. Why is it important to know the etymology of this word and what does the heart have to do with it? Fundamentally, the approach that we must always take when faced with any information regarding these topics is to **never take anything as true**. In fact, we must always trust our sensations, that is, what our 'heart' feels to be true.

As I have just told you, we already know everything, therefore every time we read or listen to something, we must take as true only the things that we 'feel' to be true. Although it may seem strange, this is the way to go towards the rediscovery of our enlightenment. Our being 'vibrates' in tune only with what it feels to be true, so we must always be guided by our sensations.

To give you an example, the first time I read a book on the Law of Attraction I was so excited by what I was discovering, that I literally had tears in my eyes. I had the distinct feeling that I had known these things all along, and I was even surprised that I had never taken into consideration what seemed so *obvious*.

The buried knowledge

Someone might ask at this point why it is so important to read books or attend seminars, if we already know everything that is inside of us. It is important because we need someone or something **to help us 'remember'**, precisely. In my previous example it was obvious, as I later realized, that I had known that information all along, but without that book it would have been difficult, if not impossible, to bring it back to the light of my awareness.

Beware of any 'guru' who wants you to believe that you are an incomplete being, and that you are always missing something in order to reach perfection. You are already a perfect Divine being, so all you need is someone to help you 'remember' that.

All the Truth is buried inside of us, under a multitude of preconceptions and beliefs that we have assimilated since our birth, through what we have been taught in school, in the family, in church, etc.

You do not have to learn anything, because your True Essence and the knowledge about Reality are is buried under a huge pile of false preconceptions, taboos, vetoes and inhibitions that make you see a reality that does not actually exist.

The bad news is that those false truths condition our lives every day, forcing us inside a prison made of imaginary bars. **The good news** is that the keys to that prison are in our hands.

Therefore, rather than learning new things, **we must demolish** this enormous pile of false knowledge that prevents our true essence from coming to the light of consciousness. Put aside rationality, because it is based precisely on that heap of false knowledge, which cannot be of any help to you. Instead, **use your heart**, your feelings, to see if something rings true within you. Always approach your personal and spiritual growth with an open mind and with the utmost curiosity, without prejudices or preconceptions, just as a child would do.

This is what Jesus meant when he said:

"Let the little children come to me, for theirs is the kingdom of heaven" (Matthew 19:14).

So, arm yourselves with a pickaxe and begin right now to strike at all your current certainties. Question everything, in order to finally bring to light your True Self, which for countless lives has done nothing but scream, begging you to finally listen to it and bring it to light.

The Road to Awakening

The path to awakening is long and winding. Let's see what its main stages are.

Sooner or later the journey of our life comes across something that maybe we did not plan or did not think was in our plans. Sometimes it happens by reading a book, sometimes by listening to someone in a video or a seminar, sometimes by reading an article in a blog, etc.

Maybe after years of so-called 'normal' life, one day something happens that changes forever the way we perceive our existence, and then everything appears under a different perspective, and nothing and no one will be able to stop our journey **towards awakening**.

The phrase "towards awakening" may seem a bit strong, apparently suitable for gurus who live on a mountain or in a monastery in Tibet. In reality it is the road that we, without distinction, will have to take sooner or later. It is a long, winding road, with ups and downs, but the interesting thing is that it is a road with no possibility of return. It may take years, decades, or entire lifetimes, but once you take that road to awakening, there is no stopping.

Sooner or later, we will all feel that normal life is not so normal anymore. It is not enough for us, and that sense of uneasiness will very soon turn into an unbridled desire to know more, about life, about why we are here, about who or what we are. And so, we set out in search of information, perhaps not yet knowing exactly what we are looking for. But the good news is that, once we take the path to awakening, the Universe will offer us, in an apparently random way, a multitude of opportunities, events and people who will facilitate our path.

The stages of the path towards awakening

Joe Vitale in his wonderful book "Zero Limits" summarizes in a very effective way, in my opinion, the different stages to awakening.

Let's see them together.

1. Victims of the World. This is the initial stage in which we all found ourselves at the beginning, and in which most people on this planet still find themselves. It is the stage in which we experience the world as an entity outside of us, unpredictable and uncontrollable. It is at this stage that we are convinced that we have no control over the world, and we feel a strong sense of fear and uneasiness. We complain, we feel resentment towards others, and we are convinced that the world has limited resources, and that therefore we must fight to get anything in life. It is unbelievable, but the vast majority of people live at this stage, and the worst part is that they believe this is the 'normal' way to live. They have not embarked on the road to awakening at all, and they do not even realize that they are living in a real hell of their own making.

2. Conscious Creators. In this second stage are those who in one way or another have become aware of the **Law of Attraction**. The first real, fundamental step towards awakening has been taken. In this stage we realize that we may have control over the events of our lives. We begin to realize that we are the creators of our reality, and that there is some way to exercise this control. We then attempt to exert control over the world through the application of a variety of techniques, such as meditation, visualization, repeating positive phrases, etc., and we even get some results. We are overjoyed by the incredible discovery, life is actually more beautiful now, but after the initial euphoria, we soon realize that something is still missing, some fundamental ingredient that is eluding us.

3. The awakening. As I have already said, it is only a matter of time, but those who undertake the road to awakening can reach this stage sooner or later. We finally realize that all the control we wanted to exercise in the previous stage is actually harmful and inevitably leads us astray. We understand that we must actually let life flow as it comes, aware of our connection with our True Self, which assists us and always chooses the best for us. At this stage we learn to live in the **here and now** and enjoy each moment, no longer influenced by the past and without any expectations for the future. We realize that only by placing our total and unconditional faith in the Divine does our life take a positive turn, miracles happen and we are pleasantly surprised. We perceive the insights that come more and more into our minds, we learn to recognize them and act accordingly. And the results occur.

The road to awakening is complete. We are one with the Universe, and we feel in the depths of our being that the world is within us. We finally stop being afraid and we really understand what it means to be in control of our life, which is simply no control.

I will leave you with a very beautiful statement by Salvatore Brizzi that sums up what we have said so far:

You are awake when what you desire no longer happens, but you desire what happens.

Does Absolute Truth Really Exist?

We believe that there is somewhere an absolute truth that reveals to us how the world really works, and shows us the right path to our spiritual journey. Let's dispel this belief once and for all.

At the time when I was donating the course "The Supreme Key" by C. Haanel on my blog Campo Quantico, I received an email from one of the readers who was reading the course handouts. The email contained the following question:

Good evening Paolo, I read with much interest the lessons about "The Supreme Key", of which I feel with confidence the truth ... but, reading for years the speeches of Osho, more recently Tolle, where the emphasis is placed on the absence of thoughts, the absence of desires, that the mind is the problem, it seems to me that instead the control of the mind, desire etc. are emphasized. Can you tell me something about this doubt of mine?

I sincerely thank Luca, the author of the email, because he gave me the cue to write this chapter and to finally clarify this controversial aspect. I want to clarify it also because I have received some time ago some criticism about one of my blog articles where I explained that you should always have positive expectations towards the desired things. The criticism centered on the assumption that *expectations are deleterious*, and that therefore we must *let everything be*.

Absolutely true, but the mistake that is made in these cases is precisely in believing that there is one truth that is the same for everyone, and that it is therefore possible to dictate very precise rules of behavior to be followed in order to continue on the correct path of spiritual growth.

The three levels of awareness

I have already explained in the previous chapter that the path of growth of each of us passes through three fundamental stages, which correspond to three different levels of awareness-knowledge.

I will summarize them quickly here:

1. The first level includes those people (the vast majority of the inhabitants of this planet) who believe they are limited to their physical body and that they live in a hostile world separate from themselves. These people will certainly not read this book, or Osho or Tolle's books.

2. The second level includes people who have discovered the existence of the Law of Attraction and begin to understand that their thoughts and attitudes somehow influence reality. To answer Luca's question, it is to this category of people that Charles Haanel addresses in his course "The Supreme Key", teaching them how to take control of the mind and direct it towards their desires.

3. On the other hand, the third level is for people (very few, to tell the truth) who have understood that the world we live in is only the result of an illusion, and that we are simply living in a huge dream. Those who have reached this level of awareness are no longer attached to earthly things, because they understand their total lack of value. It is like when we wake up in the morning and think back about the dream we just had during the night. We certainly do not take much interest in the things we dreamed, because we know they are absolutely not real.

Osho and Tolle have certainly reached this last level, and that is why they can say with the utmost authority that you have to be silent in your mind, and that it makes no sense to nurture desires for material goods.

But now I will ask you: raise your hand who, among the readers of this book, has reached such a level of "enlightenment" as to have the intimate certainty that everything we see has no real consistency, and therefore has lost interest and attachment to any material thing.

...I do not see any raised hands.

Here's what the problem is. We cannot enunciate sentences heard by others, as if they were absolute truths that must be respected by everyone, indiscriminately. There is no truth that applies to everyone. Each one of us lives within his own personal world, in which personal rules only and exclusively are valid. Those rules mark the boundary of our world, and until our level of awareness does not allow us to go beyond those limits, no one can give us pre-packaged truths of any kind, even if they were said by an enlightened people like Osho or Tolle.

Just as we cannot tell a person belonging to the first level of consciousness, that thought creates reality, because they would think we were crazy, we cannot tell a person of the second level to abandon any expectation or desire towards material things. He could not understand, convinced as he is that we can be happy only through the realization of our material desires.

We always learn to ask ourselves questions. Let's ask ourselves if what we are told represents a truth for us as well. We must not take everything for granted just because we have heard it from others. And above all, **let's not repeat it as if it were an indisputable certainty, setting ourselves up as champions of the Absolute Truth**. Surely Tolle is able to live free from any attachment, and it is also right that he shows us the way, but let's remember that until we have not yet taken and walked that same path, that truth may not represent our truth.

So, let's go forward on our spiritual path with the utmost tranquility, convinced that everything will come at the right time, without any need to rush things.

Dream and always keep a positive attitude towards life, love everything around you, and thank the Universe for all the beautiful things it has given you and will give you, including that beautiful villa with the swimming pool that you would love to own ... in spite of the Inflexible Tellers of the Absolute Truth.

It Is Not Enough to Know the Rules of the Game

We read so many books, we listen to so many teachers and gurus who tell us so many beautiful things about how to make progress on our path of personal growth, but then, at the end of the day, we realize that we cannot put into practice all those notions that we have learned. Let's see, with the help of a little story, what we can do to solve the problem.

Once upon a time there was a disciple of a Zen school who asked his Master: "Master, I have read practically all the books you have recommended, I have followed all your teachings to the letter, but I still don't see great results. Show me where I am going wrong".

The Master replied, "Get that chessboard you see on that table and bring it here." The disciple did as the Master had indicated.

"Good" - continued the Master - "now listen to me well. On this chessboard are resting black and white pieces, in equal numbers. The rule of this game is to arrange the pieces on the board making sure that on each row there is an equal number of black and white checkers. Are you ready?"

"Of course" - replied the disciple - "the rules of the game are very simple, I think I can easily do it".

The Master then took out a black cloth from a pocket of his suit and asked the disciple to use it to blindfold his eyes before starting to arrange the pieces. "But Master" - exclaimed the disciple in amazement - "how will I ever be able to place the pieces correctly on the chessboard without being able to see what I am doing?"

"Here is the answer to your question" - replied the Master with a smile – "All the books you have read and the teachings you have received have only served to provide you with knowledge about the rules that govern the world. They are indispensable rules, because without them you would not know how to face the vicissitudes of life, but they are not enough. You must also remove the blindfolds from your eyes, for despite your knowledge, you are still blind to the truth, and your eyes do not see what the world is really made of."

This short story makes us understand something very important: no matter how well we have understood the rules, **we cannot play the game of life with our eyes blindfolded**. Knowledge, though indispensable, is not enough if we continue to see things with the same eyes.

We know that the world is an illusion, and that we are creating it, but in spite of this we continue to be afraid of it, persisting with usual attitudes of complaint, anger and judgment whenever we have the opportunity. We forget that we are only ever dealing with ourselves when we see something or someone we do not like.

We need to take the blindfolds off if we really want to make progress on this path of growth. But how do we do that?

Let's get into the perspective that we are **solely responsible for everything that happens to us**, whether pleasant or unpleasant. To do this we must remind ourselves, as often as we can, that we are living in a dream, and that everything that seems real and separate from us is only **the result of a hallucination**, in which we blindly believe.

I will take this opportunity to show you a very simple technique that Osho has suggested in one of his many teachings to finally remove the blindfolds from our eyes and understand that everything we see is illusory.

OSHO: THINK THAT ALL PHENOMENA ARE DREAMS

This is an extremely powerful technique.
Begin to contemplate in this way: if you are walking down the street...
contemplate that the people you see are all dreams.

The stores and the shopkeepers...
the customers and the people who come
and go... are all dreams.

The houses... the buses...
the train... the plane... are all dreams.

You will be immediately surprised by something of enormous importance
that happens inside of you.
The moment you think
"They are all dreams" suddenly... like a flash...
something comes into your vision:
"I am a dream too".

If what is seen is a dream...
then who is this 'I'?
If the object is a dream...
then the subject is also a dream.
If the object is false...
how can the subject be the truth? Impossible.

If you look at everything as a dream... suddenly you will find something...
that escapes your being:
the idea of the self.
This is the only way to drop the ego... and the easiest.

Just try meditate in this way.
Meditate in this way over and over again...
one day the miracle will happen:
you look inside...
and the ego is not there.

The ego is a byproduct...
a byproduct of the illusion of whatever you see as real.
If you think objects are real...
then the ego can exist;
it is a byproduct.
If you think objects are dreams...
the ego disappears.

And if you constantly think that everything is a dream...
then one day...
in a dream during the night...
you will be surprised:
suddenly in the dream you will remember that this is also a dream!
And immediately...
as the memory happens...
the dream will disappear.

And for the first time you will feel deeply asleep...
but awake.
a paradoxical experience...
but of great benefit.

To remember to do this exercise, put an alarm in your phone to alert you at regular intervals, for example every two or three hours, and every time you hear it try to do the exercise proposed by Osho. Soon the blindfolds will drop fall your eyes, and you will finally be able to see what the world is really like. Guaranteed.

I Didn't Say It Would Be Easy

Too often we say that obtaining results in the field of personal growth is too difficult. It is an excuse we tell ourselves, but you will be amazed to discover the real mechanism behind this behavior.

The title of this chapter comes from a famous phrase from the very popular science fiction film **The Matrix**, where Morpheus, responding to Neo about the difficulties they encountered in the fight against their enemies, says:

I didn't say it would be easy, Neo. I just said it would be the truth.

Too often in my articles or posts about working on oneself are commented with phrases like:

"it's too hard"
"I wish it were that easy"
"I've tried, but it doesn't work for me."
...and so on.

Well, it is important to clarify one thing: I have never said that it would easy anywhere. Never. On the contrary, many times I have explained that the work on oneself is long, and that in order to obtain results one has to work very hard. It is the work of a lifetime.

In his seminars, Salvatore Brizzi usually says that if it is called *"work on oneself"* there must be a reason. If it is a job, it means that you have to do it to get some results.

The truth is that there are no shortcuts, and those who really want to take a path of personal growth will necessarily have to make a commitment to themselves to walk along that road to the end, overcoming obstacles and the inevitable uphills.

Those who write those comments do it simply as an instinctive and unconscious act to justify - to themselves - the lack of commitment in achieving their goals. Labeling something as difficult puts our minds at ease about the fact that we never really decided to take the path of personal growth. We tease ourselves by saying that *"I'd even try, but since it's hard...".*

The truth is we do not want to change

The reality is that we just say we want to grow personally and spiritually, but in reality, **we have no intention of doing so.**

This is a sneaky mechanism that we tell ourselves, a false story, made up of excuses that have the sole purpose of justifying our absolute intention **not to move one step from the current situation.** Don't tell me that you really want to improve yourself at all costs, and that you have every intention of changing your life by finally taking control of your destiny, and that you really want to make those dreams come true.

It's all bullshit.

You have a thousand reasons not to change, and your ego comes up with an excuse every time, invariably whenever you have to make a decision to do so. It has happened to all of us, especially when we would like to do some meditation exercise, that a little voice inside us tells us that we could put it off until tomorrow. What does it matter, today or tomorrow it is the same. And when we finally do that exercise, the same little voice tells us the next day that since we did it **yesterday**, maybe we can postpone it until **tomorrow**, so that **today** we are okay with our conscience.

Tomorrow does not exist, and yesterday is gone. Do you understand where the deception is?

Relax, it is not your fault

If you find yourself in any of these descriptions, do not blame yourself. You have nothing to do with it, it is not your fault. Listen carefully: **not one of the thoughts that crowd your mind belongs to you.** That's right. It is all part of the illusion in which we are immersed. You are inside a Great Simulation that you have built. It is the game that we have set up when we incarnated in order to fully experience the condition of non-God, in order to be able to conceive, through work, our true divine nature. We have been so good at building this mise-en-scene that it is really difficult to see it and get out of the labyrinth in which we have locked ourselves.

But in order to get out of the labyrinth we have to decide to see that labyrinth. The problem is that the voices in our head are there specifically to prevent us from realizing Reality, the one with a capital R, and to do this they use illusionist's tricks.

One of these is precisely *distraction*. If you have ever seen any illusionist show, you will surely know that the magician is very good at distracting your attention, so that you do not notice the trick. That's what those voices that tell us a lot of nonsense are for. They steal your attention to distract your mind, making you believe in the existence of false concepts like *'yesterday'* or *'tomorrow'*, so that you cannot see the trick.

Do you find it hard to believe? Normal, it's part of the illusion.

To get out of the Great Simulation it is necessary first of all to realize that you are up to your neck in it, but to do this you also need strong willpower to overcome this state of semi-sleep, and to work seriously to do the so-called "work on yourself". A good way to start is to stop believing that little voice that tells you *"it's hard"*, not because it is easy, but simply because it is not you talking.

Remember. I did not tell you it would be easy, **I just said it would be the truth.**

Escape Your Past to Free Your Present

It is only our mind, through the memories of our past, that obscures our vision of the present, making us live a reality that does not exist.

There is a beautiful passage in the book "A Course in Miracles", whose title is "The Shadows of the Past", which explains how our mind sees in others only a projection of what has been, making us in fact blind to the true reality, which we cannot perceive because it is obscured by our past.

Already in a previous chapter, I had the opportunity to explain that our present is nothing but the crystallization of our past thoughts, which make us live constantly far from the present. In this chapter I would like to emphasize how this constant living outside the here and now influences not only our relationship with others, but also and above all our life, creating an artificial world in which we think we see enemies that do not exist in reality.

Whenever we meet someone, we observe and judge them through the distorted lens of our past experiences. In fact, we tend to categorize people, anticipating our judgment even before we have really ascertained whether what we think about a particular person is true or false. This constant prejudice is a normal and almost an inevitable effect for anyone who identifies with their body, forgetting their true nature. This happens because our brain tends to always project the past into the present, imagining that without a cause, the only possible outcome is to obtain the same effect that was manifested in previous experiences. We tend to do this with both events and people, and by doing so we condition our lives, projecting the past inexorably into the future, making us relive it constantly.

This concept has been expressed many times in these pages, but what I want to highlight in this chapter is how this attitude conditions our reality and our relationship with others, making us forget what the real purpose of the presence of other people in our lives is.

We need to understand an important truth:

Every encounter with our neighbor is a Sacred encounter.

In the relationship with any person, we must always keep in mind that we are projecting aspects of our ego onto the other, and this happens anyway, being a law of the Universe. But if we want to grow and really become masters of our own lives, the next step is to avoid falling into the trap of judgment, and not forgetting that we are only observing a part of ourselves.

The reason why every encounter is sacred is that the moment we detach ourselves from our past, and understand that what we see is nothing more than a part of our unconscious, we are in fact bringing to light that part that had remained in the dark, because it was not recognized.

Recognition and subsequent observation have the beneficial effect of **dissolving the dark parts of our being**, thanks to the light of awareness.

So, every encounter becomes *Sacred*, because it is a precious opportunity for personal evolution, making us more and more similar to our True Self, that part of us that is not identified in the body and that knows perfectly well how things really are.

In this new perspective, every relationship with our neighbor has a whole new purpose. We are in fact completely off track if we seek in the presence of others an opportunity to be happy, or to see our merit acknowledged. These are just ego traps, and if we look to others as the source of our fulfillment, we are inexorably destined to be unhappy.

Here then we understand what the ultimate purpose of this rule is. When we finally understand that each encounter is an opportunity to see dark aspects that belong to us, we are also able to eliminate the cause of that projection. This allows us to slowly change our being from the inside, through a work of **recognition** and **forgiveness** of all that is buried in our unconscious.

But you also know that each of us creates reality with the unconscious, and so here is where the usefulness of this work is revealed in all its power.

By changing ourselves we automatically change the reality around us.

This work of cleansing makes sure that the past no longer conditions the way we perceive our present, allowing us to open the way for a **different future**, a future in which the shadows of the past fade away, and give way to all the expressed desires that could not be realized because they were 'polluted' by memories and projections of the past.

So, escape the past to free your present. **Forgive others to free yourself.** Difficult to do, perhaps, but the prize reserved for those who succeed is unparalleled.

Reinterpret Your Past to Change Your Future

We mistakenly believe that we cannot change the past. But we are wrong. Find out how you can revisit the past to change your future.

We all think that the past is something granitic, unchangeable. We believe that there is only one past, the same for everyone, and that past is indelibly carved into the fabric of time.

Nothing could be more wrong.

We have a conception of time that derives from our limited vision of reality. As I have already had occasion to say in this book, we live in a dream that we create ourselves, moment by moment, projecting our unconscious beliefs into the physical world, and then ending up believing that they are absolute truths.

The problem with time is that we believe that the past really exists somewhere, and we are constantly influenced by it. In fact, our thinking about past things condemns us to relive the same things, since thought is creative. You are what you think, and so your constant thinking about the past causes you to constantly **relive the past**.

We are much like the hamster running in the wheel, convinced we are going somewhere. In order to get out of this, we must clear the ground of some false beliefs.

Well, first of all get it through your head that **time does not exist**. You have surely already read about it in this book, but here I will reiterate the concept by saying that everything we believe is the past, actually exists only in our minds. Think about it for a moment.

Where did your yesterday go? What about your past birthday? Where are the events that happened on your last beach vacation?

They are in your head. Only in your head. There is no other place in the Universe where these events still exist or have ever existed. All that exists is the present moment, the here and now.

I know it is not easy to understand, always having believed in the existence of time as a linear continuum on which we are 'traveling' as we go ahead with our lives. We therefore think that our past exists, just as the road we leave behind us when we travel by car does. In that case we know that the road behind us exists because we can see it reflected in the rearview mirror. But think about it, the rearview mirror of our reality is represented only by our mind. Our memories are just illusions created by our brain, stored and recalled through chemical processes.

Chemical processes in our brain. The past is just that.

Quantum physics has shown that time is not an absolute and linear entity as we think of it. Did you know that a particle can under certain conditions exist simultaneously in different points of spacetime? In fact, in the microcosm time does not exist, or at least it does not exist as we imagine it.

Tired or confused? Don't give up. You are about to discover how to apply this in your life.

Changing the past is possible

So, if time is just a pious illusion, and the past exists only in our minds, what is the logical consequence? The logical consequence is that we can change our past.

Change the past? Yes, you read that correctly. If the past is only in our mind, then it is also true that we are the only and complete masters of our past, and so able to change it.

Yes, but how? Our reality is the result of our beliefs, so if we are convinced that a certain past event happened in a certain way, we mentally create our future as a logical consequence of our past. But beware: we are creating our future on the basis of something that does not exist, that is only represented in our physical brain through chemical processes.

So, we can change the consequences of the past simply...by changing the past. How to accomplish this? Well, simple, the past is just a representation in our minds. Change that representation and we will have changed the past.

Here's an exercise that I suggest you do every time you want to change something about your past that you don't like. In fact, I suggest you do it every night anyway.

Reinterpreting the past

This process, which we will call "Reinterpretation," should be done in a comfortable position, such as when you are lying in bed at night before going to sleep. Close your eyes and relax, concentrating on your breath. Try to reach a state of complete relaxation by releasing all the muscles in your body one by one, from your head down to your feet. Then think back to an event from the past day that you did not like and that you want to change. Relive it, but the way you would have liked it to have gone, not how it really went. If you had an argument with someone, for example, imagine that both of you say different words, in calmer tones, and that at the end you come to a final agreement, perhaps shaking hands or even, if you feel like it, hugging. Imagine thanking that person and using words of admiration and congratulating him.

Use this process **very carefully**. As a very powerful tool, Reinterpretation should not and cannot be used to imagine revenge or retribution against the person or people with whom you have collided. Reinterpretation only works if you use it to bring peace into your life and the lives of others. Remember, you are creating the world, and if you create discord, you will only obtain more discord.

You use Reinterpretation to 'fix' your past, and although it may seem strange or absurd to you, once you have reinterpreted a pleasant version of an unpleasant event, you have in fact changed your reality (remember that reality is only in your mind). The consequence is that you are literally **reprogramming your future** in order to bring more peace, serenity and abundance into your life.

This is how to get out of the hamster wheel. Try it to believe it.

The True Story of the Original Sin

We have always been told a false story about original sin. Let's find out what the real meaning of this ancient guilt is.

We all know the story of the original sin and Adam and Eve's banishment from Paradise. Our official religion teaches us that each one of us comes to earth with a guilt inherited from our first ancestors, and that baptism is nothing but the 'purification' and expiation of this guilt.

This absurd theory is absolutely not acceptable. We are divine beings who are having an earthly experience. We are perfect and nothing can affect our perfection. Whoever tries to make us feel less than perfect by using stories of faults and sins committed who knows when and by whom, is either ignorant or is in bad faith.

We are perfect beings, as I said, but it must also be said that what has been handed down to us about original sin, though artfully twisted, contains a very important truth that I wish to reveal in this chapter.

We commit original sin at every moment

But how, you will say, didn't you just say that we are perfect beings, and now this subtitle says that we continually commit sin? Which one is true and why?

What the Bible wanted to pass down to us is that, as divine beings, we are always connected to the One who created us (call him God, Creator, Universe, or whatever you want). In fact, we are one with Him, and have never been separated. The problem is that we believe otherwise, because we think we are separate entities living in a physical body that is also separate from the rest of the Universe.

That's what **original sin** is. Original sin is the belief that we are separate from the rest of the Universe, and that we believe in a separate world outside of us that threatens us and can harm us at any time. At one time man was a being aware of his divinity and his unity with God. But our soul only knew this at a conscious level, not by experience. Therefore, it was necessary to 'forget' our true nature and descend into the world of good and evil (in the Bible this is represented by the act of eating the apple and the subsequent expulsion from Eden).

Why did we have to do this? Because until you experience something, it is impossible to truly know it. Imagine having to explain what honey is to someone who has never tasted it. You could tell them that it is sweet (but we all know that it is not the same kind of sweet as sugar), that it has a gelatinous consistency, that it has a transparent yellow color, and we could go on and on listing all the physical and organoleptic characteristics of honey. But the person who has never tried it could never ever know what honey really is until he has tasted it, not until he has had **direct experience** of it.

And so, if we really want to give a purpose to our incarnation here on earth, the purpose could be to experience, through a dual world where positive and negative exist in all their forms, the true essence of things, so as to slowly build the awareness of being Divine, through the experience **of not feeling Divine**.

In fact, one cannot know what light is without having experienced darkness, or good without having experienced bad, generosity without having experienced selfishness... and I could go on and on.

Returning then to our original sin, we commit it whenever we think we are separate from our Creator, so we can use this journey of ours here on earth, as a reminder throughout all our earthly experiences. So, let's not waste this life. Let's become aware of our divinity and unity with the whole Universe. Only in this way can we atone for our original sin and finally take control of our lives, with full awareness of our perfection.

The Unconscious Is the Seat of Our Guilt

All of our problems stem from the fact that we feel guilty. Let's discover the origins of our guilt and how to overcome it.

Let's go back to talking about original sin and how it influences our feelings of **guilt** in our lives. In the previous chapter we saw what original sin really is, but what I want to highlight in this chapter is how that episode in which we felt separated from our Creator then determined the whole course of our lives.

What I am talking about is taken from the book "A Course in Miracles" which I highly recommend you read. This book explains that the moment we believed we were separated from the One who created us, we began to feel the guilt within us for having done so. This guilt of ours then made us see God as an enemy, convinced in our subconscious that we would be punished for it.

This is why many religions describe an irascible and vengeful God. In reality this is not the case, as God is only unconditional love. Nothing has to happen and we are not required to do anything to make him love us. But our guilt has caused us to fall into the error and belief that there is a wrathful God who punishes us for our faults.

Voltaire said:
God created man in his own image and likeness.
...and then man returned the compliment.

Remember, whenever we feel guilty about something, we also expect to be punished. And this guilt of ours has caused us to project onto the One who created us, our own faults and negative emotions.

From the same guilt also comes that restlessness that we sometimes feel, which makes us think that something unpleasant could happen to us at any moment, even if apparently our life has no particular problems. That sense of insecurity always comes from the unconscious fear of being punished by an avenging God. Official religions have made their fortune by leveraging this aspect of our psyche.

How do we manifest our guilt?

This is where things get very interesting. At the moment of separation our ego is in fact born. The ego does not exist, it is only an invention of ours that serves to justify the impression of being separated from God. Now, since it is completely impossible to bear this guilt of ours, we have to cushion it somehow, and to do so we have turned to the only entity that we feel is present, the ego.

But the ego knows very well the true origin and the ephemeral nature of our guilt, and it also knows that its survival depends on perpetuating that guilt as much as possible, so as to strengthen our idea of separation. So, what does the ego do? It apparently solves our problem by dumping our guilt outward. In fact, it deceives us into thinking that we can get rid of it simply by seeing these faults outside of us, that is, by transferring them onto others.

This is the reason why we see the ugliness of the world. They are nothing but the projections of what we feel inside. The worst that we unconsciously think of ourselves, because of our guilt, our ego makes us observe in others, so that we fall into the false belief that those attributes do not belong to us.

Whenever we notice an attribute in someone that we do not like, we must remember that we are simply seeing a characteristic of ours projected outwardly. Any person or thing that annoys us: an obnoxious person, a dishonest politician, recession, the slowness of the car ahead of us in traffic, etc., we consider a bad thing.

When we complain we are actually complaining about something that affects us, but we are not aware of it. And the origin is only due to what we think is our guilt for believing in the separation from our Creator.

A way out exists, and it is called forgiveness. We must stop complaining, and in light of what has been said in this chapter, we must remember that, that hateful person is there to remind us of this great truth, and that person is in our lives for the sole purpose of dissolving that false sense of guilt.

How? Through forgiveness of course. By forgiving that person we are actually forgiving ourselves, and we are permanently dissolving some of that guilt we have in our unconscious. The ultimate prize is the cancellation of the ego and the regaining of our freedom.

I think it is worth the effort.

The Hidden Truth behind Pinocchio's Story

Perhaps not everyone knows that the novel Pinocchio is actually an esoteric story that reveals many truths about the spiritual path of human beings.

We are all familiar with the **story of Pinocchio,** and we have certainly all admired the almost 'ingenious' gimmicks that Collodi devised to develop the story of the little wooden puppet. In reality, those gimmicks were nothing more than esoteric symbols cleverly hidden within the story to show us the journey that a human being takes throughout his or her life in order to reach awakening and pass from a simple mechanical puppet to a human being with complete self-identity.

Several times in this book I have explained that although we think otherwise, we actually live most of our lives 'asleep'. More accurately, we live in an illusion created by ourselves, and we believe that illusion to be real. Sleepiness expresses itself in different ways, first of all not remembering oneself, which has as its main symptom in the continuous noise we have in our mind, and the continuous brooding in the past or fantasizing (most of the time worrying) about the future.

This mental state makes us live continuously at the mercy of the world, since we do not have conscious control of our thoughts, we simply react to the events of life. It is no coincidence that Pinocchio is a "mechanical" puppet which is able to speak and move, but is not equipped with his own will. This is why he does all sorts of things (but above all he suffers), heedless of the advice of the Talking Cricket, who represents the voice of his Conscience.

The story of Pinocchio hides a multitude of esoteric symbols

Let's talk about the name: Pinocchio derives from the composition of the Italian words "pine" and "eye". The pine is the tree whose fruits, pine nuts, have the same shape of the pineal gland, which in the esoteric tradition represents the "third eye". The story of Pinocchio represents therefore the path towards the opening of the "third eye", therefore towards the awakening of the being.

Another strong symbolic element of the story of Pinocchio is the fact that Geppetto, his Creator, "molds" him starting from a trunk of wood. There is a strong similarity with what is written in the Bible about the Creation of man. Geppetto represents the "demiurge" (from the Greek "creator, artisan") who, in Plato's philosophy, personifies the lesser God capable of creating beings who are not aware of their own divine nature, and for this reason are subject to the snares of the material world.

The fairy is also a symbol, and represents what many call the true Self. The fairy is the one who gives life to the puppet, and then observes and assists him during all his vicissitudes, intervening only when the situation becomes serious, thus helping him to find the right way to enlightenment (which in the story is represented by the transformation of the puppet into a child in flesh and blood).

The story of Pinocchio then describes the separation of the puppet from his father (the Creator) and the descent of man to earth, therefore the removal from the one who created him. In the story, Pinocchio flees from his father to go in search of external satisfaction. This is a clear reference to the fact that man has become increasingly detached from his true nature (the Father) in order to pursue vain material achievements.

The story highlights the emptiness and futility of pursuing the "easy road" to enlightenment, represented by the many encounters that Pinocchio undergoes, which attract him towards vain chimeras, distracting him from his path. An example of all this is Toyland, a place of perdition that forges unaware people (with donkey ears) as future slaves subjected to the service of the ruling elite.

The last element of Pinocchio's story that I want to highlight in this chapter is the overturning of some conceptions that we consider 'normal' but to a careful eye they are not at all. I am speaking, for example, of the trial in which poor Pinocchio is subjected to after being robbed by the Cat and the Fox. In that apparently unreal trial, the judge condemned Pinocchio, even though he was actually the injured party. If, to an unobservant eye, the sentence might seem strange, for those of us who have read this book the meaning is obvious: since we are the ones who attract any event in our lives, the allusion that we are the only ones responsible for whatever happens in our lives is clear. As Brizzi says in his Draco Daatson's Book, "It is the victim who attracts the perpetrator, thus becoming an unwitting and consenting accomplice".

It is a story that can be read in two different ways: the first by a child, or an unconscious being who can only grasp the aspects that are in some ways senseless and incoherent, and for this reason considered amusing. The other way is to read the text in a conscious way, catching all the aspects related to the esoteric symbolism cleverly hidden by Collodi inside his novel.

For now, I will stop here, hoping to have stimulated your curiosity for further investigation.

APPENDIX: Mind-Body Alignment Techniques

This section is dedicated to the study of some techniques that allow us to facilitate all the work done so far. In this last part of the book, I will address the relationship that exists between the mind and the world around us, deepening the ways in which it is possible to influence in some manner both our body and external events in order to find the right alignment between our well-being and mental peace.

In my research I have come across many different techniques, but what I present in the following chapters are those that I have been able to experiment on myself successfully, and for this reason I re-propose them, hoping they will be of help to you. These techniques are quite well known, and most likely you already know them, but having listed them here and having described some of them in real life situations in which I was able to verify the benefits, I think they will be particularly helpful. Maybe in some cases we cannot even speak of techniques, but only of indications to face certain events of our lives.

I am sure of the fact that there is no technique that can be considered better than others. For example, when I am asked what kind of meditation I recommend, I usually answer that I am deeply convinced that meditation is like a dress. In my opinion, we have to try different ones on and then adopt the one that gives you real benefits and with which you feel more comfortable. This section should be approached in this spirit. It is only a limited and partial list of something that has worked for me. Try it out, and evaluate for yourself its validity. Like any other topic in this book, each indication should be considered as a starting point for further research, considering that most likely it will never be possible to put the word end to this wonderful and fascinating journey of discovery.

Anger Is Your Drug

Contrary to popular belief, chemical addiction does not only affect those who take drugs or alcohol, but it affects all of us, without distinction.

We tend to think that the problem of chemical addiction does not affect all of us. After all, we live regular, healthy lives, many of us even play sports, we do not use drugs, and we do not drink alcohol at all, or we only have a few drinks with meals - in short, we think we are completely unaffected by this problem. We are not. Each one of us is addicted to different chemicals, and although this may seem strange to you, keep reading and you will understand why.

In fact, addiction does not only concern chemical substances introduced from outside the body, such as drugs or alcohol; what I am talking about is a more subtle addiction, which we do not realize, but from which we are all, in varying degrees, afflicted. I am talking about addiction to chemicals that are **produced by our own body**.

Well, yes. Much of our mental habits are conditioned by a real addiction to the chemical substances that are produced by our bodies, and now I will explain how.

The materialization of emotions

Neurobiology has discovered that every emotion, such as anger, envy, fear, but also joy, euphoria, etc., is accompanied by chemical substances, called *neurotransmitters*, which are nothing but proteins that are emitted by the body in response to any emotion.

We can consider neurotransmitters as the **materialization of emotions**. What are these neurotransmitters used for? We can say with good approximation that they represent the 'food' for our cells. The cells, in fact, have on their outer membrane several receptors, each of which responds to a different neurotransmitter. The role of the receptors is to be activated by the corresponding neurotransmitter to generate a specific protein, a kind of *chemical message*, which penetrates into the cell and activates the DNA.

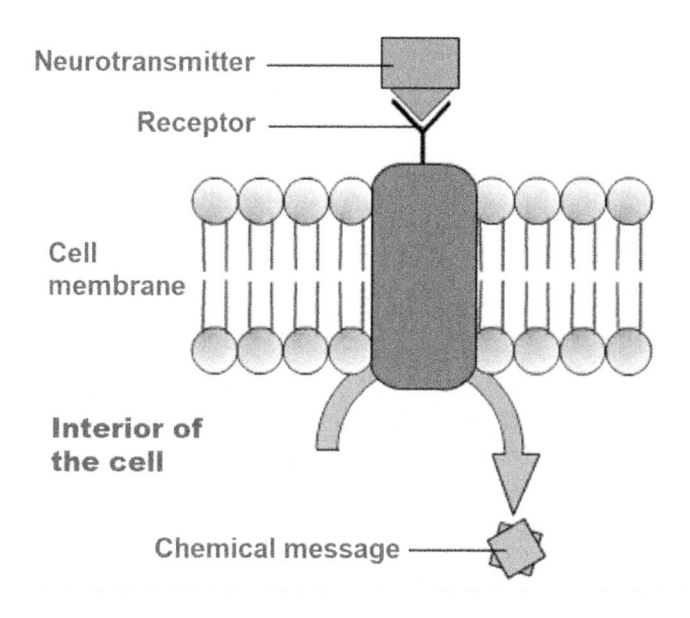

Neurotransmitter

Receptor

Cell membrane

Interior of the cell

Chemical message

Cosa What does this have to do with chemical addiction? It has everything to do with it. If we tend to have many negative thoughts such as anger, rage, fear, etc., many neurotransmitters corresponding to these emotions will be produced in our body. Our cells will then feed on these substances, putting inside them the message corresponding to the emotion connected to it.

If there are too many of them in excess of the receptors, however, at some point there is a kind of saturation, and since the cell gets used to receiving these neurotransmitters, what will happen at the next cell duplication? Simple, the two new cells resulting from the duplication will have many more receptors on their membrane to absorb the excess neurotransmitters. In other words, with each new generation of cells, the receptors corresponding to the emotions we feel deteriorating will increase, while all others will decrease and deteriorate.

This is when we enter the addiction phase. Our body, in fact, whose cells are full of a particular type of receptors, will ask for more and more neurotransmitters to satisfy the increased demand, thus triggering a spiral process from which it will be difficult to get out, exactly as it happens in any kind of chemical addiction.

That subtle pleasure...

What are the effects of this addiction? Exactly what usually happens to each of us when we cannot control our mind and let it wander in any direction. It is easy to understand that the direction chosen by the mind will be exactly the one that will satisfy the demand that the body continually makes on it, thus activating negative thoughts that will emit the corresponding neurotransmitters.

This is why we often find ourselves brooding over past episodes that cause us anger, or imagining future events in which we are going to *'tell him off'* (our boss, the neighbor who is disturbing us, the ex-partner, the mother-in-law, ...). You may also have noticed that we even feel a **subtle pleasure** in losing ourselves in thoughts that stimulate in us feelings of anger or revenge.

This is very normal, because that pleasure is a real pleasure, caused by our body that 'thanks' us for such an abundance of food for its hungry cells.

They are not just thoughts

Okay, you will say. What's wrong with that? They are just thoughts anyway. Not at all. You must realize that **you are putting dangerous toxins** inside your cells. You are inserting the chemical substances corresponding to negative feelings such as anger, resentment, hate, fear, etc. But they are not harmless. Each of these substances modifies the DNA of your cells, and surely you already know that the new cells that populate your body are generated from that DNA. All this is reflected on the health and the appearance of our body.

Every wrinkle that appears on our face corresponds to a sense of anger or worry. And in the long term, those negative feelings will inexorably turn into physical problems and diseases.

To begin detoxification, you must first have the awareness of being intoxicated. Is this enough for you to finally start taking control of your mind and shut up once and for all that stupid and harmful little voice that forces you *to think thoughts that are not your own.*

Discover How Meta-Medicine Helps Healing

Discovering the true underlying causes of any disease is of paramount importance. Meta-Medicine helps in this process. Let's see how.

Modern medicine has certainly made giant leaps, finding solutions to diseases that only a few decades ago were considered fatal. What official medicine does, however, is most often to treat the effect of the disease. What everyone does not know is that the real cause of the disease is often psychosomatic, and the disease is nothing but the external expression of an internal discomfort.

Meta-Medicine is a science that studies these primary causes. In fact, the use of Meta-Medicine helps to investigate the real reasons for which some symptoms manifest themselves, thus allowing intervention on the first cause to accelerate healing.

I would like to make a preliminary remark before moving on in this chapter. Even if Meta-Medicine helps to find and solve the causes of a disease, it cannot, **for no reason**, be used to replace official medicine. Meta-Medicine can be used to 'support' official medicine in order to facilitate the healing process.

How Meta-Medicine helps to find the primary cause

Let's start by talking about why a disease develops. As you already know, everything comes from our thoughts, therefore also diseases are attracted to us through our mental attitude.

Perhaps not everyone realizes that negative emotions, such as anger, jealousy, resentment, guilt, fear, etc. are poisonous for our organism. People who continuously feed on negative thoughts in the long run necessarily develop some form of illness. The problem is that the disease often occurs after months or years, so it is very difficult, if not impossible to trace any form of cause-effect between the thought and the corresponding physical discomfort.

It is important to trace the true cause of an illness in order to resolve it.

If you are ill, find out first what you did to become ill.
- Hippocrates

Meta-Medicine helps precisely to trace this kind of connection, giving precise indications on the cause that may have triggered a disease. Virtually every form of disease can be traced to some psychosomatic cause.

The idea to write this chapter came to me after having bought and read the beautiful book "The Great Dictionary of the Meta-Medicine" by Claudia Rainville.

Let's take a look at a few examples from the book.

Did you know that our feet represent our progress in life? The fracture of a foot, for example, indicates that the person has a great need to stop, because he/she is worried about doing something, but there is currently no possibility of stopping, if not through a physical injury. Of course, the damage is caused by our unconscious part, which responds to our thoughts by attracting the corresponding circumstances.

Or, the headache is almost always associated with a feeling of fear or danger experienced in the past, and the headache then occurs whenever we feel threatened by something or someone, or simply when certain memories resurface from deep within us.

How is Meta-Medicine applied? Practitioners do not make diagnoses or propose cures. They just ask the patient questions in order to identify the trigger and induce the person to reason about the root cause. The operator of Meta-Medicine helps the patient to become aware of the psychosomatic cause that has produced the disease, and most of the time this is of great help to reach the final healing.

The disease is just a cry for help from our body, which manifests its discomfort for something unresolved. The observation of the real cause is the means through which healing can happen, because the light of awareness illuminates the dark parts of us that only ask to be recognized.

In the case of fear, Meta-Medicine helps to get rid of it **through a process of blessing and love** towards the cause of our traumas. If it is anger, it will try to identify the cause in order to let go of it **through a process of forgiveness**, etc.

If you are interested in this topic, I invite you to read Claudia Rainville's book, which has become an irreplaceable companion for me whenever I am ill. And I must confess that as far as I am concerned, Meta-Medicine always helps me to identify the real cause of the problem.

Heal Yourself. Now It Is Possible with EFT

EFT is a very effective technique to heal yourself with just the use of your hands.

Today you can heal yourself from several ailments, both physical and emotional, simply by using a technique called EFT (Emotional Freedom Techniques). This technique allows you to heal yourself through the simple tapping of certain parts of the body with the fingers of your hands.

EFT is an innovative technique that is part of the Energetic Psychology, a collection of mind-body approaches to understand and improve human functioning.

We often hear about techniques to **heal oneself**, perhaps with nutrition, or complex physical exercises, but none of those seen so far, in my opinion, are more simple, harmless and effective than EFT.

Of course, it is easy to be skeptical of certain techniques, but this time I can say that the method has a solid theoretical basis, combining some psychotherapeutic techniques with the principles of acupuncture and applied kinesiology.

The Theory

EFT was born in 1995, and the theoretical principles on which it was based at the beginning have gradually been replaced by more modern and plausible principles. The explanation commonly accepted today starts from the assumption that the human body is crisscrossed by countless "energy pathways" that interact with our cells, organs, and even thoughts and feelings. You know very well that the mind plays a crucial role in creating reality, including our physical health.

These so-called "energy pathways" are constantly being traversed by energy flows that power all the cells in our bodies. When one or more of these pathways are "obstructed", generally because of negative thoughts or attitudes, then the flow of energy is hindered in its normal course, and consequently some parts of the body are affected, manifesting an ailment, which as we have said can be indifferently physical or psychic.

Intervening on some points of our body that are located at the intersections of these energy pathways is possible to restore the normal flow of energy, thus bringing the body back to its normal functioning. A very famous technique to intervene on these points is acupuncture, a millenary technique invented in China. This technique, however, although effective, cannot be used without the help of specialized personnel, and only by the use of special needles prepared for this purpose.

Thanks to EFT it is now possible to heal oneself by intervening on these sensitive points of the body simply by using the fingers of one's own hand, therefore in complete autonomy, in a non-intrusive way and above all without the use of any specific tool.

The practice: healing yourself with EFT is very simple

The technique is really within everyone's reach. As we have said, it involves tapping some specific points of your body (especially head, face and neck) with your fingers.

The technique requires that during this tapping you repeat some specific phrases related to the problem to be solved, such as:

"Even if I have problem X... I love and accept myself anyway", or

"Even though I have problem X... it's nice to know/feel that I have all the resources to change."

Unlike acupuncture, where the patient passively "suffers" the insertion of the needles, and his mind is free to wander everywhere, in EFT the patient plays an active role, both physical (by tapping) and mental (by the repetition of phrases). This allows you to focus on solving the problem, and thus, to be in my opinion, much more effective in healing oneself.

So, what else are you waiting for? You can watch one of the many existing videos on YouTube about the subject (just search for the word "EFT") and start applying this wonderful healing technique right away.

An Almost Magical Purification System

Here is an extraordinary Hawaiian purification system to enjoy a wonderful life in which everything is possible.

I would like to begin this chapter with a sentence that in my opinion contains one of the most profound truths:

All men mistake the limits of their field of vision for the limits of the world
- Arthur Schopenhauer

Indeed, we are all convinced that what we see is all that exists. By now it should be clear to the readers of this book that there is much more beyond the visible world, especially after learning of the amazing discoveries of quantum physics. But the knowledge that we create the world with our thoughts and beliefs does not help us at all. In fact, we are absolutely unable to change our lives, even knowing at a conscious level that reality is only an illusion created by ourselves.

A purification system to change our life

That's where the problem lies, in the fact that we know it only on a conscious level.

Our being is composed of a conscious part that constitutes only 5% of our true self. The remaining 95% is made up of an unconscious part, which in fact is precisely the part that acts in the world bringing to us things and events that we attract according to our innermost and hidden beliefs, of which we often know absolutely nothing.

That's the key. If we could clean up our subconscious, we could surely live a more joyful life, but above all a more conscious one, taking back the reins of our destiny.

So, we must necessarily resort to some sort of inner **purification system** that can help us to dissolve all the wrong beliefs that we have created over the years, since our birth.

This purification system fortunately exists and it is called **Ho'Oponopono**.

Ho'Oponopono is a very ancient prayer/mantra, belonging to the ancient traditions of the indigenous peoples of the Hawaiian Islands. The key to its effectiveness as a purification system comes from its meaning. In fact, Ho'Oponopono translated means "to put things in the right place".

Which things? The ones inside our unconscious, of course, but as you all know (otherwise you wouldn't be reading this book) the moment we are able to change internally, the external world is forced to change accordingly.

How do you use Ho'Oponopono?

Okay, but how do you use this purification system? Very simple. It involves repeating to yourself (or out loud if you prefer) these exact words:

I love you,
I'm sorry,
Please forgive me,
Thank you.

Is that all? Yeah, that's it. Nothing else. Repeat it for at least 10-15 minutes at different times of the day, for example when you go to bed at night or when you wake up in the morning, or when you take a shower. Better yet, if you can, try to replace that little voice that talks to you incessantly with this powerful purification system. You will reap tremendous benefits. Joe Vitale, one of the performers in the movie "The Secret" wrote an entire book about this purification system, entitled "Zero Limits". A best seller that I absolutely recommend.

OK, but what should we repent and ask forgiveness for? Of nothing in particular. This mantra simply helps to reconcile us with the Universe through the complete recognition that everything has been created by our subconscious, and if there is something that we do not like in this world, we take full responsibility and ask the Universe (or God, the Creator, the Supreme, ... you choose) forgiveness for all the ugliness in the world. Those simple words contain some of the highest concepts, such as Love, Forgiveness and Gratitude. If we put them together and pronounce them with the right conviction, they represent a very powerful mix.

It may seem strange or impossible, but the system really works. The mere fact of recognizing that we are in some way the artisans of our world, purifies us internally, allowing our unconscious part to be cleansed and consequently the external world begins to reflect this internal cleansing.

Trying is believing, although I am sure you are not among those who, as Schopenhauer says, mistake the limits of their field of vision for the limits of the world.

Make the Law of Attraction Work without Limits

The Law of Attraction does not work unless you first cleanse your unconscious of past memories. Reach the zero point to live without limits.

How many of you have seen the movie "The Secret", read a multitude of books on the Law of Attraction and maybe even attended more than one seminar on the subject, but then tried to apply all the methods you learned but simply nothing happened?

I see a forest of raised hands. The reason is very simple. We receive from the Universe what was imprinted inside our unconscious, and the conscious part has practically no effect on the events of our life. Do you want to live your existence **without limits**? Stop chasing the gurus who promise you that you can achieve anything with just the power of imagination, or by writing a few sentences on a sheet of paper.

First we need to fully understand what it means to live 'without limits'. It is not as they have led you to believe, we cannot achieve what we desire on a conscious level, but only what is aligned with our 'being'. In short, we must first *be* what we wish to *become*. But what does this mean? Only when the three parts that make up our being, namely our unconscious, our conscious and our True Self (also called superconscious) are aligned towards the same goal, then our life really starts to 'spin' and the term living without limits becomes a possible reality.

You must understand that our True Self has access to all the infinite creative power of the Universe. We already know that for the Universe nothing is impossible, and we can draw at will from this incredible power to achieve unlimited living.

But how? Only when all three components of our being are aligned towards the same goal, that is, towards the fulfillment of the mission that has been assigned to us in this life.

Okay, but now let's see how things really are. Whether you like it or not, the real protagonist is our unconscious, which is constantly connected with the Superconscious and makes continuous requests, which are regularly fulfilled by our True Self. This is the part that comes into play when we say that we attract to ourselves what we believe. We only really believe what is imprinted in our unconscious, and as a result we create the world in 'our own image and likeness'. This is the true essence of the Law of Attraction, but few people know this, and perhaps no one has ever told them.

Let's clean the unconscious to have a life without limits

So, what can we do? Visualizing villas with swimming pools and luxury cars without having intervened in some way on one's unconscious is completely useless. We have to clean it of the noise, which is represented by the weight of our memories, guilt, remorse, etc., so as to eliminate the interference of the past. Those who do not do this essential work on themselves will inevitably continue to drag the past into their future. Memories are like a program that has been imprinted in the unconscious by all our past experiences and all that we have believed in since childhood.

It is only a program, and as such it cannot create anything new. It is the mechanical part of us that projects outward all that it contains within it (the past) in the form of events. Every event or person in our life is nothing but the 'materialization' (or projection) of our internal memory. Our true nature without limits is constantly obscured by the past, a weed to be eradicated in order to bring out the beautiful garden that is within us.

But how to do this? It may not be easy if we do not know the right techniques. In this book we have presented several, all very valid, but it is also very important to ask our Divine part, which is our true essence, to help us in this work of cleansing. We cannot do it alone. And a good technique is that of **Ho'Oponopono**.

So yes. In order to live without limits we must first return to 'zero level', the one we were in when we first came into the world. Only in this way will we be able to listen to the voice of the Divine within us, which manifests itself through intuitions, that are nothing more than ideas uncontaminated by the past. If you practice Ho'Oponopono constantly, you will only 'cleanse' yourself of the past, eliminating the background noise and creating a vacuum within you. The space that is created at that point can be filled by the Divine presence, which has been waiting for this possibility since time immemorial. And then you will find that, as if by magic, you will begin to have more and more insights and new ideas. Those ideas will come to suggest to you how to achieve the things you desire. All you have to do is follow them without interfering with your conscious mind, which as we have just seen is contaminated by the noise of the past, then you will have a clear path to follow and actions to take.

This is how to make the Law of Attraction work at its best. And this is how to really live a life without limits.

A Demonstration of the Power of Ho'Oponopono

Here is a real demonstration of the power of Ho'Oponopono that happened to me.

I will take up the topic of self-purification to give you a real demonstration of how powerful this method is in purifying the subconscious and how it can have a real impact on our existence.

This is an episode that happened to me a few days ago, which I want to share with you to give you a real example of the **power of Ho'Oponopono**. You surely remember that this purification practice derives from an ancient Hawaiian practice that allows you to cancel all the memories of the past that influence our subconscious, and consequently change our life for the better.

I have read a lot about this practice, and I have been practicing it for a long time, but until now I had not had a real experience of the power of Ho'Oponopono, not until the episode that happened to me.

My practical experience of the power of Ho'Oponopono

A little over a month ago I slipped in the bathroom and unfortunately fractured a toe on my right foot. As prescribed by the doctor who had given me treatment after the accident, after about 30 days I went to the clinic to have the necessary x-rays to verify that the fracture had healed properly.

That morning, at around 12 o'clock, I went to the radiology department of the hospital where I had an appointment. As soon as I arrived, I noticed that in the waiting room there were several people waiting, who were nervously talking to each other complaining about the extreme slowness with which they were calling the people waiting for X-rays. As I approached, I heard that some of them had been waiting for over 2 hours. There was a very tense atmosphere.

Okay, that is normal in Italian public hospitals, you might say. But it was not for me, as I have learned in these situations to be aware of the fact that it is I who create my own reality, be it good or bad.

I could not therefore blame someone 'outside' of me. It was clear that I had created that situation, because of some 'memory' from the past that was materializing on an unconscious level in that particular situation.

I then remembered the power of Ho'Oponopono to 'clean' the subconscious from the dross of the past, and consequently the possibility to modify one's own reality (remember? The external reality is only a reflection of the internal one). So why not test whether what I had read about the power of Ho'Oponopono was true? Sitting in a corner of the waiting room I started to recite Ho'Oponopono to myself, trying to focus on the fact that I and only I was responsible for that situation.

That was the desired effect!

Well, after a few minutes from my decision, I heard that the people were entering at intervals of about 4-5 minutes from each other and, what was really incredible, only 20 minutes later I heard my name called! It was my turn, just after 20-25 minutes from my arrival, when, as I had already, said the people who arrived before me had waited for several hours.

The atmosphere was suddenly "lighter" and there was a completely different air from the one I had experienced when I first arrived. I let you imagine my joy, not so much because I was able to finish in such a short time, but especially because I had finally had direct and evident proof of the immense power of Ho'Oponopono.

I invite you then to experience for yourself, through constant commitment, the enormous power of Ho'Oponopono in giving you full control of your existence. It is a life-changing experience, believe me.

Bibliography

Braden G., "The Divine Matrix: Bridging Time, Space, Mira-cles, and Belief" (Hay House Inc., 2008)

Brizzi S., "Draco Daatson's Book" (Gateways Books & Tapes, 2016)

Capra F., "The Tao of Physics: An Exploration of the Parallels Between Modern Physics and Eastern Mysticism" (Shambhala, 2010)

Cason T., "All Things EFT Tapping Manual: Emotional Freedom Technique" (Little Sage Enterprises, 2015)

Castaneda C., "The Teachings of Don Juan" (University of California Press, 2016)

Dispensa J., "Becoming Supernatural: How Common People Are Doing the Uncommon" (Hay House Inc., 2019)

Dyer W.W., "Living the Wisdom of the Tao: The Complete Tao Te Ching and Affirmations" (Hay House Inc., 2008)

Dyer W.W., "The Power of Intention" (Hay House Inc., 2005)

Foundation for Inner Peace, "A Course in Miracles: Combined Volume" (Foundation for Inner Peace, 1975)

Goddard N., "Feeling is the Secret" (CreateSpace Independent Publishing Platform, 2010)

Goddard N., "The Power of Awareness: Unlocking the Law of Attraction" (Independently published, 2020)

Goddard N., "Your Faith is Your Fortune" (Merchant Books, 2018)

Hill N., "Think and Grow Rich" (Sound Wisdom, 2016)

Lipton B.H., "The Biology of Belief: Unleashing the Power of Consciousness, Matter & Miracles" (Hay House Inc., 2016)

Maharaj S.N., "I Am That" (The Acorn Press, 2012)

Marrone P., "Ancient Wisdom: The Monk With No Past" (Independently published, 2020)

Osho, "Love, Freedom, Aloneness: The Koan of Relationships" (St. Martin's Griffin, 2002)

Ruiz D.M., "The Four Agreements: A Practical Guide to Personal Freedom" (Amber-Allen Publishing, 2018)

Tolle E., "The Power of Now: A Guide to Spiritual Enlightenment" (New World Library, 2004)

Troward T., "The Hidden Power" (Kessinger Publishing, LLC, 2010)

Vitale J., "The Attractor Factor: 5 Easy Steps for Creating Wealth (or Anything Else) from the Inside Out" (Wiley, 2006)

Vitale J., "Zero Limits: The Secret Hawaiian System for Wealth, Health, Peace, and More" (Wiley, 2008)

Walsch N.D., "Conversations with God: An Uncommon Dialogue" (Hodder & Stoughton, 1997)

Zeland V., "Reality Transurfing 1: The Space of Variations" (O Books, 2008)

Zukav G., "Dancing Wu Li Masters: An Overview of the New Physics" (HarperOne, 2009)